Economic Policies, Governance and the New Economics

International Papers in Political Economy Series

Series Editors: **Philip Arestis** and **Malcolm Sawyer**

This is the seventh volume of the new series of *International Papers in Political Economy* (*IPPE*). The new series will consist of an annual volume with four to five papers on a single theme. The objective of the *IPPE* will continue to be the publication of papers dealing with important topics within the broad framework of Political Economy.

The original series of *International Papers in Political Economy* started in 1993 and has been published in the form of three issues a year with each issue containing a single extensive paper. Information on the old series and back copies can be obtained from Professor Malcolm Sawyer at the University of Leeds (e-mail: mcs@lubs.leeds.ac.uk)

Titles include:

Philip Arestis and Malcolm Sawyer (*editors*)

THE EURO CRISIS

NEW ECONOMICS AS MAINSTREAM ECONOMICS

21st CENTURY KEYNESIAN ECONOMICS

PATH DEPENDENCY AND MACROECONOMICS

CRITICAL ESSAYS ON THE PRIVATISATION EXPERIENCE

POLITICAL ECONOMY OF LATIN AMERICA
Recent Economic Performance

ALTERNATIVE PERSPECTIVES ON ECONOMIC POLICIES IN THE EUROPEAN UNION

FINANCIAL LIBERALIZATION
Beyond Orthodox Concerns

International Papers in Political Economy
Series Standing Order ISBN 978–1–403–99936–8

You can receive future titles in this series as they are published by placing a standing order. Please contact your bookseller or, in case of difficulty, write to us at the address below with your name and address, the title of the series and one of the ISBNs quoted above.

Customer Services Department, Macmillan Distribution Ltd, Houndmills, Basingstoke, Hampshire RG21 6XS, England

Economic Policies, Governance and the New Economics

Edited by

Philip Arestis
Director, Department of Land Economy, University of Cambridge

and

Malcolm Sawyer
Professor of Economics, University of Leeds, UK

palgrave
macmillan

First published 2013 by
PALGRAVE MACMILLAN

Palgrave Macmillan in the UK is an imprint of Macmillan Publishers Limited, registered in England, company number 785998, of Houndmills, Basingstoke, Hampshire RG21 6XS.

Palgrave Macmillan in the US is a division of St Martin's Press LLC, 175 Fifth Avenue, New York, NY 10010.

Palgrave Macmillan is the global academic imprint of the above companies and has companies and representatives throughout the world.

Palgrave® and Macmillan® are registered trademarks in the United States, the United Kingdom, Europe and other countries.

ISBN 978–1–137–02350–6

This book is printed on paper suitable for recycling and made from fully managed and sustained forest sources. Logging, pulping and manufacturing processes are expected to conform to the environmental regulations of the country of origin.

A catalogue record for this book is available from the British Library.

A catalog record for this book is available from the Library of Congress.

Typeset by MPS Limited, Chennai, India.

Contents

List of Figures

List of Tables

Preface

This is the ninth volume of the series of *International Papers in Political Economy (IPPE)*. The series consists of an annual volume with five to seven papers on a single theme. The objective of the IPPE is the publication of papers dealing with important topics within the broad framework of Political Economy.

The original series of *International Papers in Political Economy* started in 1993 until the new series began in 2005 and was published in the form of three issues a year with each issue containing a single extensive paper. Information on the old series and back copies can be obtained from the editors: Philip Arestis (e-mail: pa267@cam.ac.uk) and Malcolm Sawyer (e-mail: mcs@lubs.leeds.ac.uk).

The theme of this ninth volume of six papers is Economic Policies, Governance and the New Economics. The papers in this volume were initially presented at a one-day conference in Cambridge, UK, 12 April 2012. The conference was organized by the Department of Land Economy under the aegis of the Cambridge Trust for New Thinking in Economics, entitled *Economic Policies, Governance and the New Economics*. The Cambridge Trust for New Thinking in Economics fully supported and financed the conference. The papers were subsequently presented at the 9th International Conference, entitled *Developments in Economic Theory and Policy*, held at Universidad del Pais Vasco, Bilbao, Spain, 28–9 June 2012, which fully supported and funded the special session to which the papers included in this volume were presented. We are grateful to the organisers of the Bilbao conference and to the Cambridge Trust for all the help and funding provided.

Notes on the Contributors

Philip Arestis is Director of Research, Cambridge Centre for Economics and Public Policy, Department of Land Economy, University of Cambridge, UK; Professor of Economics, Department of Applied Economics V, University of the Basque Country, Spain; Distinguished Adjunct Professor of Economics, Department of Economics, University of Utah, USA; Senior Scholar, Levy Economics Institute, New York, USA; Visiting Professor, Leeds University Business School, University of Leeds, UK; Professorial Research Associate, Department of Finance and Management Studies, School of Oriental and African Studies (SOAS), University of London, UK; and holder of the British Hispanic Foundation 'Queen Victoria Eugenia' British Hispanic Chair of Doctoral Studies. He is Chief Academic Adviser to the UK Government Economic Service (GES) on Professional Developments in Economics. He has published as sole author or editor, as well as co-author and co-editor, a number of books, contributed in the form of invited chapters to numerous books, produced research reports for research institutes, and has published widely in academic journals.

Luiz Fernando de Paula is Professor of Economics at the University of the State of Rio de Janeiro and Fellow Research in Economics at CNPq, Brazil. His research interests are in the areas of macroeconomics, Post-Keynesian theory, international financial flows, banking and monetary economics. He has published as sole author or editor, as well as co-author and co-editor, a number of books and in a lot of refereed journals such as the *Brazilian Journal of Political Economy*, the *Cambridge Journal of Economics, ECLAC Review, Investigación Económica,* and the *Journal of Post Keynesian Economics.*

Fernando Ferrari-Filho is Professor of Economics at the Federal University of Rio Grande do Sul and Fellow Research in Economics at CNPq, Brazil. His research interests are in the areas of macroeconomics, Post-Keynesian theory, financial and currency crises and the international monetary system. He has published as sole author or editor, as well as co-author and co-editor, a number of books and papers in the following journals: the *Journal of Post Keynesian Economics,* the *Journal of Economic Issues, Investigación Económica,* and the *Review of Political Economy,* among others.

Jesus Ferreiro is Associate Professor in Economics at the University of the Basque Country, in Bilbao, Spain, and an Associate Member of the Centre for Economic and Public Policy, University of Cambridge. His research interests are in the areas of macroeconomic policy, labour markets and international financial flows. He has published a number of articles on those topics in edited books and in refereed journals such as the *American Journal of Economics and Sociology, Economic and Industrial Democracy, Économie Appliquée, Ekonomia, European Planning Studies,* the *International Journal of Political Economy,* the *International Labour Review,* the *International Review of Applied Economics,* the *Journal of Economic Issues,* the *Journal of Post Keynesian Economics,* and *Transnational Corporations.*

Valpy Fitzgerald is Professor and Head of the Department of International Development at the University of Oxford. He is also Professorial Fellow of St Antony's College Oxford and Visiting Professor of International Finance at the Universidad Complutense, Madrid. He has in recent years conducted advisory work for international agencies on: international investment regulation (Organisation for Economic Co-operation and Development, OECD); debt sustainability (United Nations Conference on Trade and Development, UNCTAD); macroeconomic policy and children (United Nations Children's Fund, UNICEF); and financial development (United Nations-Department of Economic and Social Affairs, UN/DESA). His areas of expertise are: financial and trade linkages between industrial and developing countries; macroeconomics of Latin America; conflict and reconstruction; history of economic thought. He was educated at Oxford (PPE, BA 1968) and Cambridge (Economics, PhD 1972).

Aline Gomes is Assistant Researcher at the Faculty of Economics, University of the State of Rio de Janeiro, Brazil. She was CNPq fellowship junior researcher in 2009–2010, and worked as Assistant Researcher in the Division of Research and Economic Analysis of the Brazilian Development Bank (BNDES) in 2010–12. Her research interests are in the areas of macroeconomics, banking, financial markets and Brazilian economy.

Patricia Peinado is Assistant Professor of Macroeconomics and Microeconomics at the University of the Basque Country. She was awarded both her BA and PhD in Economics by the University of the Basque Country. Her research interests are in the areas of social security, welfare state, public policy, ageing economics, gender economics, applied econometrics and finance. She has published in journals such as *Feminist Economics, Panoeconomicus* and the *Journal of Pension Economics and Finance.*

Malcolm Sawyer is Professor of Economics, Leeds University Business School, University of Leeds, UK. He was until recently Pro-Dean for Learning and Teaching for the Faculty of Business, University of Leeds, UK. He is managing editor of the *International Review of Applied Economics*, on the editorial board of a range of journals and editor of the series New Directions in Modern Economics. He has published widely in the areas of Post-Keynesian and Kaleckian economics, industrial economics and the UK and European economies. He has authored 11 books and edited 18, has published over 70 papers in refereed journals and has contributed chapters to over 100 books.

Felipe Serrano is Professor of Economics at the University of the Basque Country, in Bilbao, Spain. He is the Head of the Department of Applied Economics V at the University of the Basque Country. His research interests are in the areas of social security, the welfare state, labour market, innovation and economic policy. He is the author of a number of articles on those topics in edited books and in refereed journals such as *Economies et Sociétés, Ekonomia, European Planning Studies,* the *Industrial and Labor Relations Review,* the *International Labour Review,* the *International Review of Applied Economics,* the *Journal of Economic Issues,* the *Journal of Pension Economics and Finance,* and the *Journal of Post Keynesian Economics.*

Howard Stein is a professor in the Department of Afroamerican and African Studies at the University of Michigan and a Fellow of the African Studies Center Community at the University of Leiden. He has held academic posts in Africa, Asia and a number of European countries. He is the editor or author of more than a dozen books and collections and has published widely in scholarly journals. His research has focused on foreign aid, finance and development, neoliberalism, health and development, industrial policy and rural property right transformation. His most recent books include *Beyond the World Bank Agenda: An Institutional Approach to Development* (2008), *Good Growth and Governance in Africa: Rethinking Development Strategies* (2012), co-edited with Akbar Noman, Joseph Stiglitz and Kwesi Botchway; and *Gendered Insecurities, Health, and Development in Africa* (2012), co-edited with Amal Fadlalla.

John Weeks is Professor Emeritus of the University of London (School of Oriental and African Studies). His two most recent books are *Capital, Exploitation and Economic Crisis* (2011) and *The Irreconcilable Inconsistencies of Neoclassical Macroeconomics* (2012). In an importance recent theoretical contribution he demonstrated flawed logic in the Mundell–Fleming macro model (*Review of Political Economy,* forthcoming). He is Visiting

Professor at Kadir Has University in Istanbul and Senior Research Fellow at Institute for African Economic Studies, Addis Ababa University. In recent years he has written an economic recovery programme for Sierra Leone while being advisor to the Minister of Finance and Economic Development (2009), and contributed to the construction of a short-run forecasting for the Central Bank of Kenya (2010–11). Under the auspices of the United Nations Development Programme he led macroeconomic diagnostic missions to Moldova (2005), Vietnam (2004) and Zambia (two, 2006 and 2007). His commentary on current economic events can be found at http://jweeks.org.

1

The Great Recession, Capital Market Failure and International Financial Regulation

Valpy FitzGerald
University of Oxford

1.1 Introduction[1]

For at least a decade before the onset of the 'great recession' in 2007 it had been clear that systemic global capital market failure is a far more significant driver of the crisis than government monetary or fiscal policy. Some initial steps have been taken towards re-regulating national financial markets to increase stability and reduce uncertainty, but at the international level there is little progress despite initial commitments by the governments responsible for the greater part of the world economy (G20, 2009).

Although there is clear historical evidence that financial crises are closely linked to capital mobility (Reinhart and Rogoff, 2009), G20 policy statements do not address this as a multilateral issue. None the less, in effect almost all governments and central banks have acted so as to reduce mobility by protecting national banking systems while increasing risk aversion among financial intermediaries has led to increased home bias among investors.

If there is a parallel with the Great Depression of the 1930s, it is not to be found in the restrictions on imports because global trade liberalization and the construction of the World Trade Organization (WTO) at the end of the twentieth century have largely eliminated the power of governments to raise tariffs or apply import quotas. Competitive devaluation between economic powers is unviable in a world of flexible exchange rates where major nominal parities are no longer set administratively, although excessively low (or even negative) real interest rates have the effect of avoiding – or rather attempting to avoid – currency overvaluation; they are weak instruments at best. Rather the parallel is to be found in attempts of national regulators to protect their domestic banking systems through prudential regulation (IMF, 2012a). This in turn has reduced the negative impact of capital flows: not through capital controls as such but rather through the socialization of national balance sheets – the accumulation of foreign exchange reserves and bank bailouts.

Cross-border capital flows have grown enormously over the past three decades and have become more volatile and riskier rather than stabilizing in a mature market as standard theory would predict (Milesi-Ferretti et al., 2011). Surges of capital occur sequentially, and are persistent. Further, both surges and sudden stops are becoming increasingly globally synchronized. A number of factors contribute to these trends, including structural changes, the rapid expansion of financial markets, the rise of large cross-border institutions, and the acceleration of financial interconnections among countries. While the crisis showed that both advanced economies and emerging market economies (EMEs) could face risks from capital flows, the differing pattern of flows among these two groups determined the types of risks that manifested themselves (IMF, 2011a, b; IMF, 2012c).

Transactions among a small set of large advanced economies account for the majority of flows and stocks of external assets, and embed potentially important risks. While net flows are not so large among advanced economies relative to their GDP as those for developing, the former account for the bulk of gross global capital flows. This trend has been largely driven by the acceleration of portfolio investment flows which have proven to be the most volatile in recent years; the other investment segment mainly reflects banking-related flows, mostly driven by European banks. Additionally, a few advanced economies account for the bulk of global investment outflows and are also home to 'systemically important financial institutions' (SIFIs) and global capital markets, which makes them important sources and transmitters of global shocks.

In contrast to the large advanced economies, capital flows to EMEs and small developed economies (notably the European periphery) are larger on a net basis relative to host GDP, directly affecting macroeconomic stability through the funding channel. Not only is macroeconomic stability in these economies vulnerable to even temporary halts in flows, but in recent years the risks have compounded by increased volatility, and, until recently, greater recourse to debt financing in foreign currency. For instance, banks domiciled in advanced countries overwhelmingly participated in foreign currency financing in EMEs, but a much smaller group extended loans in domestic currency.

This paper sets out to explore the implications of these large fluctuations in international capital flows unrelated to the current account financing that had concerned John Maynard Keynes and his colleagues at Bretton Woods seven decades ago. The analytical relationship between global capital market failure and macroeconomic instability is outlined in section 1.2 of this paper, by drawing on concepts of credit market rationing, portfolio home bias, uncovered interest rate parity and the nature of the risk premium. In section 1.3 the very different responses of advanced economies as a group and EMEs to the crisis – reflecting lessons learned from recent past as well as distinct fiscal constraints – are explored in the context of the framework of section 1.2 – where it is shown that the level of national indebtedness has a crucial influence on both output (and employment) and the risk premium and thus the behaviour of capital flows. Both groups have in effect engaged in extensive socialization of macrofinancial fixed assets and liabilities such as external reserves and major bank liabilities (and in the case of housing, assets as well) in addition to the traditional sovereign debt, essentially as a means of national institutional insurance against sudden changes in global risk aversion.

Section 1.4 discusses the treatment of risk aversion in the standard literature in view of its importance in both theory and practice as set out in the previous two sections. A fundamental breach is revealed between mainstream economists' belief in the stability of the risk aversion parameter (derived from the derivatives of the foundational utility function itself) on the one hand, and financial analysts' conventional wisdom and measurement of its path-dependent instability on the other. Thus not only is financial socialization in the face of unstable global risk aversion best understood in an explicitly Keynesian framework, but also Keynes's own brief yet influential references to 'animal spirits' can be fruitfully seen as an expression of this concept of risk appetite. For it is the case that not only is financial socialization in the face of unstable global risk aversion best understood in an explicitly Keynesian framework, but also Keynes' brief yet influential references to 'animal spirits' can also be best understood in this context. Section 1.5 concludes with some implications of this argument for future steps in the pressing task of reform of the international financial architecture seventy years after the first attempt.

1.2 Global capital market instability

Financial markets are inherently unstable, because the assets being traded are claims on future income and these in turn depend not only upon unknown future events but also upon market participants' view of the likelihood of such events. International markets are even more unstable because they lack both the regulatory systems to maintain bank integrity on the one hand, and the macroprudential policy measures to ensure market stability on the other that characterize national systems.

This instability causes crises in ways that other international markets (such as those for commodities) do not, even though they too can exhibit large price fluctuations. This is because financial flows reflect adjustments in stocks – that is, balance sheets. Markets can only truly clear when participants (banks, households, firms and governments) have reached their desired balance sheet positions, and this may take some time. Indeed, because the potential equilibrium foreseen by market participants is itself always shifting, this process can take years to complete – if it occurs at all. The real effects of these adjustments on output, investment, employment and trade can be large and politically difficult to adsorb. Further, balance sheet adjustments by one sector – particularly banks – can have enormous effects on other sectors (households, firms and governments) as leverage changes. Last but not least, market expectations as to the value of particular asset classes, or the future of the world economy or as to the behaviour of other economic (and political) actors – can all shift considerably and rapidly in response to changing risk aversion, itself a response to political and market shocks.

In other words the extent of cross-border financing is not mainly reflected in *net* capital flows but rather in gross flows and balance sheet positions (Borio and Disyatat, 2001; Milesi-Ferretti et al. and others, 2011). This much is evident from the US balance of payments, as is illustrated by Figure 1.1. The current account imbalance has averaged about 3 per cent of US GDP over the past 15 years, with the band of variation lying between 2 and 5 percentage points; while the exact size of the deficit clearly reflects the long-term demand cycle as would be expected. In the case of the USA (with no significant foreign exchange reserves) the net capital inflows match the current account deficit by construction. In marked contrast, the gross capital flows are not only much larger (outflows averaging 10 per cent and inflows 7 per cent of GDP over the period) but also fluctuate enormously and erratically in the short run and thus clearly respond to factors other than trade and factor payments in the current account. In particular, the 'great recession' has seen gross inflows fall from 20 per cent of GDP in mid-2007 to 2 per cent in 2009, and then recover to 10 per cent by the end

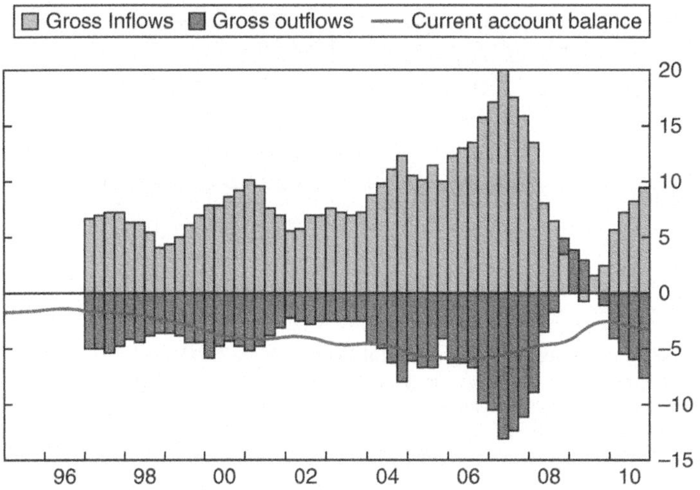

Figure 1.1 US gross capital flows, 1995–2010
Source: Borio and Disyatat (2011).

of 2010; while the figure for net capital flows (the current account balance) has moved steadily from 4, though 3 to 2 per cent of GDP as the economy decelerated.

Other parts of the world economy with structurally surplus current account positions (traditionally Germany, Japan and OPEC, of course, but more recently also East Asia) exhibit a similar pattern, although in reverse, with gross capital flows behaving quite differently from net flows in terms of both size and fluctuations. Figure 1.2 shows these gross flows as a percentage of GDP in 'Emerging Asia', where the compensating items are not only the current account balance but also the change in reserves. Over the period since the 'Asian Crisis' reserve accumulation has more or less balanced current account surpluses (a deliberate policy stance), so net capital movements have been effectively near-zero. None the less, gross capital flows have been very large – reaching US$750 billion in 2007 after a five-year build-up during the global boom – only to collapse to pre-boom levels in 2008. Again, as in the case of the USA, capital flows are clearly being driven by forces other than the need to fund a current account imbalance.

This instability in capital flows and spreads, originating in global financial markets, has profound consequences for host economies themselves; particularly since all but the largest open economies are driven by the capital account. This is for at least four reasons: first, because the

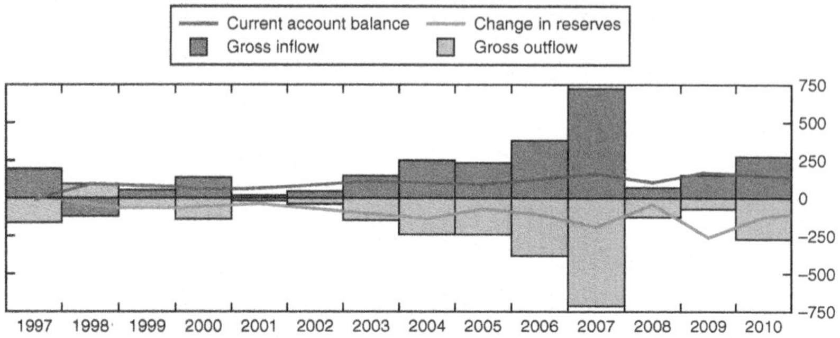

Figure 1.2 Emerging Asia gross capital flows, 1997–2010
Note: Emerging Asia comprises Chinese Taipei, Hong Kong SAR, India, Indonesia, Korea, Malaysia, the Philippines, Singapore and Thailand.
Source: IMF World Economic Outlook

level of interest rates at which government and national corporations can borrow is effectively set externally through the global level of interest rates along with financial markets expectations on exchange rate movements and credit risk assessments; secondly, because the level of investment and the long-run capital stock is determined in relation to global capital markets (see the end of this section); thirdly, because the short-run level of output is affected by the level of bank credit, and the expansion of output and investment is dependent on domestic bank credit creation; and fourthly, because the real exchange rate (and thus both export incentives and the real wage rate) is set by the scale of capital flows, and it is the size of capital flows which determines the size of current account flows, rather than the reverse. Moreover, in each case, investor risk tolerance is crucial in determining the outcome, as will be demonstrated below. As will be discussed in section 1.5 of this paper, this dynamic is fundamentally different from the 'Bretton Woods' era of the post-Second World War decades, when countries' balance of payments accounts were driven by trade (that is, the current account) and capital accounts adjusted to accommodate current account imbalances.

The systemic nature of this instability is best understood by reference to the theory of credit market rationing. Adapting and extending an extremely useful model by Folkerts-Landau (1985), consider a competitive international banking market with many (non-collusive) bank lenders and borrowers and an initially upward-sloping supply schedule of bank loans or bond purchases in the space of the interest rate and the volume of lending. Banks are price-takers in deposit markets but set lending rates (that is, spreads above the international 'base' rate, taken to be the US federal bond rate for the appropriate maturity) to maximize expected returns. Higher lending rates have an adverse selection effect on borrowers and thus increase default risk along with higher levels of indebtedness – because the incentive to default rises with both debt level and interest rate – so the supply schedule will be backward-sloping beyond a certain point. This effect is not just due to imperfect information in the sense of data on the borrower as such, but is clearly exacerbated by the belief that other lenders will respond in a similar way. We assume a conventional downward-sloping demand curve for bank loans from households, firms and governments because borrowers are deterred from increasing their debt levels as the cost of financing that debt rises.

Figure 1.3 depicts this international loan (*L*) market in a situation where equilibrium in the market arises with credit rationing. Banks are willing to lend up to the point (r^*) where its returns on loans (*rL*) is maximized. At this point the amount of funds on offer to the country (*L*) is less than the demand (*L′*) and thus there is rationing process. Note that if the loan demand schedule shifts down, or asset demand shifts up sufficiently, then an un-rationed equilibrium point can occur but this is not generally the case in practice except for 'borrowers of last resort' such as the USA or the UK (IMF, 2011c) – or perhaps, in the not too distant future, the European Community itself. Under these

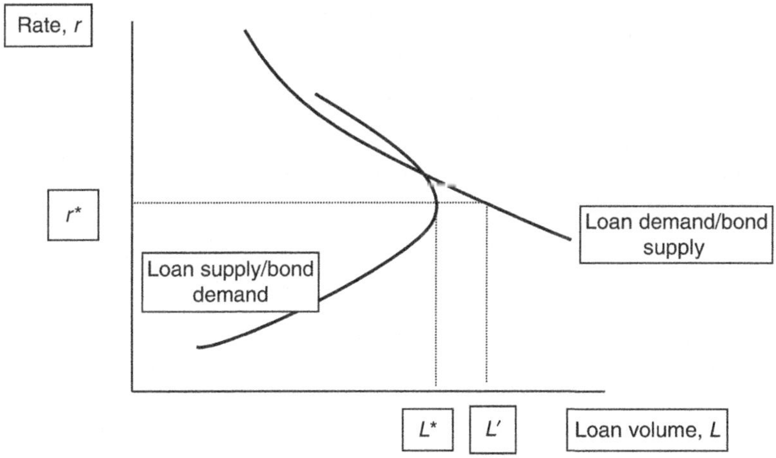

Figure 1.3 Credit rationing in the global debt market

circumstances, shifts in the supply of loans schedule (or demand for assets) determine the flows that take place, not changes in demand or the interaction between the two.

The peculiar shape of the supply function is the consequence of default risk being a function of the interest rate itself. We can see this by going beyond Folkerts-Landau (1985) to define the income (Z) from new bank lending as the difference between gross interest income (rL) received and expected capital losses from defaults on these new loans (pL) for a given default probability (p):

$$Z = rL - pL \qquad [1]$$

Default probability (p) is perceived by the banks as directly proportional (γ) to the level of debt service (rD) on outstanding debt (D) which results from debt accumulated in previous periods (D_0) and the new loans (L) so that

$$p = \gamma rD \qquad D = D_0 + L \qquad [2]$$

and by substituting [2] into [1], equation [3] is derived showing bank income Z as a function of the interest rate r and the loan level L:

$$Z = rL - \gamma r\,(D_0 + L)L \qquad [3]$$

This quadratic relationship between bank profits (Z) and the new loan book (L) in [3] to a particular class of borrower is clearly maximized where

$$\frac{\partial Z}{\partial L} = r(1 - \gamma D_0 - 2\gamma L) = 0 \qquad [4]$$

So that by rearranging [4] we have a solution for the equilibrium level of lending (L^*) in terms of existing debt (D_0)

$$L^* = \frac{1 - \gamma D_0}{2\gamma} \qquad [5]$$

Note that this result implies that the determinant of the credit-rationed equilibrium loan level is the previous debt level (D_0) and the banks' perception of the effect of debt on default probability (γ), an increase in either of which will reduce lending levels. The demand for loans (L') is not relevant.

The interest rate at this rationed equilibrium (r^*) is not determined by the intersection of the demand and supply schedules for loans either, because this is a rationed equilibrium: in other words, demand for loans is unsatisfied at equilibrium, as Figure 1.3 shows. The interest rate is determined as a spread (s) over the international rate $\bar{r}$; this spread in turn being determined by competition between banks eliminating excess gains at the margin (this arbitrage process is discussed further below) to the point where it is equal to the default risk (p)

$$s = r^* - \bar{r} = p \quad r^* = \bar{r} + p \qquad [6]$$

In other words, the spread can be seen as an insurance premium against default. However, this premium (and thus the spread) cannot rise beyond a certain level because of the reversion of the loans supply schedule, as we have seen. In practice – as is evident from recent events in Southern Europe – the point at which this occurs appears to lie somewhere between 5 and 10 per cent. Substituting [2] into [6] gives [7] which is the solution for the equilibrium interest rate r^* in terms of the base rate ($\bar{r}$), previous debt levels (D_0) and the banks' perception of the borrower's likely default behaviour (γ)

$$r^* = \frac{\bar{r}}{1-\gamma(D_0 + L^*)} = \frac{2\bar{r}}{1-\gamma D_0} \qquad [7]$$

These results become even stronger if we allow for risk aversion among lenders (on which more later in this section) or if the relationship between debt and default probability in equation [2] is non-linear, which is logically the case at higher debt levels or in situations of generalised crisis.

So far we have been considering international bank lending and, by implication, borrowing by sovereigns or major corporates. However, very similar factors enter into portfolio investments by institutions such as pension, mutual or hedge funds. Moreover, risk aversion becomes an explicit factor in determining capital flows, while banking models such as the one discussed above implicitly assume risk neutrality among lenders.

Consider a home investor holding home (h) versus foreign (f) securities. Her objective function is to maximize the expected value (V) of a portfolio W where V is increasing in the mean of wealth but decreasing in its variability. The mean and variance of wealth are written in terms of real wealth (W) and an expectations operator, $E(.)$ conditional on information known in time t and var (.) is the variance–covariance matrix operator.

$$\begin{aligned} V &= V[E_t\,(W_{t+1}),\ var(W_{t+1})] \\ V' &> 0 \\ V'' &< 0 \end{aligned} \qquad [8]$$

The investor maximizes V with respect to a vector of portfolio shares, simplified here to the proportion (P) held in foreign securities. The lack of perfect correlation between home and foreign securities ensures a non-linear relationship between home and foreign returns: this is logically necessary because if their risk were identical, then the whole portfolio would be assigned to whichever had the higher expected return.

$$\begin{aligned} E_t\,(W_{t+1}) &= W_t\,[\{(1 - P\}\{1 + E_t\,(r^h_{t+1})\} + P.E_t\,(r^f_{t+1})] \\ var(W_{t+1}) &= W_t^2\ var[(1 - P)r^h_{t+1},\ P.r^f_{t+1}] \end{aligned} \qquad [9]$$

and substituting [9] into [6] and maximizing the resulting expression with respect to P yields the first order condition, where σ_h^2 and σ_f^2 are the respective variances of home and foreign returns to home investor, σ_{hf} the covariance between these two returns and λ is the parameter of relative risk aversion ($\lambda = -2V''W_t\ /\ V'$). We then derive

$$P_t^f = \frac{[E_t(r^f_{t+1}) - E_t(r^h_{t+1})]\,/\,\lambda}{\sigma_f^2 - \sigma_h^2} + \frac{\sigma_h^2 - \sigma_{hf}}{\sigma_f^2 - \sigma_h^2} \qquad [10]$$

Equation [10] is straightforward to understand – it is a demand function for foreign assets and thus the determinant of gross capital outflows from the home country and inflows to the host country. The first RHS term is the demand arising from the higher return from the foreign security: this clearly falls with rising risk aversion λ and rises with the returns r. The second term is the portfolio share that minimizes the variance of the wealth portfolio. Note here that covariance *between* markets (σ_{hf}) is a vital aspect of 'contagion' from the point of view of investors – either arising from 'real' factors (such as trade or investment links) or from anticipation of the reaction of *other* investors to this asset class.

The key point here is that the demand for foreign portfolio assets will clearly depend in great part upon 'fundamentals' (that is, r_f and σ_f^2) but also upon variables in the *home* market such as risk aversion and home volatility (λ, r_h and σ_h^2, and thus σ_{hf}). The empirical evidence indicates that the latter is at least as important as the former. This is perhaps more important than the widely observed – yet largely unexplained – existence of 'home bias' itself: that for reasonable values of risk aversion λ the share of foreign – and even more so, of emerging market – assets that is observed in institutional portfolios is much lower than [10] suggests that should be the case (Lewis, 1999; Babilis and FitzGerald, 2005).

One possible explanation might be thought to be found in a Bayesian approach where the investor has prior views about means and returns, updates these views as she observes new data and then makes the portfolio allocation decisions (Klein and Bawa, 1977). However, numerical simulation using data for US mutual funds of this process indicates that only if the investor holds implausible prior views can home bias be generated: while an investor with no (or diffuse) prior views about foreign returns would arrive an allocation not far from the optimal (Lewis, 1999).

The explicit inclusion of risk aversion in the standard portfolio model, which then enters into the asset demand function, implies that we should do the same for the rationed bank lending model discussed above, because remuneration incentives can make bankers risk seeking, while their shareholders and regulators are likely to be risk averse – and all three can change opinion through the cycle. This would mean explicitly introducing risk aversion λ into Equation [1] as well

$$Z = rL - \lambda pL \quad [1a]$$

And thus transforming Equation [4] for the equilibrium loan level into

$$L^* = \frac{1 - \lambda\gamma D_0}{2\lambda\gamma} \quad [4a]$$

And that for the equilibrium interest rate in Equation [7] into

$$r^* = \frac{2\bar{r}}{1 - \lambda\gamma D_0} \quad [7a]$$

Thus when international investor risk aversion (λ) rises, the equilibrium loan level (L^*) will fall: in terms of Figure 1.1, this would mean that the entire loan supply schedule shifts – and thus the equilibrium L^*, r^* position in Figure 1.3 moves to the north-west with higher rates and lower flows. In other words, changes in both the yields *and* the flows observed will reflect changes in both default probability *and* risk aversion.

The macroeconomic implications of this result for the host economy are severe in an integrated global capital market. With a liberalized capital account, arbitrage by domestic and foreign investors will ensure that *uncovered interest rate parity* obtains. In other words, the domestic interest rate (i_d) is necessarily equal to the sum of the world interest rate ($i_\$$), the expected rate of depreciation of the nominal exchange rate ($\dot{E}$) and the default risk premium (ρ). This premium is itself the product of the default risk (p) and the risk aversion parameter (λ) for international investors – sometimes known (in its inverse form) as 'risk appetite' or 'risk tolerance'.

$$i_d = i_\$ + \dot{E} + \rho \qquad [11]$$

$$\rho = p\lambda \qquad [12]$$

Equation [11] states that if the domestic interest rate is above (below) the international rate once adjusted for expected losses either through exchange rate changes or default, then capital will flow in (out) until that equilibrium is reached. This in turn means that a government can only exercise two out of the following three policy options: (i) open capital account (the equality itself); (ii) independent monetary policy (i_d); or (iii) independent exchange rate policy ($\dot{E}$); because setting any two – given the world interest rate ($i_\$$) and the default premium (ρ) risk – will determine the third. In consequence, this result is commonly known as the 'trilemma', the 'iron triangle' or the 'impossible trinity'. In practice, this has meant that as most governments have been wedded until recently to inflation targeting as the basis of monetary policy on the one hand, and open capital accounts on the other: exchange rates (and thus export competitiveness) have not been a policy variable (FitzGerald, 2008).

Equation [12] is self-explanatory, except that it should be borne in mind that the default probability is what the market considers it to be (which is the function of ratings agencies) and thus exogenous factors such as contagion from related economies may enter into the estimation, as well as the sustainability of debt in view of future current account imbalances on the one hand and anticipated government macroeconomic policy on the other. Equation [12] also reflects the facts (discussed further in section 1.4 below) that international investors are *not* risk neutral ($\lambda = 1$); and that risk aversion/tolerance/appetite varies widely over time in a path dependent manner (FitzGerald, 2007).

An important consequence is that any increase in the *international* interest rate ($i_\$$) or *international* risk aversion (λ) will immediately increase the host interest rate (i_d) or force a depreciation of the currency ($\dot{E} < 0$). The 'dollar' interest rate paid by the country ($i_{\$d}$) in Equation

[13] is no more than the domestic rate adjusted for exchange rate changes, and thus equal from [11] to the world rate plus the default premium. Rearranging [13] and substituting into [12] reveals in Equation [14] the spread (s) on international debt markets between the domestic dollar rate and the base international rate, to be no more than the risk premium – that is, the product of default risk and risk aversion.

$$i_{\$d} = i_d - \dot{E} = i_\$ + \rho \qquad [13]$$

$$S = i_{\$d} - i_\$ = \rho = \lambda p \qquad [14]$$

Last but not least $\dot{E}$ and ρ are *not* independent variables. A fixed exchange rate regime (i.e. $\dot{E} = 0$) would at first sight seem to reduce the spread (s), and indeed it often does in the short run. However, a fixed exchange rate also reduces the authorities' capacity to adjust the domestic economy, and thus increases the debt servicing capacity – by increasing exports for example – and can thus increase default probability (p).

We can assess the longer-run effect on output and incomes of a small open economy of this arbitrage as follows, leaving aside exchange rate movements for the moment. Consider a simple aggregate model of an economy with a familiar production function, where output capacity (Y) depends on the stock of capital (K) and labour (N).

$$Y = AK^{\alpha} N^{1-\alpha} \qquad [15]$$

This production function then determines the rate of return (r) as the marginal product of capital in the conventional way

$$r = \frac{\partial Y}{\partial K} = \alpha A \left(\frac{K}{N}\right)^{\alpha - 1} \qquad [16]$$

And finally, the open capital account ensures that r equals the international interest rate ($i_\$$) plus the risk premium from [13].

$$r = i_\$ + p\lambda \qquad [17]$$

Substituting [17] into [16] and then into [15] solves simply for the level of output Y

$$Y = N\left(\frac{\alpha A}{i_\$ + \lambda p}\right)^{\frac{\alpha}{1-\alpha}} \qquad [18]$$

In other words, any increase in the *international* interest rate ($i_\$$) or *international* risk aversion (λ) will depress the level of output (Y) in the host economy.

In short, international asset demand is of its nature unstable – reflecting home as well as host macroeconomic fluctuations on the one hand and changes in investor risk aversion on the other – and this instability has severe external effects on output as well as on capital flows and interest rates worldwide.

1.3 The contrasting response of advanced and emerging market economies

Policy reactions to the current 'great recession' have been clearly distinct in developed and developing countries. In particular, as Figure 1.4 demonstrates, the advanced economies suffered real falls in consumption at the height of the crisis in 2008–9, and subsequently little or no recovery. Meanwhile, while consumption growth slowed in emerging economies, it did not actually fall and recovered much more rapidly. A very similar pattern is evident in investment behaviour, with large absolute declines in developed countries and continued growth in emerging economies – apart from at the height of the crisis. As I will argue below, this difference was largely the result of radical policy differences between the two groups, both during the recession crisis itself and in the previous decade.

Behind this policy difference lies a surprising divergence in underlying macroeconomic balances between developed and developing countries

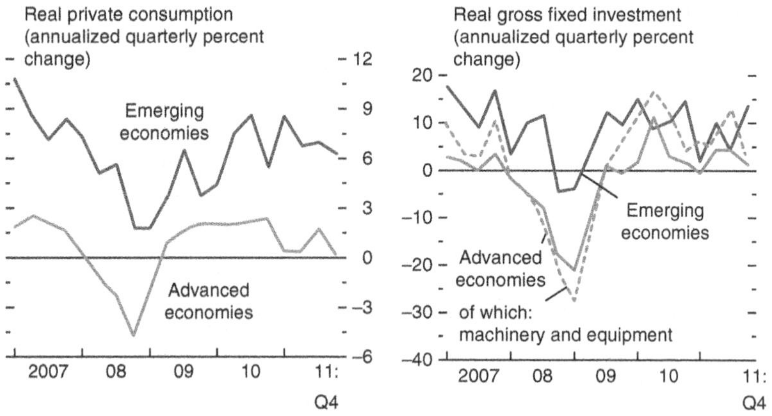

Figure 1.4 Consumption and investment in developed and developing economies, 2007–11
Source: IMF (2012a).

since around 2000. In great part the different developing country response is due to the emerging market financial crises of the late 1990s (themselves closely related to the impact of unstable capital flows) and the inability – or unwillingness – of international financial institutions to either stabilize the international economy or support individual countries in difficulties. On the one hand, developing country debt ratios (see Figure 1.5 below) declined rapidly to about half their previous level; while domestic savings rates almost doubled. In marked contrast, debt levels in developed countries continued on the upward trend they had exhibited since the mid-1970s while savings rates declined steadily. The origins of this trend are to be found in a complex combination of demographic transition, resistance to tax reform and withdrawal of state support for investment; but the consequence has been to reduce the scope for fiscal policy as a macroeconomic policy instrument during the 'boom years' so that it became unavailable during the 'bust'.

The bottom line, however, was that for the first time in recent economic history developing countries were better placed than developed ones to weather a global financial storm.

In terms of policy responses to the crisis, the developed economies have adopted three main lines of action. First, they have all in effect socialized non-performing bank loans – particularly those in the housing sector where the welfare (and thus the political) consequences of widespread default leading to property losses were too great. Secondly,

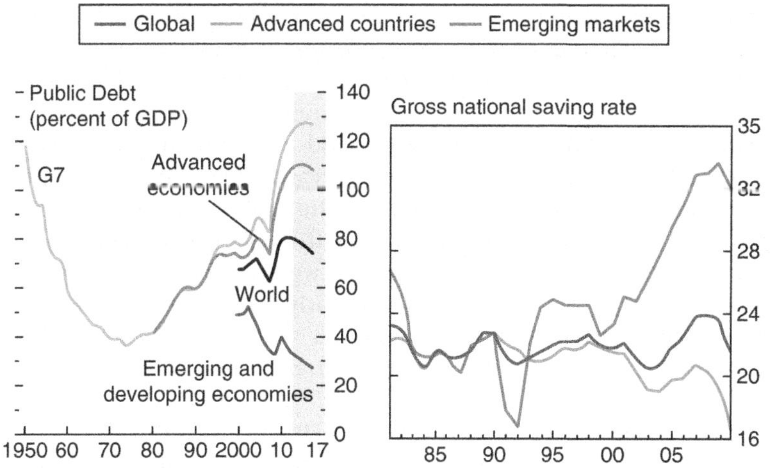

Figure 1.5 Debt and saving in developed and developing countries, 1980–2010
Source: IMF (2012b).

they have bailed out systemically important banks by extending large public credit lines and entering into various forms of equity participation both explicitly and implicitly – through independent stabilization agencies. Thirdly, they have combined expanded liquidity provision from central banks with fiscal consolidation based more on expenditure cuts than tax revenue increments. This last is in part due to the existing debt overhang, as Figure 1.5 illustrates, but is also due to ideological fiscal positions. It would appear that a heterodox approach to the public ownership of non-performing assets is politically acceptable when support for the banking and real estate sectors is required. But when issues of education or employment are concerned (or indeed taxes on wages as opposed to profits) then enhanced orthodoxy is still the political consensus. This inconsistency clearly reflects relative political lobbying power but also demonstrates the fear induced in national politicians by the prospect of being excluded from global capital markets.

Meanwhile, there has been only slow progress towards re-regulating the financial sector in order to prevent excessive risk-taking after the excessive liberalization of the previous two decades which brought about the present crisis. However, because this rebalancing has been mainly focussed on the protection of major national banks and although it has led to stronger bank balance sheets, it has also involved a reduction in credit for productive investment (ICB, 2012).

As indicated above, the developing economies – particularly the larger and/or stronger among them in Asia and Latin America – drew upon hard lessons learned during the 1990s and thus benefitted from the increased policy space created by lower debt levels and high levels of foreign exchange reserves. The function of these reserves had also changed radically. Traditionally, these reserves had been seen as a means of buffering imports from fluctuations in export earnings, and thus of maintaining the level of production and employment. However, the liberalization of capital markets in the early 1990s meant that these reserves became a means of stabilizing the capital account rather than the current (that is, trade) account of the balance of payments. Or, to put it another way, foreign reserves were needed to underpin the domestic money supply – and particularly bank deposits – and protect production and employment from a sudden conversion of liquid domestic financial assets into foreign currency assets and thus destabilizing credit fluctuations (IMF, 2012c).

None the less, in the short run, capacity is given and the effect of capital flows is felt either on output and employment through the bank credit channel, or on the exchange rate and thus the real wage. Within a given long-run capacity Y (which depends upon previous investment as in [14] above), output (Q) will be constrained not only by capacity but in practice by credit supply – itself affected by bank liabilities and thus foreign borrowing – or else foreign exchange availability as the authorities regulate aggregate demand in order to ensure that reserves are not depleted.

Consider a simple model of a small (that is, price-taking) open economy starting from the balance of payments with exports (X), imports (M), changes in reserves (R) and net capital flows (F) in Equation [19]

$$X + F \equiv M + \Delta R \qquad [19]$$

The 'modern' rule as discussed above is that foreign exchange reserves should be equal to a fixed proportion (φ) of external liabilities, so that the *change* in reserves must be in this proportion to net capital flows (F), which in turn of course can be either positive (net inflow) or negative (net outflow):

$$\Delta R = \varphi F \qquad [20]$$

Finally, exports are a linear function of world demand (Z) and the real exchange rate (e); and imports are a linear function of domestic output ($Q < Y$) and the real exchange rate

$$X = x_1 Z + x_2 e$$
$$M = m_1 Q - m_2 e \qquad [21]$$

The impact of a change in capital flows (F) depends upon what the government policy is for macroeconomic management in response to external shocks. One option is for the government to attempt to achieve a target real exchange rate (e^*) in order to maintain export competitiveness. In this case, output (Q) becomes a function of the capital flow – which we can visualize as working through increased (decreased) foreign deposits in domestic banks, which then serves to expand (contract) credit to consumers and producers.

Substituting [20] and [21] into [19] and rearranging yields output (Q) as a function of capital flows (F); with a marginal effect or multiplier which can be quite large in practice given that the import propensity (m_1) has values in practice of the order of 0.2–0.4

$$Q = \{(1 - \varphi)F + x_1 Z + e^* (x_2 + m_2)\}/m_1$$
$$\partial Q/\partial F = (1 - \varphi)/m_1 > 0 \qquad [22]$$

This volatility of output will also be reflected proportionately in employment levels – albeit at a stable real wage because the real exchange rate is fixed (FitzGerald, 2008). However, the higher the marginal reserves requirement (φ) the lower the impact will be, which reflects the 'sterilization' approach adopted by a number of developing countries. Full sterilization ($\varphi=1$) would, of course, mean no multiplier effect at all because all the capital flows are absorbed by the reserves.

Alternatively, if full employment output ($Q^* = Y$) itself is targeted by the authorities then the real exchange rate adjusts to capital flows. We substitute [20] and [21] into [19] again, but rearrange to yield the real exchange rate (e) as a function of capital flows (F); as shown in Equation [23]

$$\begin{aligned} e &= \{m_1 Y - (1-\varphi)F - x_1 Z\} \,/\, (x_2 + m_2) \\ \partial e / \partial F &= -(1-\varphi)/(x_2 + m_1) < 0 \end{aligned} \qquad [23]$$

Here the real exchange rate appreciates (e falls) with increased capital inflows, or depreciates (e rises) with outflows. Again the multiplier effect is potentially quite large for plausible trade elasticities, but also the effect can be migrated by higher reserve requirements (φ) as before.

This in turn means that real wages are increasing (decreasing) with the appreciation (depreciation) – albeit at full employment. The fact that overvaluation from capital inflows is politically popular among organized workers and consumers, and undervaluation resulting from outflows unpopular, is merely a reflection of this distributional logic. However, if real wages are to be stabilized, and thus the real exchange rate, then employment will fluctuate with output as in Equation [22] and this will prejudice those at the margin of the formal sector labour force, who are likely to be the poorer workers (and women).

The unattractive nature of these choices had led most developing countries to adopt some form of capital controls before the crisis in order to reduce capital account volatility. In effect, this means breaking (or at least seriously distorting) the uncovered interest rate parity condition in Equation [8] above, and thus regaining control over monetary and exchange rate policy. These were gradually put in place in the early 2000s (FitzGerald, 2005) in response to the shocks of the previous decade, and are generally not of an administrative nature – although it should be noted that those countries which still maintained such controls (particularly India and China) did not dismantle them. Several even imposed transaction taxes designed to bear most heavily on short-term capital inflows and outflows; but while these could reduce excess volatility they were of insufficient size to buffer large shocks.

In consequence most countries have introduced prudential measures in their banking systems designed to prevent currency mismatch in balance sheets and thus excess exposure to exchange rate fluctuations on the one hand, and sudden withdrawal of deposits by non-residents on the other.

Last but not least, developing countries have managed to maintain public expenditure levels (IMF, 2012b), and thus the gradual extension of universal benefits to their populations, which has had the effect of buffering consumption levels. Private investment has been maintained by low real interest rates and continued public investment expenditure.

Summing up this 'new model' of national macrofinancial management we can detect two major changes. On the one hand, the active management of macroeconomic balance sheets (government, banks and the external account) through the socialization of both assets and liabilities has given greater space to maintain production and employment. This can be seen as a form of self-insurance which while certainly more costly than the potential for collective insurance from international financial institutions, is clearly far more reliable. On the other hand, this model is the equivalent of tariff protection during past global recessions, for two reasons: first, because as pointed out above, the major international instability are now transmitted through the capital account of the balance of payments and not through the current (trade) account; and secondly, because trade protection through tariffs or quotas is in effect outlawed by the World Trade Organization (WTO) membership.

To understand the implications of this contrasting stand it is also necessary to refer back to the models discussed in the previous section. First, from the point of view of host country policy relevant policy variables are clearly total factor productivity (*A*) and default risk (*p*) in Equation [18] above. For developing countries rapid growth is a major driver of the political economy and there are coherent strategies to raise total factor productivity (*A*) through the provision of infrastructure and education. This contrasts markedly with the situation in developed countries, where there are no growth strategies as such with investment almost entirely reliant on market forces and public expenditure devoted to welfare and defence. Large budget cuts clearly limit the scope to raise *A* in the longer run. The only option therefore appears at first sight to be raise income (*Y*) by reducing the default probability (*p*) through fiscal austerity. This is the origin of the proposed 'growth through austerity' strategy, although there is little or no evidence to suggest that it is effective once the negative effects on demand and efficiency (*A*) have been taken into account (Perotti, 2011). What is more, although reduced primary budget deficits can logically reduce the pressure on debt service by both making debt service easier and reducing the need for further borrowing; this could better be achieved by increasing tax pressure – particularly on assets held outside the tax jurisdiction (FitzGerald, 2012).

Alternatively, governments can reduce the risk of default (particularly in the view of international investors) by increasing their holdings of foreign reserves so as to provide more liquidity for debt service, thus reducing p. This also has the effect of supporting the exchange rate, and thus reducing the probability of depreciation – in other words reducing $\dot{E}$ in Equation [11]. Indeed one of the key indicators in practice of p used by bond traders is the 'quick ratio' between short-term debt – less than one year – and reserves: in other words, φ in Equation [20].

Another option, as explained above, is to regulate capital markets in such a way that uncovered interest arbitrage in Equation [11] does *not* hold – in other words, various forms of capital controls ranging from taxes on short-term capital movements to prudential regulation of the foreign exchange exposure of bank balance sheets (FitzGerald, 2005).

Second, there is no reason why the debt level determined by markets as discussed in section 1.2 above should correspond to that which is optimal from a macroeconomic point of view. There are thus good theoretical reasons for intervening in capital markets to allow this level to be reached. The optimal debt level from the point of view of the borrowing country depends largely upon the extent to which the borrowing results in productive investment that will raise the capacity to repay in subsequent years. Consider a country with welfare (W) – technically this would be GNP as opposed to Y as GDP – defined as output (Y) minus debt interest costs (iD). Debt also plays a role in capital formation and thus affects Y positively, but with declining marginal effect, so that while the first derivative of wealth is positive, its second is negative. This formulation is useful because the two constraints reflect declining absorption capacity (that is, the marginal productivity of additional borrowing) and debt overhang effects respectively

$$G = Y - iD \qquad [24]$$

The first derivative of [24] is positive because $Y'(D) > i$ but the second derivative is negative because $Y''(D) < 0$ due to declining returns to debt-led investment. In models of this type, a large 'inherited' debt and consequent repayments – plus the consequent attraction of default – will create a 'debt overhang' (Obstfeld and Rogoff, 1996). Inherited debt will reduce optimal investment due to the 'tax' on returns arising from service obligations on old debt. This reduces the future ability to repay and increases the benefits of default; both of which will reduce the willingness of lenders to extend further loans. By extension, reducing the debt burden will increase investment and future ability to repay. This outcome reflects the situation in Equations [5] and [7] in section 1.2 where the level of lending *and* the lending rate are strongly affected by the prior debt level. Under these circumstances it is in the interest of lenders to unilaterally write off a proportion of the debt in order to secure full service on the rest. However, it is very difficult to achieve this in practice due to the problem of coordination between debtors – with a strong incentive towards 'free riding', particularly in bond markets, where US law (unlike the UK) protects minority bond holders.

Under these conditions, the optimal debt level from the point of view of the borrowing country can only be defined as that value which maximizes the level of national welfare (G). Differentiating [24] with respect to the debt level (D) we obtain

$$\frac{\partial G}{\partial D} = \frac{\partial Y}{\partial D} - \left(i + D\frac{\partial i}{\partial D}\right) - 0 \qquad [25]$$

In other words, debt should be contracted up to the point where the marginal addition to output equals the marginal addition to interest costs. Obviously, the higher the interest rate (i), the lower the resulting optimal debt level, while the larger the positive impact of that debt on output, the higher the optimal debt level. As we have already explored the effect of debt on interest rates ($\partial i/\partial D$) in Equations [7] and [7a], the key issue here is the effect of debt on investment ($\partial Y/\partial D$). For simplicity we examine the particular case where the domestically funded capital (K_1) is already installed, there is no previous debt, and the authorities contemplate moving in one period to the optimal debt level, by providing extra capital stock (K_2) funded by external debt

$$K = K_1 + K_2 \qquad [26]$$

External debt (D) is then contracted. A fixed proportion (μ) of this is used to fund the installation of new productive capital directly in the public sector or indirectly by funding private investment; the rest goes on other activities such as social investments (health, social care and education), coverage of current deficits or non-economic infrastructure

$$J = \mu D \qquad [27]$$

The installation cost of this productive investment (J) is assumed to be a quadratic function of the investment rate in order to reflect 'congestion' costs of high levels of new investment (K_2) relative to the existing installed capital (K_1) or alternatively the limits on public capacity to manage new projects:

$$J = K_2\left(1 + \pi\frac{K_2}{K_1}\right) \qquad [28]$$

We assume a fixed capital–output relationship for simplicity:

$$Y = aK \qquad [29]$$

So we can now specify the objective function (G), aggregate output less interest charges, by substituting [26]–[29] into [24]

$$G = Y - iD = aK - \frac{iJ}{\mu} = a(K_1 + K_2) - \frac{i}{\mu}K_2\left(1 + \pi\frac{K_2}{K_1}\right) \qquad [30]$$

Differentiating [30] with respect to K_2 yields the optimal solution in terms of the ratio (ω) between the debt-funded new capital and the existing stock:

$$\begin{aligned} \frac{\partial G}{\partial K_2} &= a - \frac{i}{\mu}\left(1 + 2\pi\frac{K_2}{K_1}\right) = 0 \\ \omega &= \frac{\hat{K}_2}{K_1} = \frac{1}{2\pi}\left(\frac{a\mu}{i} - 1\right) \end{aligned} \qquad [31]$$

Note that the optimal capital structure coefficient (ω) can in principle be negative – which would imply accumulating foreign assets instead of borrowing abroad (as many natural resource exporters now do and even some successful manufactures exporters such as China).

Substituting this result for the optimal capital structure in [31] back into [28] and [29] gives us the optimal debt and output levels respectively

$$\begin{aligned} \hat{D} &= \frac{J}{\mu} = \frac{\hat{K}_2}{\mu}\left(1 + 2\pi\frac{\hat{K}_2}{K_1}\right) = K_1\frac{\omega}{\mu}(1 + \omega\phi) \\ \hat{Y} &= a(K_1 + \hat{K}_2) = aK_1(1 + \omega) \end{aligned} \qquad [32]$$

And we can now derive the optimal debt–output ratio (θ) that maximizes national welfare from [32] as

$$\theta = \frac{\hat{D}}{\hat{Y}} = \frac{\omega(1+2\omega\pi)}{a\mu(1+\omega)} \qquad [33]$$

Clearly θ is increasing in ω, and thus the optimal debt–output ratio will be lowered by an increase in the interest rate (i) as we would expect, but will be *raised* by an increase in the proportion of debt funds allocated to productive investment (μ) or by an increment in the overall productivity of capital (a). It is precisely this longer-run 'developmental' approach to debt management that the larger and stronger emerging market countries (that is, those less under the spell of IMF doctrine) have adopted – and which is patently lacking among the more advanced economies, even where such an approach is clearly necessary for longer-term structural adjustment and employment sustainability as in Southern Europe.

There is thus a strong argument for monetary authorities in small open economies to adopt a counter-cyclical monetary stance in response to capital flows. This would involve real exchange rate targeting, bank credit regulation and an active fiscal stance and can be shown effective in supporting growth and investment (FitzGerald, 2005). In consequence, it is not surprising that most host governments have had to intervene (in many cases disguised as fiscal or regulatory measures) in the market in order to reduce the volatility of capital flows. These controls are now usually based on price measures, particularly taxes, while quantitative instruments have become less common. Open market operations have also proved quite successful in this regard, and can be complemented by the active use of reserve requirements and public sector deposits. Domestic regulatory systems for banks and securities markets (including corporate borrowing abroad) are also important supportive instruments.

1.4 Changing risk aversion, capital market instability and Keynes

Explanations of changes in asset prices as being due to exogenous changes in risk appetite, a Keynesian concept, have been popular in the financial community and have received steadily more attention over the past decade as the nature of capital market crises has become more problematic. The terms 'risk appetite' and 'risk aversion' are used interchangeably, the former being more common in the financial community, and the latter in academic research: increasing risk appetite means declining risk aversion; decreasing risk appetite indicates increasing risk aversion; in other words, one is essentially the inverse of the other.

In marked contrast, the idea that price changes might reflect exogenous changes in risk aversion has not been a popular approach in the mainstream academic literature. Two types of arguments have been made against this approach. The first is methodological. The risk aversion parameter (λ), of course, is derived from the first and second derivatives of the utility function with respect to income: so to allow changes in risk aversion in both directions over comparatively short spaces of time negates an essential axiom – constant preferences – that underpins the whole of neoclassical microeconomics. Further, because the 'new consensus macroeconomics' (for example, Obstfeld and Rogoff, 1996) relies on these same micro-foundations to construct intertemporal behaviour based on the representative agent, then this construct too is fatally undermined.

The arguments for considering risk tolerance as a variable that changes over time in response to recent events, reinforced by endogenous market characteristics related to investor behaviour, is clearly a major difficulty for neoclassical theory not only because it questions microeconomic foundations because also because the proposition that the underlying utility function can be inferred from the financial market via the mean–variance portfolio model is a basic tenet of efficient markets theory (Levy and Markowitz, 1979). The key characteristic of this and similar utility functions is that the parameter λ is constant and fairly near to unity.

The second argument is based on the essential observational equivalence of changes in prices due to changes in asset riskiness and changes due to changing risk aversion; and that the latter cannot be distinguished from the former. However, recent experimental evidence does suggest that state-dependent preferences can lead to changing risk aversion. State-dependent preferences refer to decision making in the face of uncertainty, where the states resolving the uncertainty are of direct concern to the decision maker, and affect his or her evaluation of the consequences. The presence of state-dependent preferences raises fundamental issues concerning the representation of the decision maker's preference relations and, in particular, the definition and interpretation of subjective probabilities (Karni, 2008).

Rabin (2000) points out that within the expected-utility framework, the only explanation for risk aversion is that the utility function for wealth is concave: a person has lower marginal utility for additional wealth when she is wealthy than when she is poor. Rabin (op. cit.) provides a theorem showing that expected-utility theory is an utterly implausible explanation for appreciable risk aversion over modest stakes: within expected-utility theory, for *any* concave utility function, even very little risk aversion over modest stakes implies an absurd degree of risk aversion over large stakes. Indeed, what is empirically the most firmly established feature of risk preferences, *loss aversion*, is a departure from expected-utility theory that provides a direct explanation for modest-scale risk aversion. Loss aversion in this context means that people are significantly more averse to losses relative to the status quo than they are attracted by gains, and more generally that people's utilities are determined by *changes* in wealth rather than absolute levels (Kahneman and Tversky, 1979).

On the second empirical point, the form (rather than the parameters or stability) of the standard utility function does not correspond well to the real world – at least that of finance. For instance, Siegmann (2003) takes both a traditional risk measure and a downside risk measure and shows that they will give very different portfolio outcomes depending upon the initial conditions. His example is that many UK defined benefit pension funds base their investment strategy on asset-capital management (ACM) which borrows techniques from operations research in order to address the fact that pension funds cannot suffer a huge loss (given their fixed obligations to pensioners) even when they frequently make small amounts of money on their investments.

As Misina (2003) points out, operational measures of risk appetite are based on the assumption that changes in asset prices can in practice be decomposed into a part that can be attributed to changes in riskiness and a part attributable to changes in risk aversion, and that some quantitative measure can capture these effects in isolation. Indices of this type index are widely used in the financial community, and are based on rank correlation between assets riskiness and excess returns. Exogenous changes in risk aversion have been used to explain the financial crises of the late 1990s in foreign exchange markets and to elucidate the mechanisms that lead to financial contagion (Kumar and Persaud, 2002).

Last but not least, the incentives faced by fund managers themselves (such as quarterly performance bonuses based on performance relative to the industry average) are widely considered to exacerbate herding behaviour. Herding can be attributed to: first, payoff externalities where payoff to an agent adopting an action is positively related to the number of agents adopting the same action; second, principal–agent considerations such that a manager, in order to maintain or gain reputation when markets are imperfectly informed, may prefer either to 'hide in the herd' to avoid evaluation or 'ride the herd' in order to improve reputation; and third, information cascades where later agents, inferring information from the actions of prior agents, optimally decide to ignore their own information (Devenow and Welch, 1996).

The parallel, of course, is with John Maynard Keynes' well-known view of the stock market as being like a newspaper beauty competition where brokers price shares not on the basis of what they believe their fundamental value to be (that is, future yield discounted to the present), but rather on what they judge everyone else believes their value to be, or even what everybody else would predict the average assessment of value to be (Keynes, 1936, p. 156).

It is thus necessary to construct a practical model of risk tolerance and asymmetry – which the mean variance model misses – through the cycle with risk tolerance rising suddenly in a crisis. Specifically, Kumar and Persaud (2002) argue that most of the indicators used to proxy risk tolerance in the literature confuse the level of risk itself with risk tolerance: asset prices (or yield spreads) are in practice a function of both underlying risk and risk tolerance, this latter containing structural components (the underlying utility function and financial market structure) and a time-varying element reflecting shorter-term factors such as so-called 'wake-up calls'. This formulation has the attractive property that changes in risk tolerance have a greater impact on the price of more risky assets, and thus help explain the magnified effects on international capital markets discussed above. The 'wake-up calls' in turn are related to the fact that the market tends to move as a whole due not so much to changing information about a particular asset, as to changing perceptions about how asset information is to be *interpreted.*

Kumar and Persaud (2002) consider a situation where the interest rate spread (s) in Equation [14] above is normally distributed with mean $\bar{s}$ and variance (σ^2), where risk aversion λ is known. The investor's utility (U) of a given portfolio position (W) is given by

$$U = W\left\{E(\bar{s}) - \frac{\lambda}{2}var(s)\right\} \qquad [34]$$

Assuming that investors are already at their efficient portfolio position, then the first order condition for the optimum is given by

$$\bar{s} - \lambda\sigma^2 = 0 \qquad [35]$$

Thus not only does real risk (σ) or 'fundamentals' affect the spread, but so does exogenous change in investor risk tolerance/aversion (λ). Empirically, Kumar and Persaud (2002) estimate risk appetite by calculating excess returns (the difference between spot rates and forward rates from the previous period) on emerging market currencies over ten years. Their risk appetite index exhibits marked quarterly and annual cycles, and troughs that appear to be correlated with major market discontinuities. Froot and O'Connell (2003) take a similar approach in comparing the equity portfolios of global and local investors, showing that relative risk tolerance of the latter varies widely and cyclically over time.

The most widely used indicator of risk appetite is the Morgan Stanley 'Global Risk Demand Index', which is based on the rank correlation between the riskiness of returns (σ) on a range of asset classes and excess returns (r) : the software for this has actually been patented (Fornasari, 2009). The patent states that the Index specifically distinguishes between the two concepts: 'risk aversion represents willingness to take risk, whereas risk represents the distribution of possible investment outcomes' (p. 1). Figure 1.6 below is taken from the patent application (p. 10): it shows a 'risk demand index' which corresponds in effect to the inverse of risk aversion ($1/\lambda$) used in this paper normalized on the mean for the period. As can be seen, the large variations reflect major international events (both economic and political) that have contagion effects over global markets. They all appear to be asymmetric in the sense that the falls are sudden and the recoveries more gradual taking about a year in each case to regain the mean.

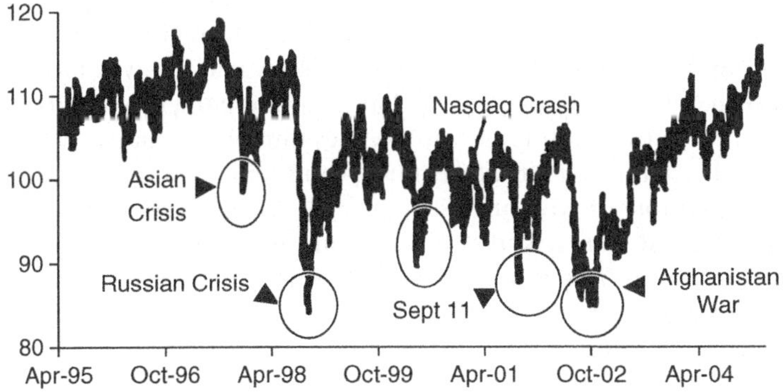

Figure 1.6 Global risk appetite, 1995–2004
Source: Fornasari (2009, p. 10).

This measure of risk aversion or appetite has been used to assess the impact of global capital market instability on developing countries in the highly influential annual IMF *Global Financial Stability Report* (e.g. IMF, 2012a) and is considered to be a major form of external shock (Dungey et al., 2003). These path-dependent variations in the collective risk aversion in reaction to exogenous shocks as demonstrated in practice by the market.

I would go so far as to argue that risk appetite as understood by capital market participants and their regulators – if not by neoclassical economists – is essentially equivalent to what Keynes (1936) meant by 'animal spirits':

> Even apart from the instability due to speculation, there is the instability due to the characteristic of human nature that a large proportion of our positive activities depend on spontaneous optimism rather than mathematical expectations, whether moral or hedonistic or economic. Most, probably, of our decisions to do something positive, the full consequences of which will be drawn out over many days to come, can only be taken as the result of animal spirits – a spontaneous urge to action rather than inaction, and not as the outcome of a weighted average of quantitative benefits multiplied by quantitative probabilities. (pp. 161–2)

This is almost the exact opposite of what his favourite pupil Ramsey (1926) meant when reducing uncertainty to risk by considering empirical choices as if investors were betting, and founded the theory of subjective probability. Starting from the notion that gambling choices are influenced by, or 'reflect', differing degrees of belief, this approach sets out to infer those beliefs from the actual choices. In effect, this reduces uncertainty to risk by allowing that decision making was faced with unknown outcomes but assuming that the underlying probability distributions are known. John Maynard Keynes himself, of course, was at the time of the *Treatise on Probability* (1921) and remained thereafter firmly in the tradition of Knight (1921, p. 233) in distinguishing between measurable risk (or 'risk proper') and un-measurable uncertainty (or 'true uncertainty') as fundamentally distinct concepts in theory and practice (Rosser, 2001).

Mainstream economics, unfortunately, subsequently adopted the Ramsey notion – as indeed it did his other two brilliant insights into taxation and intertemporal macroeconomics (FitzGerald 2012). Following Arrow (1951) towards the merging of uncertainty and randomness, then not only does uncertainty become a subcategory of (measurable) risk but also the economist can logically generate a decision procedure based on empirical observation. Ideally, such observation could discover regularities similar to the known mathematical properties of random physical systems such as Brownian motion. But on financial markets investors *are already* betting and react to uncertainty in a path-dependent manner, so we cannot state that because they make bets they are reducing uncertainty to risk. Rather the opposite: uncertainty influences their bets and allows risk aversion to be inferred from the *time-varying* price premium paid for differential risk across the *same* assets.

Although the concept of uncertainty is used (particularly in relation to interest rates and consumption and investment decisions) in the Keynes's (1936) *General Theory*, it is not directly explained. Moreover, it is uncertainty not just about future events, but also about the opinion of the market:

> There is, moreover, a further ground for liquidity-preference which results from the existence of uncertainty as to the future of the rate of interest, provided that there is an organised market for dealing in debts. For different people will estimate the prospects differently and anyone who differs from the predominant opinion as expressed in market quotations may have a good reason for keeping liquid resources in order to profit, if he is right, from its turning out in due course that the [expected present value of future debt options] were in a mistaken relationship to one another (Keynes, 1936, p. 95)

However Keynes (1937) reaffirms in his earlier belief a year later his 'General Theory of Employment' (Keynes, 1936):

> By, uncertain knowledge, let me explain, I do not mean merely to distinguish what is known for certain what is only probable. The game of roulette is not subject, in this sense, to uncertainty; nor is the prospect of a Victory bond being drawn. Or, again, the expectation of life is only slightly uncertain. Even the weather is only moderately uncertain. The sense in which I am using the term is that in which the prospect of a European war is uncertain, or the price of copper and the rate of interest twenty years hence, or the obsolescence of a new invention, or the position of private wealth owners in the social system in 1970. About these matters there is no scientific basis on which to form any calculable probability whatever. We simply do not know. Nevertheless, the necessity for action and for

> decision compels us as practical men to do our best to overlook this awkward fact and to behave exactly as we should if we had behind us a good Benthamite calculation of a series of prospective advantages and disadvantages, each multiplied by its appropriate probability, waiting to be summed. (pp. 213–14)

It is true, as Dow and Dow (2011) point out, that the term 'animal spirits' has returned to policy and public discourse in a way different than that used by Keynes (1936) himself: the new behavioural economics literature uses the term to refer to a range of behaviour which falls outside what is understood as rational in neoclassical utility maximisation. This treatment follows from the mainstream dichotomisation between rationality and irrationality, and is fundamentally incorrect. I would agree with this appreciation, because in the context of the discussion of financial market behaviour in this paper, it is clear that individual investors are behaving rationally, even though the aggregate outcome in terms of the asset bubbles, international instability and unemployment and poverty is socially irrational.

Unfortunately, Keynes (1936) only uses the term 'animal spirits' three times, in Chapter 12 of *The General Theory,* which deals with the decision by entrepreneurs to invest in real capital:

> Most, probably, of our decisions to do something positive, the full consequences of which will be drawn out over many days to come, can only be taken as a result of animal spirits – of a spontaneous urge to action rather than inaction, and not as the outcome of a weighted average of quantitative benefits multiplied by quantitative probabilities. ... Thus if the animal spirits are dimmed and the spontaneous optimism falters, leaving us to depend on nothing but a mathematical expectation, enterprise will fade and die; – though fears of loss may have a basis no more reasonable than hopes of profit had before. ... But individual initiative will only be adequate when reasonable calculation is supplemented and supported by animal spirits, so that the thought of ultimate loss which often overtakes pioneers, as experience undoubtedly tells us and them, is put aside as a healthy man puts aside the expectation of death. (pp. 161–2)

Dow and Dow (2011) argue that in consequence animal spirits refer to an innate capacity or instinct or disposition of the entrepreneurs who characterized 'old-fashioned capitalism'. As the key element in the investment decision, therefore, animal spirits were central to Keynes's theory of effective demand and his identification of underemployment equilibrium as the norm. However, they claim that animal spirits was the name Keynes gave to the psychological urge to action which explained decisions being taken in spite of uncertainty. In other words, animal spirits were neither rational nor irrational, and thus beyond analysis. However, unlike Dow and Dow (2011), I would suggest that Keynes (1936) did not mean – or did not mainly mean at least – by this concept the sociological or historical propensity to invest of a particular national bourgeoisie, which leads them to be sufficiently optimistic about future returns to overcome uncertainty. This characteristic seems to correspond rather more to what his mentor Alfred Marshall termed 'initiative' (Marshall, 1919). Animal spirits for Keynes are explicitly volatile and implicitly observable, and thus should be expressed in modern technical terms by a variable that reflects the balance between uncertain (future) gains and certain (present) costs. As his conceptual point of reference in the practical world was obviously finance, then shifting risk aversion is probably closer to what Keynes was really thinking about.

What this in turn implies is that what *is* radical about Keynes's concept of animal spirits is that it essentially undermines the basis of neoclassical utility theory: that is, by implication the path-dependent variation of risk aversion means that the utility function itself cannot be taken as stable and exogenous to the market. Moreover, we understand little more than in Keynes's (1936) day about *how* information is actually used by fund managers in their investment decisions. In particular, perceptions of risk cannot reliably be based on econometric analysis of past trends, due to both the lack of data and the persistence of structural breaks. In terms of the psychology of decision making 'people evaluate the probability of events by the degree to which these events are representative of the relevant model or process' and perceptions of risk under circumstances that are difficult to imagine or have not been experienced before are systematically underestimated, while by extension the probability of recurrence of recent major events (particularly if themselves unexpected) is overestimated (Kahneman et al. 1982, p. 97).

A possible approach in the Keynesian tradition to the sudden shifts in risk tolerance that are the topic of this section might well be to adapt De Grauwe's (1996) model of the 'band of agnosticism' in exchange rates within which demand is stable, but once breached leads to large demand shifts. This reflects 'rational behaviour in an uncertain world' (pp. 181–206). He argues that 'the idea that economic agents compute a future exchange rate based on a model they believe in, then telescope it back into the present, is of little use in a world where economic agents have great difficulty in working out what the true model of the world is' (op. cit., p. 189). Further, 'the band of agnosticism is also a breeding ground for fads which, in the absence of credible alternatives, are elevated to important theories' (op. cit., p. 202) so that 'movements of real exchange rates are, within certain bounds, inexplicable' (op. cit., p. 209). In short, investor uncertainty is about models rather than information – about how to use the data available rather than the data itself.

In relation to the topic of this chapter, this approach to uncertainty in international finance means that the public institutions required for stability are those that can reduce risk aversion: both the level, so that poor countries, new technologies and small firms can gain access to capital markets; and, above all, its volatility for the reasons discussed here. Where the future is uncertain, institutions that are bound by fixed rules – such as central banks with rigid inflation targets – are actually counterproductive: in the best case their interventions become pro-cyclical; in the worst case their inaction in crises causes even more uncertainty. Coping with uncertainty (not eliminating it or reducing it to measurable risk) means having institutions that markets will trust to intervene on a discretionary basis on behalf of the general good when unforeseen circumstances occur as they certainly will. This is, of course, not a new point, as Keynes himself considered that public institutions provided a mechanism for actively promoting public-spirited behaviour, which would address the consequences of uncertainty in the economy and in society, albeit on the basis of uncertain knowledge (Dow, 2013).

1.5 Concluding remarks

There are three central policy conclusions that can be drawn from this chapter: (i) that uncertainty is a key determinant of macro asset/liability balances, whose adjustment causes instability; that this uncertainty is expressed in changing risk aversion; and that the function of international *institutions is to reduce asset uncertainty as a public good;* (ii) that therefore prudential macro-regulation (building on bailouts and reserve management) requires bank balance sheet socialisation so as to restore the social function of banks to convert liquid liabilities to illiquid fixed assets; even though profit incentives *and* regulatory prudence work against this; and (iii) that from hard experience on the one hand and less devotion to orthodox economics on the other, developing countries have much to teach developed ones in terms of macroeconomic management in an unregulated global economy. The present volume is concerned with developments in economic policy as well as theory, which has been the main thrust of this chapter, so these conclusions address international financial policy issues – albeit in a tentative fashion because events are unfolding by the day and specific recommendations are almost certain to be outdated by the time of publication.

What little recent progress there is in international financial regulation has been through the Basel III framework, which is explicitly designed to strengthen systemically important banks (SIBs) by reducing their risk taking and increasing their ratio of equity to loans (Basel Committee on Banking Supervision, 2012). But there is little cross-border coordination of these efforts, despite the general recognition that capital market instability is a global issue, and the clear evidence gathered by the Bank of International Settlements (BIS) that on a country-by-country basis, 'monetary and financial regimes failed to restrain the build-up of unsustainable credit and asset price booms' (Borio and Disyatat, 2011, p. 1).

Gallagher (2012) traces the history of governing global capital flows and presents a useful political economy framework for understanding the three distinct eras in the modern governance of global capital. The framework emphasizes how power, interests, ideas, and institutions interact to shape each era in different combinations to yield different outcomes. He argues that what used to be a regime of 'cooperative decentralization' has become a patchwork of overlapping and inconsistent governance structures that pose significant challenges to nations attempting to regulate global capital flows for stability and growth.

Despite this evidence, the G20 debate still focuses on 'global current account imbalances' and, by implication, on trade disequilibria rather than capital account shocks, and regards exchange rate movements as related to trade competitiveness rather than to asset price volatility. Clearly, there is a relationship between the two sides of the balance of payments, and, in particular, persistent current account deficits (surpluses) will inevitably lead to unsustainable external sovereign liability (asset) positions in the long run – as Ferreiro, Peinado and Serrano (2013) point out in this volume. None the less, the volatility of capital flows is far greater than that of trade flows and it is the national *balance sheet* instability that these cause, with consequent impacts on domestic credit, output and employment, that is the driver of financial crises (Borio and Disyatat, 2011).

There is little disagreement that the volatility of capital flows is indeed a major issue. Dell'Ariccia (2012), in a report for the IMF Executive Board, assesses the effectiveness of macroeconomic and macroprudential policies – such as capital and liquidity requirements, limits on asset concentration and loan eligibility criteria – in reducing the risk of a crisis after credit booms or, at least, limiting its consequences. He argues that it is difficult to tell 'bad' from 'good' booms in real time. He suggests that 'good' booms can lead to financial deepening but that 'bad' booms tend to be larger and last longer (roughly half of the booms of more than six years end up in a crisis). However, Dell'Ariccia (op. cit.) finds that fiscal consolidation during the boom years can help create fiscal room to support the financial sector or stimulate the economy if and when a bust arrives; while macro-prudential tools have at times proven effective in containing booms, and more often in limiting the consequences of busts, thanks to the buffers they helped to build.

While monetary policy is, in principle, held by most economists to be the natural lever to contain a credit boom, this chapter has tried to show in practice the integrated global capital market (and the related concerns of interest rate determination, credit channel effects and exchange rate volatility) severely limit – if not eliminate – its effectiveness in small open economies, whether developed or developing. In addition, fiscal overhang in the form of large debt burdens or a combination of inflexible statutory commitment to expenditures combined with political resistance to progressive tax reform renders fiscal policy almost powerless to either halt a boom or take effective counter-cyclical action beyond the very short term after a bust.

At the global level, as the IMF (2011b) explains, the international regulatory and supervisory architecture is complex, not legally binding on its own, and its implementation is up to national authorities. Moreover this architecture is itself presently in a state of flux as major reforms prompted by the crisis are being decided. In addition to the Group of Twenty (G20), the Financial Stability Board (FSB) plays an important coordinating role for national regulation and supervision policies; while the Bank of International Settlements (BIS) coordinates central banks. The FSB comprises high-level officials from central banks, regulators, and treasuries from 24 jurisdictions and the European Central Bank (ECB) and EU, six international standard-setting, regulatory, and central banking bodies, and four international financial institutions – including the IMF. The FSB coordinates the international work of national financial authorities and international standard setters in regulation and supervision. BIS membership comprises 58 central banks and hosts regular meetings of central bank heads and other officials to discuss a variety of issues of interest to the central banking and regulatory community; while also serving as a 'bank for central banks'.

None the less, public intervention – by the IMF itself or by a consortium of G3 central banks – could do a great deal to reduce the externality caused by fluctuating G3 demand for emerging market assets. I do not wish to suggest that fundamentals are unimportant; but which fundamentals are considered relevant and in what way depend more upon the view of home investors than on the actions of host governments. On a parallel with traditional central bank intervention in advanced economies, such a consortium could conduct open market operations in these bonds in order to stabilize their price, and by acting as 'market makers' would encourage more home investors to enter the market. In particular, pension funds could benefit far more than they do at present from the high yields on these assets over the long run. It is of interest in this context that the Asian central banks are engaged in building a joint system of this kind based on their foreign exchange reserves built up as a crude insurance against financial crisis; but this does not address the root cause of asset demand instability.

Such a consortium would not be a modern version of Keynes' International Clearing Union because his (and at least initially that of His Majesty's Treasury) aim was to regulate trade between nations and address both currency instability and the lack of global liquidity (Keynes, 1942–3; 1969). The fixed exchange rates (for international trade at least) against 'bancor' and centralisation of surpluses in the ICU; the taxing of these to incentivize import demand and finance deficit countries; and the currency depreciation of deficit nations against bancor to encourage their trade adjustment; were all concerned with *current* account imbalances (Piffaretti, 2009). However, as this chapter has shown, global instability is a matter of gross capital flows, and these require a different approach. What is more, trade issues are now negotiated within the WTO, while international payments integrity is underpinned by the Bank of International Settlements. Moreover, international liquidity *per se* is not the current issue it was during the post-Second World War 'dollar shortage'. In other words, there is no lack of international money as such, but rather an unwillingness to lend due to risk aversion and debt default expectations on the one hand, and a lack of effective prudential regulation of international banks on the other.

None the less, even though international capital market shock transmission has clearly been identified by the IMF a central problem of the world economy, Dell'Ariccia (2012) points out that 'circumvention has often been a major issue, underscoring the importance of careful design, coordination with other policies (including across borders), and close supervision to ensure the efficacy of these tools, there are no proposals under serious discussion in the G20 about how international coordination might be achieved' (p. 4). This may well be, of course, because such 'circumvention' takes place through 'offshore' financial centres where the international assets (and liabilities) of major investors are held – which in turn would require the thorny issue of income tax evasion to be addressed (FitzGerald, 2012). The full inclusion of all large financial assets under a global system of prudential regulation and taxation would thus have enormous advantages in terms of both global macroeconomic stability (and thus growth and employment) stability on the one hand; and in terms of a substantial increase in fiscal resources available not only for counter-cyclical demand management but also for radical reduction in the income inequalities that have accompanied global financial liberalization on the other hand.

Finally, in view of the distributive consequences of asset price instability and unstable credit flows, it would be necessary to protect not only vulnerable small open economies, but also vulnerable households and firms. This would involve the insulation of long-term household financial services (particularly mortgages and pensions) – which also provide finance to the small firms that are the basis of most employment in both developed and developing countries – from short-term speculative forces. In other words, a return is needed to the segmented financial markets which characterised all capitalist economies before the radical liberalisation of the last three decades.

Notes

1. Previous versions of this paper were presented at conferences and workshops in Oxford, Cambridge, Helsinki, Paris and finally Bilbao. At these meetings a series of very useful comments were made which nudged me away from the original empirical focus on international regulatory and macrofinancial policy towards explaining the underlying analytical basis for my interpretation of the issues. The result is still an incomplete argument, especially the somewhat speculative remarks towards the end, but may be seen by readers – particularly those of a Keynesian persuasion – as having some interest. I would like to give special thanks to Philip Arestis and Malcolm Sawyer, the editors of the present volume, for their patient editing of this paper, which has served to increase its clarity – or at least to reduce its opacity.

References

Arrow, K.J. (1951) 'Alternative Approaches to the Theory of Choice in Risk-Taking Situations', *Econometrica* 19(4): 401–37.

Babilis, S. and FitzGerald, V. (2005) 'Risk Tolerance, Home Bias and the Unstable Demand for Emerging Market Assets', *International Review of Applied Economics* volume 19(4): 459–76.

Basel Committee on Banking Supervision (2012) *Progress report on Basel III implementation,* Basel: Bank of International Settlements.

Borio, C and P. Disyatat (2011) 'Global Imbalances and the Financial Crisis: Link or No Link?', *BIS Working Paper No 346,* Basel: Bank of International Settlements.

De Grauwe, P. (1996) *International Money*, 2nd edn, Oxford: Oxford University Press.

Dell'Ariccia, G. and others (2012) 'Policies for Macrofinancial Stability: How to Deal with Credit Booms', IMF Staff Discussion Note SDN/12/06, Washington, DC: International Monetary Fund.

Devenow, A. and I Welch (1996) 'Rational Herding in Financial Economics', *European Economic Review,* 40: 603–15.

Dow, S. (2013) 'Keynes on Knowledge, Expectations and Rationality', in R. Frydman and E. S. Phelps (eds), *Rethinking Expectations: the Way Forward for Macroeconomics,* Princeton, NJ: Princeton University Press.

Dow, A and S. Dow (2011) 'Animal Spirits Revisited', *Capitalism and Society,* 6(1): 1–23.

Dungey, M., R. Fry. B. Gonzalez and V. Martin (2003) 'Characterizing Global Investors' Risk Appetite for Emerging Market Debt During Financial Crises', *IMF Working Paper WP/03/251,* Washington, DC: International Monetary Fund.

Ferreiro, J., P. Peinado and F. Serrano (2013) 'The Global Imbalances as Constraints to the Economic Activity in the World Economy', this volume.

FitzGerald, V. (2005) 'Policy Issues in Market Based and Non-Market Based Measures to Control the Volatility of Portfolio Investment', in C.J. Green, C. Kirkpatrick and V. Murinde (eds) *Finance and Development: Surveys of Theory, Evidence and Policy,* Aldershot: Edward Elgar, pp. 241–74.

FitzGerald, V. (2007) 'International Risk Tolerance, Capital Market Failure and Capital Flows to Emerging Markets', in G. Mavrotas and A. Shorrocks (eds), *Advancing Development: Core Themes in Global Economics,* Basingstoke: Palgrave Macmillan for UNU/WIDER.

FitzGerald, V. (2008) 'Stabilization Policy and Structural Adjustment', Chapter 56 in A.K. Dutt and J. Ros (eds), *International Handbook of Development Economics,* Cheltenham and Northampton MA: Edward Elgar.

FitzGerald, V. (2012) 'Global Capital Markets, Direct Taxation and the Redistribution of Income', *International Review of Applied Economics,* 26(2): 241–52.

Folkerts-Landau, D. (1985) 'The Changing Role of International Bank Lending in Development Finance', *IMF Staff Papers,* 32: 317–63.

Fornasari, F. (2009) 'Global Risk Demand Index', Patent No US7,617.143 B2, Alexandria, VA: US Patent Office.

Froot, K.A. and P.G.J. O'Connell (2003) 'The Risk Tolerance of International Investors', *NBER Working Paper No 10157,* Chicago: National Bureau for Economic Research.

G20 (2009) 'Enhancing Sound Regulation and Strengthening Transparency', G20 Working Group 1 Final Report. Available at www.g20.org.

Gallagher, K. (2012) 'The Global Governance of Capital Flows: New Opportunities, Enduring Challenges', *PERI Working Papers Series No 283,* Amherst, MA: University of Massachussets.

ICB ('Vickers Report') (2012) *Final Report and Recommendations,* London: Independent Commission on Banking.
IMF (2011a) *Recent Experiences in Managing Capital Inflows – Cross-Cutting Themes and Possible Framework,* Washington, DC: International Monetary Fund.
IMF (2011b) *The Multilateral Aspects of Policies Affecting Capital Flows,* Washington, DC: International Monetary Fund.
IMF (2011c) *Global Financial Stability Report*: Chapter 2 'Long Term Investors and Their Asset Allocations – Where Are They Now?'. Washington, DC: International Monetary Fund.
IMF (2012a) *Global Financial Stability Report,* Washington, DC: International Monetary Fund.
IMF (2012b) *World Economic Outlook,* Washington, DC: International Monetary Fund.
IMF (2012c) *Liberalizing Capital Flows and Managing Outflows,* Washington, DC: International Monetary Fund.
Kahneman, D., and A. Tversky (1979) 'Prospect Theory: An Analysis of Decision Under Risk', *Econometrica,* 47 (March): 263–91.
Kahneman, D., P. Slovic and A. Tversky (1982) *Judgement Under Uncertainty: Heuristics and Biases,* Cambridge: Cambridge University Press.
Karni, E. (2008) 'State-dependent Preferences', *The New Palgrave Dictionary of Economics,* 2nd edition, Basingstoke: Palgrave Macmillan.
Keynes, J.M. (1921) *A Treatise on Probability,* London: Macmillan.
Keynes, J.M. (1936) *The General Theory of Employment, Interest and Money,* London: Macmillan.
Keynes. J.M. (1937) 'The General Theory of Employment', *Quarterly Journal of Economics,* 51: 209–23.
Keynes, J.M. (1942–3; 1969) 'Proposals for an International Clearing Union' reproduced in J.K. Horsefield (ed.) *The International Monetary Fund 1945–65,* Vol. III. Washington, DC: International Monetary Fund, pp. 3–36.
Klein, R.W. and V.S. Bawa (1977) 'The Effect of Limited Information and Estimation Risk On Optimal Portfolio Diversification', *Journal of Financial Economics* 5: 89–111.
Knight, F.H. (1921) *Risk, Uncertainty, and Profit,* Boston and New York: Houghton Mifflin.
Kumar, S.M. and A. Persaud (2002) 'Pure Contagion and Investors' Shifting Risk Appetite: Analytical Issues and Empirical Evidence', *International Finance,* 5: 401–26.
Levy, H. and H.M. Markowitz (1979) 'Approximating Expected Utility by a Function of Mean and Variance', *American Economic Review,* 69: 308–17.
Lewis, K. (1999) 'Trying to Explain Home Bias in Equities and Consumption', *Journal of Economic Literature,* 37: 571–608.
Marshall, A. (1919) *Industry and Trade,* London: Macmillan
Misina, M. (2003) 'What Does the Risk-Appetite Index Measure?', *Working Paper 2003-23,* Ottowa: Bank of Canada.
Milesi-Ferretti, G.M., S. Strobbe and N. Tamiresa, (2011) 'Bilateral Financial Linkages and Global Imbalances: a View on The Eve of the Financial Crisis,' *IMF Working Papers 10/257,* Washington DC: International Monetary Fund.
Obstfeld, M. and K. Rogoff (1996) *Foundations of International Macroeconomics,* Boston: MIT Press.

Perotti, R. (2011) 'The "Austerity Myth": Gain Without Pain?', *BIS Working Paper No 362*, Basel: Bank of International Settlements.

Piffaretti, N. (2009) 'Reshaping the International Monetary Architecture: Lessons from Keynes' Plan', *Policy Research Working Paper WPS5034*, Washington, DC: World Bank.

Rabin, M. (2000) 'Risk Aversion and Expected-Utility Theory: A Calibration Theorem', *Econometrica*, 68(5): 1281–92.

Ramsey, F.P. (1926) 'Truth and Probability', published 1931 in R.B. Braithwaite (ed.), *Foundations of Mathematics and other Logical Essays 1931*, London: Kegan, Paul, pp. 156–68.

Reinhart, C. and K. Rogoff (2009) *This Time is Different: Eight Centuries of Financial Folly*, Princeton: Princeton University Press.

Rosser, J.B. (2001) 'Alternative Keynesian and Post Keynesian Perspectives on Uncertainty and Expectations', *Journal of Post Keynesian Economics*, 23(4): 545–66.

Siegmann, A. (2003) 'Shortfall Allowed: Loss Aversion and Habit Formation', *WO Research Memoranda*, no. 741, Netherlands Central Bank (DNB).

2

A Progressive International Monetary System: Growth-Enhancing, Speculation-Reducing and Cross-Country Equity

John Weeks
School of Oriental and African Studies, University of London

2.1 Introduction

After the government of the United States unilaterally ended the post-war monetary system of fixed exchange rates and capital controls in 1970, discussion waxed and waned over what should replace it. The various ad hoc responses have left the world in a global system strong on instability. This instability results from the combination of capital account deregulation and so-called flexible exchange rates. This combination brought on the domination of global capital flows over global trade. One of the great ironies of the age of 'globalization' is that as global trade grew rapidly its global importance declined.

This paper argues, as Keynes did, that the central focus of international monetary reform should be on fostering growth, not price stability. This focus implies the complete transformation of the International Monetary Fund, which since its creation has taken an approach to the cross-country adjustment of imbalances that is essentially demand depressing. This pro-cyclical approach to international adjustment realized is latent potential to undermine global growth in the euro crisis of the 2010s.

Fostering strong growth requires tight control over speculative activity, which represents the financial sector's contribution to pro-cyclical instability. This control necessitates a suitable international currency of account and store of value. Closely related to the global currency, the international economy needs a new arrangement for stable exchange rates that ends the current dysfunction of excessive reserve accumulation. Finally, a progressive global system would incorporate a mechanism for the governments of deficit countries to adjust their imbalances without relying on the putative goodwill of the governments of large, surplus countries.

The global financial crisis of the 2000s represented the bitter fruit of decades of gathering instability in world markets. This growing instability resulted from successive waves of financial deregulation by national governments in the United States and Europe. The long-term global instability results from the combination of removing national restrictions on financial institutions and, earlier, the end of internationally managed exchanged rates. These policy changes allowed the dominance of finance over production, transforming the focus of profit making from production to speculation. Therefore, at the top of the international reform agenda should be the reassertion of public control of financial markets, national and global.

The paper begins with a discussion of the major aspects of the dysfunctionality of global markets. I then present the framework for the analysis of so-called open economies. Especially important are the dichotomy between 'fixed' and 'flexible' exchange rates and the Mundell–Fleming adjustment process. This discussion leads to the conclusion that exchange rate flexibility is positively correlated with internal and external instability.

If nominal exchange rate variability generates macro instability, then rational macro policy requires that exchange rates be purposefully managed to reduce nominal variations. This inference immediately encounters a major policy challenge. If rational policy requires exchange rate management, what is the appropriate mechanism to achieve and maintain external balance that does not foster competitive currency devaluations? The question can be restated as: what is the 'new Bretton Woods' system that could facilitate both strong growth and adjustment for external balance? The negative part of the answer is provided by the European Union. The combination of growth and external balance cannot be achieved through a punitive adjustment regime that imposes austerity upon countries with external deficits. Adjustment, both internal and external, should occur within a counter-cyclical policy framework at the national and global levels.

The counter-cyclical policy framework comprises a set of complementary measures, two proposed by Keynes almost seventy years ago. These two are an international banking institution that manages a global currency serving as unit of account and store of value. This institution would replace the International Monetary Fund, and the global unit of account would replace national currencies as international reserves. This framework for a growth-fostering international monetary system requires that the global currency be combined with sanctions that place the primary adjustment responsibility on the governments of countries with current account surpluses. These sanctions would not in themselves be sufficient to eliminate unsustainable current account deficits in all countries. Sanctions on surplus countries should be reinforced by a 'stand-alone' mechanism for adjustment by governments of deficit countries. The key features of this adjustment mechanism would be transitory import restrictions and export subsidies. The global formalization of this 'stand-alone' mechanism implies that the international bank would incorporate functions now assigned to the World Trade Organization.

2.2 International financial dysfunction

2.2.1 Concepts and definitions

It is appropriate to begin by clarifying key terms that are central to my analytical discussion. First, considerable confusion and unnecessary complexity result from the uncritical use of the common dichotomy between 'fixed' and 'flexible' exchange rates. These adjectives are typically used to suggest that across countries exchange rate regimes can be usefully divided between those in which the public authorities formally set a currency rate *vis-à-vis* some major currency, then take whatever steps that are necessary to maintain that rate until unable to continue to do so. This is contrasted to a 'flexible' regime in which the authorities maintain a hands-off approach, leaving the determination of the currency rate to private trading ('the market').

This dichotomy exists only in the imaginary world of neoclassical economics, having no empirical relevance. Some degree of intervention by public authorities characterizes all national currency regimes,[1] as reference to a table at the end of the IMF *Annual Report* verifies (for example, IMF 2007, Appendices, page 10). The suggestion that some currency rates are established through private trading without public intervention is false. The analysis of trade and capital flows that employs the fixed-flexible dichotomy is also false. I shall refer to currencies as 'pegged' rather than 'fixed' or 'flexible', and the peg can be associated with various degrees of discretion and intervention.

Second, the frequently used term 'balance of payments deficit (surplus)' is, strictly speaking, an oxymoron. In its place I use the term 'unsustainable balance of payments'. The terms 'surplus countries' and 'deficit countries' will refer to the current external account. Finally, the term 'adjustment' is used for the process by which the unsustainability of a balance of payments position is reduced. Also when 'Contractionary adjustment' occurs, greater sustainability is achieved through reducing output, and 'expansionary adjustment' describes the opposite process.

2.2.2 Indicators of dysfunction

In order to avoid a repetition of the instability of the 1930s (Arndt, 1963), the Bretton Woods conference at the end of the Second World War established an international exchange rate regime in which the dollar served as the major reserve currency, and the governments of other countries pegged their currencies to it. This arrangement, combined with regulation of capital flows in most countries, severely limited speculation on currencies. As a result, the pegged system implied that governments did not have to hold reserves as a defence against speculative attack. Therefore, the end of the Bretton Woods pegged system, combined with reduction in the regulation of capital flows, led to a trinity of maladies, destabilizing exchange rate speculation, massive short-term capital flows, and excessive accumulation of reserves.

A common belief is that the years since the end of fixed exchange rates and regulated capital flows brought improved economic growth and greater international trade. If this were true it should manifest itself in the performances of the most developed countries, whose governments actively embraced the deregulation agenda. The empirical evidence does not support either improved growth rates or the faster expansion of trade. Figure 2.1a shows GDP growth rates for the World Bank category 'high-income countries', with its three major components, for the European Union, the United States and Japan. For all of these, the fastest growth rate was during the 1960s and the slowest during the 2000s. For the entire forty years there is a slight but statistically significant downward trend in the growth rate for Japan, the European Union and the United States, as well as for the high-income group as a whole. These growth rates suggest at the least that the less regulated post-Bretton Woods international economy did not foster stronger macroeconomic performance.

More striking is the evidence on the growth of trade for the high-income countries. Because for all decades but the 2000s the trade of these countries was overwhelmingly among themselves, implying that export and import growth were approximately the same. Figure 2.1b measures trade growth by exports, beginning with the 1970s because of incomplete data for the previous decade. In all cases the fastest export growth occurred during the 1970s, and the slowest in the 2000s. An enthusiast for global deregulation might object that the decade comparisons are

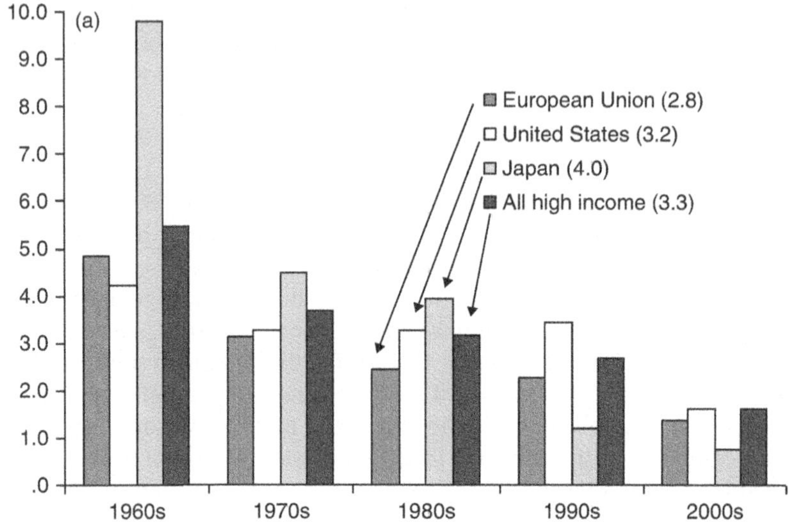

Figure 2.1a GDP growth rates by decade, high-income countries, 1961–2010
Notes: 'Decades' refers to years 1–10, i.e., 1961–1970. 'High income' is the World Bank category. Overall average in parenthesis in legend.
Source: *World Development Indicators (2012).*

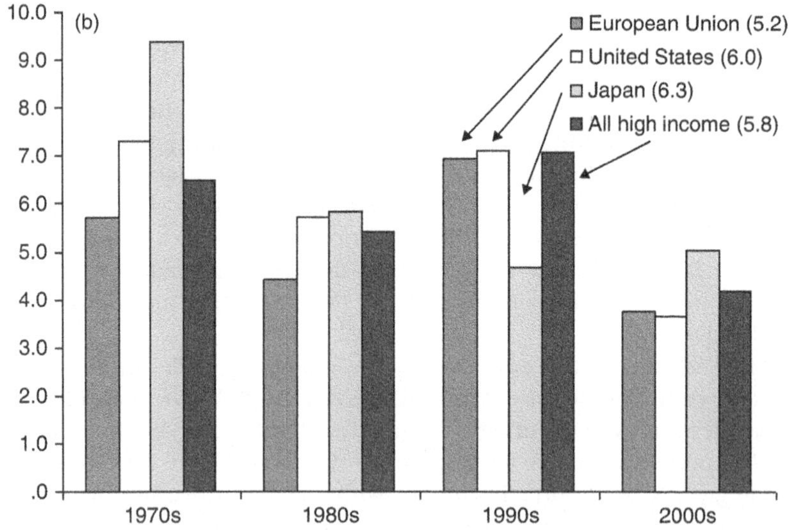

Figure 2.1b Export growth rates by decade, high-income countries, 1961–2010
Notes and source: See Table 2.1a.

inappropriate, because they are distorted by the severe downturn at the end of the 2000s. This objection would be valid if that downturn could be interpreted as an abnormal or random shock to the global economy. However, this interpretation would assume what it sought to prove, that the contraction of the 2000s as well as previous ones were unrelated to the characteristics of the post-Bretton Woods global economy.

Having assessed two major indicators of global economic performance of the real economy, I consider financial flows. Figure 2.2 shows the absolute value of net capital flows across 12 European Union countries for three decades in current and constant prices. The rate of increase was quite literally exponential, an annual average of US$14 billion for the 1990s, $84 billion during the 1990s, and $272 billion in the 2000s. The distribution of these flows indicates the dominance of finance over trade. Of the 12 countries, the one with the largest annual average inflows for the 2000s was Ireland, the smallest with a population less than five million.

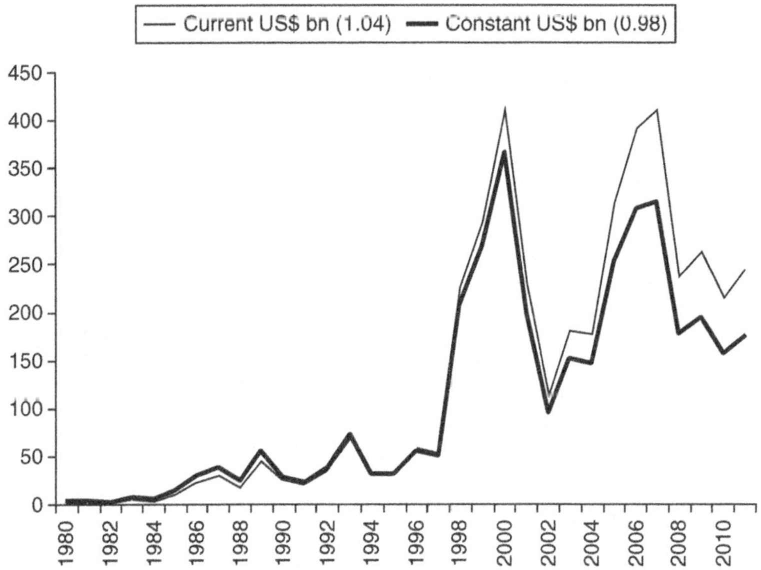

Figure 2.2 Net portfolio flows, 12 European Union countries, 1980–2011 (current & constant prices, US$ billions, absolute value)

Notes: Countries: Austria, Belgium, Denmark, Finland, France, Germany, Ireland, Italy, Portugal, Spain, Sweden, United Kingdom.

Source: IMF, *World Economic Outlook (2011)*, data base.

Figures 2.3a and 2.3b show net private capital flows to developing countries in four regions, also in current and constant prices. As for the European Union countries, the flows are striking for their increase in magnitude and volatility. Deflating by the average price level for the 32 years,[2] the sum of the absolute value of the flows for the four regions was an annual US$8 billion for the 1980s, rising to $39 billion for the 1990s, $58 billion for the 2000s, then US$136 billion for 2010–11. Equally striking are the coefficients of variation, which exceed two for all regions, and are only marginally reduced for three regions by deflation, and increased in the fourth (North African and the Middle East). For individual countries the variation was much larger.

Only the most ideologically blinkered analysis would fail to appreciate the difficulties that large and volatile capital flows present for macroeconomic management. The two most obvious are exchange rate effects and the impact on the domestic monetary base. As discussed in other papers, short-term capital movements destabilize economies

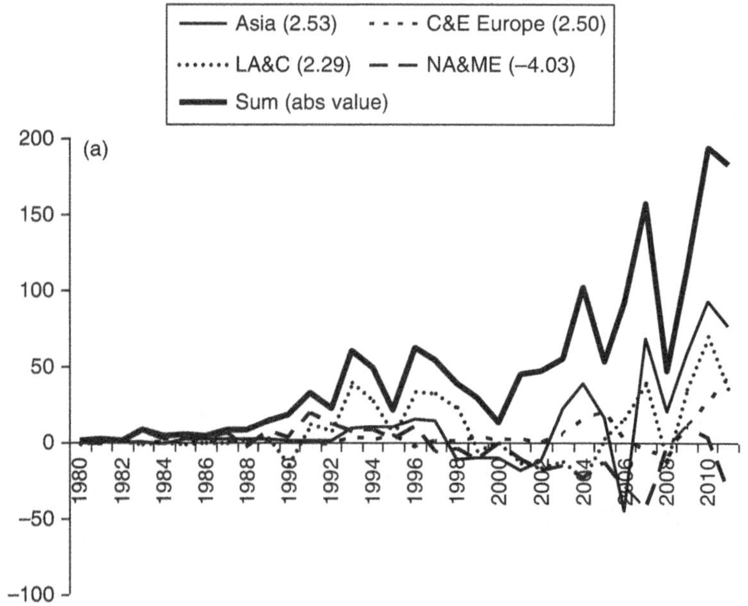

Figure 2.3a Net portfolio capital flows, four developing regions, 1980–2011 (current prices, US$ billion, sum in absolute value)
Notes: Coefficient of variation in parenthesis in legend.
Source: IMF, *World Economic Outlook (2012)*, data base.

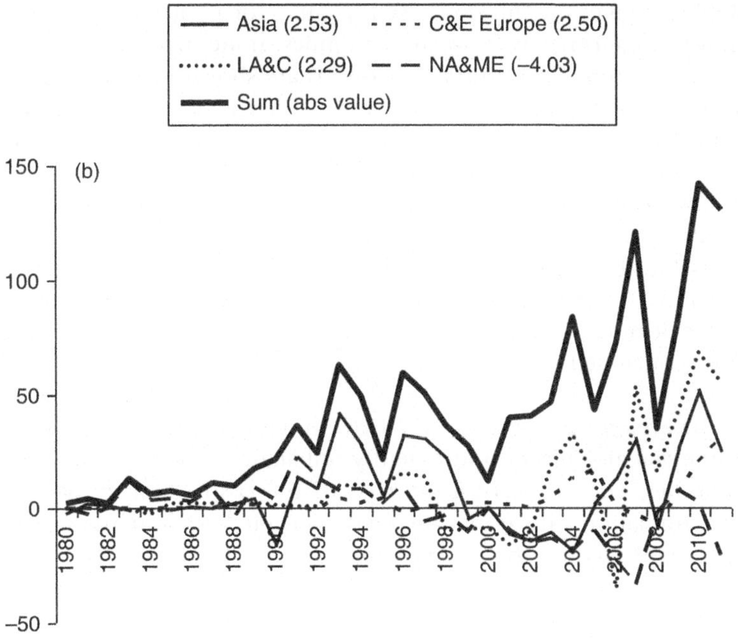

Figure 2.3b Net portfolio capital flows, four developing regions, 1980–2011 (constant prices, US$ billion, sum in absolute value)

Notes: Coefficient of variation in parenthesis in legend. The deflator is the developed country consumer price index, period average.

Source: IMF, *World Economic Outlook (2012)*, data base.

through both inflow and outflow. Inflow can result in exchange rate appreciation that undermines export performance, and outflow can force governments to take emergency measures such as increasing interest rates that are contractionary. Central banks typically attempt to manage the monetary base by sterilizing capital flows. These attempts are unlikely to be effective if the bond market and foreign exchange markets are narrow, which is common in small open economies.[3]

Policymakers in small open economies learned quickly that the large and volatile capital flows, and the exchange rate speculation associated with them, require central banks to hold substantial reserves above what would be implied by short term import requirements (see Fischer, 2001). This 'self-insurance' is a necessary form of market intervention in the absence of capital account regulation. The increase in the hoarding of reserves by central banks has been astonishing.

Table 2.1 gives the thirty-year trend values for 12 developing and four developed countries with open economies, none of which are part of a currency union. The thirty-year trends are shown in Figures 2.4–2.7, divided by region (except for the last, which is developed countries). Of the 16 countries, the trend value for reserves, measured in months of imports, is positive and significant for all but one, Chile. The cross-country thirty-year average of reserve holding is 4.3 months, while the average for 2011 was 50 per cent higher – at 6.3. The most extraordinary case is Brazil, where the central bank held 4.2 months of imports in 2000 and 13.2 months in 2009, an increase of 300 per cent.

After documenting the same trends through the mid-2000s, Rodrik (2006) concluded,

> ...[D]eveloping countries [*sic!* Governments of] have responded to financial globalization in a highly unbalanced and far from optimal manner. They have over-invested in the costly strategy of reserve accumulation and under-invested in capital-account management policies to reduce their short-term foreign liabilities. (p. 12)

Table 2.1 Forex reserves in months of imports and trend, 1981–2010

Country	Months of imports			
	Mean	**2011**	**Trend (%)**	**Significant at**
Argentina	5.5	7.8	2.8	.00
Brazil	5.7	11.9	5.1	.00
Chile	6.0	3.8	–0.1	Non significant
Mexico	2.6	4.2	2.9	.01
Indonesia	4.1	6.6	3.0	.00
Korea, Rep.	4.0	6.6	8.3	.00
Malaysia	4.5	6.1	2.1	.00
Thailand	5.0	9.2	3.2	.00
Egypt	6.1	6.7	6.1	.00
Morocco	4.6	6.7	8.7	.00
South Africa	2.1	4.7	3.6	.00
Zambia	1.6	3.3	3.5	.01
Australia	2.6	4.2	2.9	.00
Canada	4.1	6.6	3.0	.00
Denmark	4.0	6.6	8.3	.00
Sweden	4.5	6.1	2.1	.00
Average	4.2	6.3	4.1	

Notes: Trend is the coefficient from a simple logarithmic regression. The mean is in months of imports.
Source: World Bank, *World Development Indicators* (2012) online database.

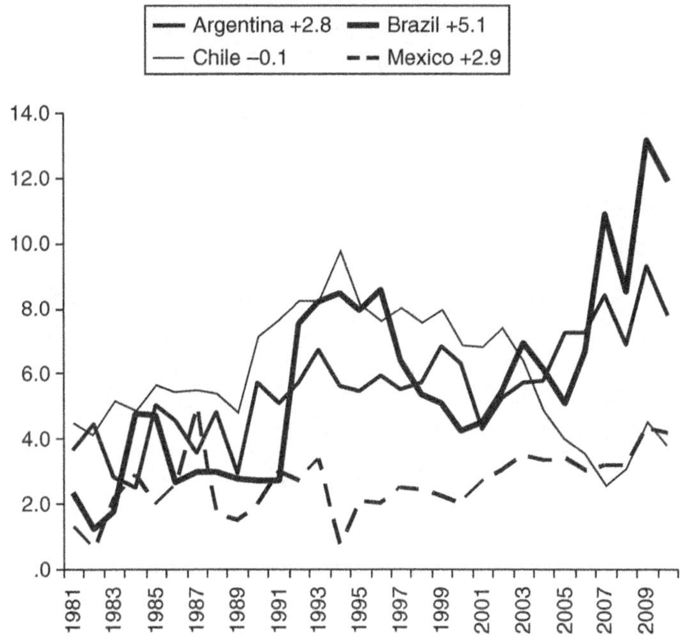

Figure 2.4 Forex reserves in months of imports, four Latin American countries, 1981–2010
Source: *World Development Indicators (2012).*

In addition to the obvious demand-restraining effect of reserve accumulation, holding foreign exchange idle rather than importing capital goods is growth depressing on the supply side. The loss of aggregate demand and wasted resources are unnecessary because the same policy outcome, protection against the volatility of capital flows, could be achieved through an alternative market intervention, capital account regulation. Below I discuss the 'Bancor' system of international monetary regulation, designed by Keynes (1943) in the early 1940s. In that system, capital controls hold a central role, in part to avoid the dysfunction shown in Figures 2.4–2.7.

The ideology of efficient markets successfully diverted attention from these major malfunctions of international money flows. Taken together, the large, volatile capital flows and the reserve hoarding to protect against them represent the dominance of finance over production at the global level. Domestically, this dominance takes the form of a rising share for the financial sector in national income, associated

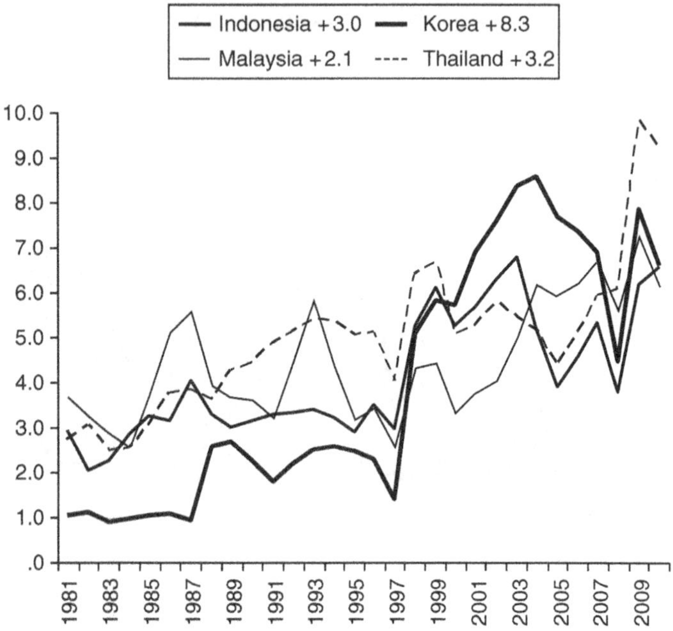

Figure 2.5 Forex reserves in months of imports, four Asian countries, 1981–2010
Source: World Development Indicators (2012).

with a decline in the commodity-producing sectors. The international analogue is the sharp decline in trade relative to money flows. The impact of this dominance of money over trade is the determination of exchange rates by money markets for high- and middle-income countries. As a consequence the exchange rate does not serve as an effective or efficient allocating mechanism between tradables and non-tradables.

2.2.3 Mechanisms of international dysfunction

From a neoclassical perspective the large variation in capital flows shown in Figures 2.2 and 2.3 would not be interpreted as dysfunctional instability, but quite the opposite. In a world of rational agents and efficient markets, cross-border capital flow serves as an equilibrating force. The argument is that unexpected 'shocks' may cause trade and current account imbalances, but these are temporary if governments do not interfere in markets. Relative prices should change, especially but only the nominal exchange rate, provoking an adjustment process to remedy the imbalances. Among countries with national currencies the main

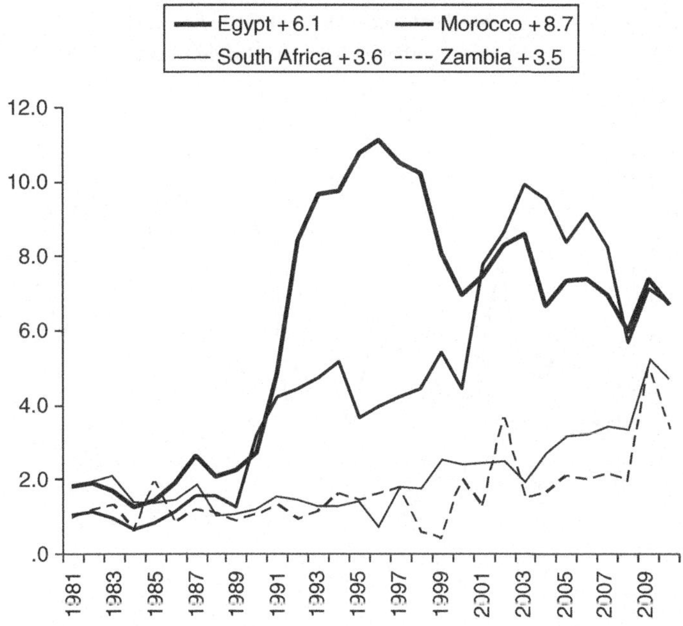

Figure 2.6 Forex reserves in months of imports, four African countries, 1981–2010
Source: *World Development Indicators (2012).*

adjustment mechanism would be the nominal exchange rate that is the relative price of tradable and non-tradable commodities and services.

Among countries using the same currency, most notably the euro zone, the adjustment would be less straightforward, but should be equally effective if markets are efficient. In this case the capital flows would stimulate changes in relative factor prices, thus adjusting the international competitiveness of traded commodities. This adjustment mechanism would be manifested in different inflation rates among countries.

If this line of argument were correct, one would expect that the large capital flows would be associated with less variation in trade and current account balances across countries. To state the matter simply, if capital flows facilitate external balance, then an increase in capital flows should be accompanied by a reduction in external balances across trading partners. This relationship can be empirically in terms of the standard deviation of external balances across countries.

Figure 2.8 shows this statistic for the trade balances of 25 countries over forty years, with the countries selected on the condition that they we market economies during the entire period. These countries

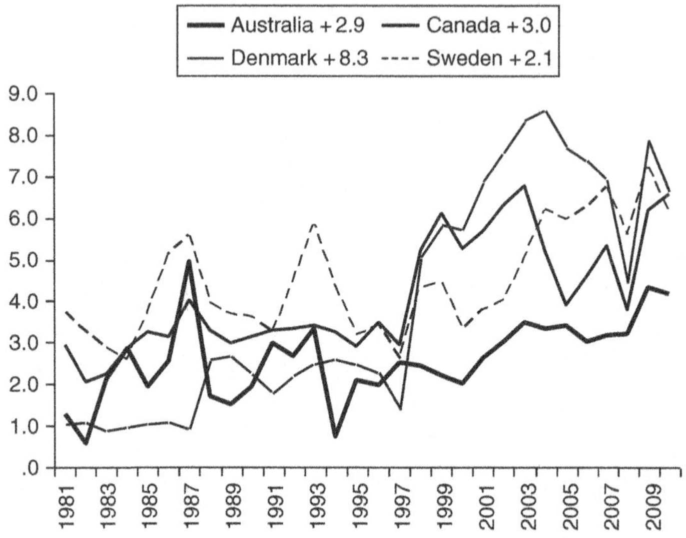

Figure 2.7 Forex reserves in months of imports, four high-income countries, 1981–2010
Source: *World Development Indicators (2012).*

accounted for the vast majority of world trade until the mid-1990s when China became a major importer and exporter. Both a division into subgroups and for the 25 countries together, the statistical result is unambiguously clear: trade balances diverged substantially. The conclusion is especially strong for the ten European Union countries whose trade is overwhelming among themselves, and whose standard deviation rose from about four at the end of the 1980s, to over eight in the 2000s. For the ten middle-income countries, the standard deviation across their trade balances increased from less than three in the mid-1990s to consistently close to eight at the end of the 2000s.

The story for current accounts is even more extreme, as Figure 2.9 makes clear. Across the European Union countries the standard deviation rose continuously from the late 1980s, quadrupling in value. For all 25 countries, a scatter diagram between the standard deviation of current accounts and real capital flows shows a strong positive correlation, and an even stronger correlation for capital flow and the variation in trade balances.[4]

While it is possible that for some countries capital flow has served as a mechanism for the adjustment of external balances, the prima facie

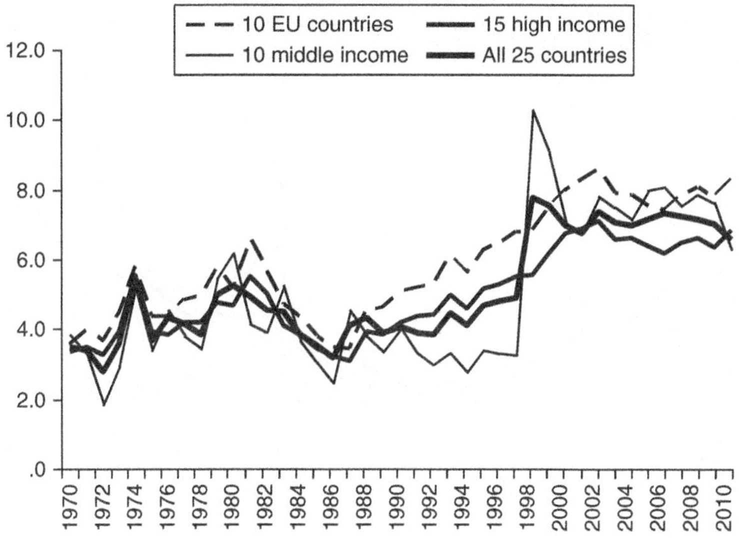

Figure 2.8 Standard deviation across the trade balances of 25 countries, 1970–2010

Notes:

10 EU: France, Germany, Greece, Ireland, Italy, the Netherlands, Portugal, Spain, Sweden, the United Kingdom.

15 high-income: 10 EU plus Australia, Canada, Japan, New Zealand, the United States.

10 middle-income: Argentina, Brazil, Chile, Mexico, India, Indonesia, Rep Korea, Malaysia, Philippines, Thailand.

Source: *World Development Indicators (2012)*.

evidence is to the contrary. Far from contributing to external balance, the substantial increases in flows of portfolio capital have been associated within greater variation in external balances across countries. The explanation for this outcome is not difficult to find. In general trade and current account surpluses result in pressure for nominal exchange rate appreciation. The anticipation of that appreciation induces flows of speculative funds seek a quick return in currency markets. External deficits can generate the opposite, signalling the likelihood of currency depreciation that prompts capital flight.

The central purpose of a rational and equitable international financial system would be to reduce in unregulated currency markets the dysfunctional tendencies that cause instability to reinforce itself. In an earlier era when trade flows had greater importance than financial flows, it was possible for exchange rate adjustment to have limited but substantial success in reducing trade and current account imbalances.

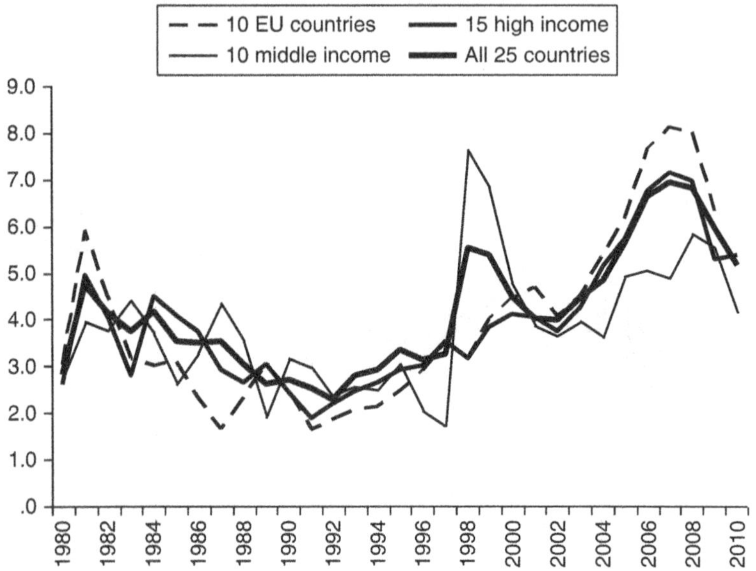

Figure 2.9 Standard deviation across the current accounts of 25 countries, 1980–2010
Notes and source: See Figure 2.8.

In that simpler world of fixed exchange rates and capital controls, devaluation impacted primarily on the relative profitability of tradables and non-tradables. With the deregulation of currency markets, the link between exchange rates and trade became overwhelmed by the interaction between exchange rates and capital flow. The task of international monetary reform can be summarized in a phrase: to re-establish the importance of trade over capital flows, of production over finance at the international level.

2.3 Analytical framework

2.3.1 Price and quantity adjustment

The existing and dysfunctional international monetary system has its analytical foundation in Walrasian general equilibrium theory. This is a *price-determined system* in which general equilibrium necessarily implies full employment, in the absence of private or public price 'distortions'. Within this global full employment the exchange rate is the price that determines the distribution of domestic resources between tradable and non-tradable commodities. This approach to external adjustment cannot be separated from the Walrasian general equilibrium system as a whole.

In this price-determined framework, all markets clear in an instantaneous process. No exchanges occur at prices other than those in the price set which would prevail at full employment (no 'false trading'). Consumers and producers take prices as signals to determine the quantities they buy and sell. It follows that any action by private or public agents to inhibit market adjustment in prices will result in an outcome below full employment. Assuming there to be no private constraints to *instantaneous* price adjustment (for example, no market power by private agents), the full employment equilibrium price set is unique, and all markets are fully developed; it follows that the role for public policy is extremely limited. The price-determined framework implies that fiscal and monetary policies should be neutral and no interventions in the foreign exchange market.

Fiscal policy should not alter the incentives of private agents from making the choices that would yield the general equilibrium price set. This implies that taxes should not affect private agents' decisions between income and leisure, which precludes income taxes. Neither taxes nor expenditures should affect the relative profitability of commodities, implying for the external sector no tariffs, export levies or subsidies. Government should not 'distort' capital markets by competing with private agents for funds, which means no funding of the fiscal deficit through bond sales. To keep capital markets free of 'distortions', governments should not apply regulations or restrictions on international flows of funds.

The theoretical basis for this idealized price determined framework is quite weak. It cannot be demonstrated that there is a real world process that ensures the realization of the full employment price set.[5] Nor can it be demonstrated that the full employment price set is unique. The latter is a quite serious problem, because if the price set is not unique, the concept of 'distortions' is called into question. A distorted outcome is defined in relation to a non-distorted one. If there is more than one non-distorted outcome, one cannot be sure that the prices in an economy with public sector interventions are substantially different from some non-distorted outcomes.[6]

While price-determined systems may seem abstract curiosities, they are the basis for any statement that governments 'distort' markets. One cannot allege the existence of distortions without simultaneously asserting the existence of a unique non-distorted economy. Consider the apparently simple statements 'tariffs distort profitability between importables and exportables', and 'capital controls reduce allocative efficiency'. The validity of these statements requires the prior demonstration of the existence of a unique full-employment general equilibrium. Since this cannot be demonstrated even in theory, the correct statements would be 'tariffs alter profitability between importables and exportables', and 'capital controls alter the allocation of investment'. The practical difference between using the two words, distort or alter, is the core of policy. If public sector actions distort the economy, which results in inefficiency, they should be avoided or minimized. If the actions alter the economy, then a subjective policy assessment is required to determine whether the alteration is a net benefit to society.[7]

If we move from the ethereal world of the abstract to the characteristics of real economies, it should be obvious that the price-determined framework is not applicable. The severe recession that began at the end of the 2000s renders price-constrained arguments absurd. Because national economies are demand constrained, the existence of a general equilibrium price set becomes a moot point. Relative prices, domestic and global, change as the level of aggregate demand rises and falls. Therefore, relative prices are not 'signals' to producers and consumers, but result from the production and consumption decisions themselves. Since prices do not determine quantity choices by consumers and producers, they are derivative *from* them; they are not signals of efficient allocation. In other words, producers and consumers are not price-takers. This implies that public sector interventions, including those on trade and cross-border capital flows, should be judged pragmatically in terms of social cost and social benefit.

2.3.2 Fixed and flexible exchange rates

The theoretical and practical weakness of general equilibrium theory implies that no a priori argument can be made for a flexible exchange rate regime. However, it might be argued that the apparently intractable adjustment problems within the euro zone imply that a broader system of fixed exchange rates would suffer from many of the same difficulties. In order to assess this anti-fixed exchange rate argument it is necessary to clarify terms and concepts.

Textbooks and reports of international agencies frequently begin discussions of managing external balance by positing a dichotomy between 'fixed' and 'flexible' exchange rates. An exchange rate is typically defined as 'fixed' if the government specifies a rate to other currencies or a major currency, and takes the actions necessary to maintain that rate. The 'necessary' actions would be an instruction to the central bank to use foreign currency reserves to purchase the domestic currency when pressure for depreciation is anticipated, or to sell domestic currency for foreign currencies to avoid an appreciation. A move from one fixed rate to another is a 'revaluation' or a 'devaluation'.

Defining a fixed rate is straightforward. Considerably more problematical is to define a 'flexible' rate. It is often defined as an exchange rate system or regime in which the central bank does not intervene, 'in which the values of participating currencies are free to change in relation to one another according to market demand and supply for each currency'.[8] This definition is non-rigorous and unclear. It could be interpreted as explaining currency movements in terms of flows that reflect the supplies and demands in a market at any moment in time. This is not the case even in the abstract, as demonstrated by the more elaborate definition of a flexible exchange rate that uses the synonymous term, 'floating exchange rate':

> [The] movement of a foreign currency exchange rate in response to changes in the market forces of supply and demand [is] also known as *flexible exchange rate.* Currencies strengthen or weaken based on a nation's reserves of hard currency and gold, its international trade balance, its rate of inflation and interest rates, and the general strength of its economy. (http://www.allbusiness.com/glossaries/flexible-exchange-rate/4958219-1.html)

If there are no interventions to limit convertibility, the price of a currency in terms of other currencies is determined by its stock as well as its flow, its domestic 'price' in terms of commodities, and the conditions prevailing in the national economy. By the end of the twentieth century it became part of conventional wisdom that a flexible exchange rate was not determined by flows alone ('supply and demand'). It results from portfolio adjustments to desired stocks of different assets that determine those flows.[9] Defining a flexible exchange rate as 'market determined' has no clear meaning.

In much of open economy macroeconomics the nature of exchange rate regimes is asserted rather than explained. A fixed exchange rate is one that changes by administrative action, and a flexible exchange rate is one that adjusts instantaneously to equilibrate the trade deficit (or current account). How a flexible rate achieves this equilibration is typically left to the reader's imagination. These two exchange rate concepts are polar opposites. Actual economies can have fixed exchange rates, and during 1946–70 all countries in the world with few exceptions pegged their currencies to the US dollar directly or indirectly.[10] No real world equivalent exists for an exchange rate that instantaneously equilibrates a country's trade balance.

Such exchange rate behaviour can be established only as a special case in abstract theory. The absence of a real world analogue can be verified in the annual reports of the International Monetary Fund, where country exchange rate policies are categorized. The table of exchange rate regimes reports that of 166 country currencies, 23, or 14 per cent, were of the type that approximated the theoretical category of 'floating'.[11] While these 23 currencies accounted for the vast majority of international trade,[12] there is no evidence that 'floating' resulted in a tendency, instantaneous or otherwise, to equilibrate either the trade account or the balance of payments.

Governments in all countries with their own currencies intervene in foreign exchange markets to some degree. Therefore, the policy choice for exchange rate policy is not fixed or flexible, but the degree of intervention. While this may seem obvious, it has an extremely import implication. The usual discussion of the advantages and disadvantages of different exchange rate policies presumes the fixed/flexible dichotomy. For example, Salvatore (2004), whose book has one of the most balanced presentations of fixed and flexible rates, summarizes as follows:

> In general, advocates of flexible exchange rates argue that such a system is more efficient than a system of fixed exchange rates to correct balance-of-payments disequilibria...[T]hey stress that by allowing a nation to achieve an external balance easily and automatically, flexible rates facilitate the achievement of internal balance and other economic objectives....[A]dvocates of fixed exchange rates argue that by introducing a degree of uncertainty not present under fixed rates, flexible rates reduce the volume of international trade and investment, are more likely to lead to destabilizing speculation, and are inflationary...

After this apparently agnostic summary, he writes,

> Under a flexible exchange rate system, only the exchange rate needs to change to correct a disequilibrium in the nation's balance of payments...
>
> A flexible exchange rate system also means that the nation need not concern itself with its external balance and is free to utilize all policies... to achieve its purely domestic goals of full employment

> with price stability, growth, an equitable distribution of income, and so on. (p. 599)

The statements that with flexible rates 'only the exchange rate needs to change' for balance of payments bliss, and that 'the nation need not concern itself with its external balance' read like a parody of neoclassical theology. Even a fervent advocate of flexible rates, the International Monetary Fund, would not take such a sanguine view.[13] The potential difficulties arising under a flexible exchange rate can be highlighted by tracing the steps from a balance of payments deficit to its elimination through automatic exchange rate adjustment. For simplicity, assume that a country's external account consists only of commodity imports and exports. Let an external 'shock', such as a change in world prices, result in a trade deficit:

1. The trade deficit provokes a nominal depreciation of the domestic currency with respect to the currencies of its major trading partners;
2. The depreciation must cause a shift in relative prices within the country, with the prices of tradables rising relatively to non-tradables; and
3. The elasticity of supply of exports (positive) and elasticity of demand of imports (negative) must be sufficiently large to eliminate the trade deficit within a short time period so that the depreciation is not so large as to provoke inflationary instability.

In the absence of capital flows, the first step can be accepted as automatic. The second is contingent upon the degree of price competitiveness in domestic markets. The third would depend upon the nature of a country's imports and exports. If domestic relative prices are slow to adjust and short-term import and export elasticities were low, the result could be a continuously depreciating exchange rate with no improvement in the trade balance. Even if one ignores the inflationary effect of the depreciation, which is considered below, the failure to close the trade gap would lead to the central bank exhausting its foreign reserves. Once imports could no longer be financed, the trade balance would adjust through a contraction of real output that would reduce import demand.

Specifying the steps from a trade deficit to current account equilibrium reveals the underlying premises of the flexible exchange rate mechanism. It assumes that: (1) the domestic and world economies are price constrained, which logically implies global general equilibrium full employment, as well as for the country under analysis; and (2) that changes in production and consumption are instantaneous. In other words, a flexible exchange rate regime brings automatic balance of payments adjustment if and only if markets behave according to the rules of Walrasian General Equilibrium.

The essential role of Walrasian clearing is obvious in the Mundell–Fleming (MF) model, for half a century the standard framework to analyze open economies. Because of the general acceptance of this model, it must be briefly addressed in any critique of exchange rate adjustment. The model has some elements that superficially qualify it as 'Keynesian', most obviously a less-than-full-employment framework. It is essentially neoclassical, because the most important adjustment mechanism in the model occurs through changes in relative prices, not through quantity adjustment.

The *faux* Keynesian element in the model is the *ceteris paribus* determination of output and employment by nominal demand, either through a change in expenditure in the real system (private investment, exports and public expenditure), or through changes in the nominal money supply impacting on real variables. These are carry-overs from the neoclassical synthesis version of the 'Keynesian' closed economy. The putative contribution of the MF model beyond the standard neoclassical model is balance of payments adjustment through changes in the nominal exchange rate. The fixed/flexible dichotomy is the core of the 'contribution'.

Even if one abandons a simplistic flow treatment of the exchange rate for stock adjustment discussed above, the MF model is fatally flawed. The dichotomy in between fixed and flexible exchange rates is transparently tautological in the model. The definition of the former is obvious, and the latter is defined as an exchange rate that instantaneously equilibrates the external sector without any elaboration on the process. The central analytical and empirical issue in open economy analysis, whether and how quickly changes in the nominal exchange rate will stabilize the balance of payments, is ignored.

But even accepting the unlikely and theoretically suspect instantaneous adjustment does not allow the MF model to escape the inconsistencies of its internal logic. When a country has a trade deficit, the nominal exchange rate must depreciate. This logically requires the domestic price level to rise by an amount determined by the pass-through rate of import prices. This price increase implies that the change in the real depreciation is less than the nominal, and the extent to which the real depreciation adjusts the external balance depends on the sum of the trade elasticities (the Marshall–Lerner condition).

The logical inconsistencies can be demonstrated with simple algebra. With the small country assumption and using the standard one commodity model, I measure exports (X), imports (Z) in constant price units. Exports are determined by the real exchange rate, and the imports by the real exchange rate and the level of real output. For simplicity I assume the marginal propensity to import equals the average. Real output is Y, and E^* is the real exchange rate, the nominal exchange rate divided by the price level, E/P, measured in units of the domestic currency to some composite world currency. The interest rate on the foreign debt is r, the stock of foreign debt is K (public and private), and debt service is rK. The foreign exchange equivalent of the debt service is rkE. Assuming no other short-term financial flows, the current account is:

$$
\begin{aligned}
CrA &= (X - Z) - rK \\
X &= X^o + a_1 E^* \\
Z &= a_2 E^* + a_3 Y \\
CrA &= (X^o + a_1 E^*) - (a_2 E^* + a_3 Y) - rK
\end{aligned}
$$

Other things equal, the change in the price level equal equals the pass-through effect of depreciation, equal to the marginal propensity to import out of national income. If the marginal propensity equals the average, then,

$$
\begin{aligned}
\Delta P/P &= p = a_3 P \\
E^* &= E/P \\
\Delta E^* &= (1 - a_3)\Delta E \\
e^* &= (1 - a_3)\Delta E/E, \quad \text{and} \quad e = e^*/(1 - a_3)
\end{aligned}
$$

The elasticities of export supply and import demand with respect to the real exchange rate are ε_1 and ε_2, and their sum is ε_T.

$$
\begin{aligned}
\varepsilon_1 &= (\Delta X/\Delta E^*)(E^*/X) \\
\varepsilon_2 &= (\Delta Z/\Delta E^*)(E^*/Z) \\
\varepsilon_1 + \varepsilon_2 &= \varepsilon_T
\end{aligned}
$$

A deprecation improves the trade balance if $\varepsilon_T > 0$ (the Marshall–Lerner condition defined for quantities).[14] Finally, the share of debt service in national income is k ($k = rK/Y$). Substituting,

$$
\begin{aligned}
d[CrA] &= [(X^o + a_1 E^*) - (a_2 E^* + a_3 Y)] - rKE \\
&= [(a_1 - a_2)dE^* - a_3 dY] - rKdE \\
&= (\varepsilon_1 - \varepsilon_2)e^* - [k]de \\
&= \varepsilon_T(1 - a_3)e - [k]de
\end{aligned}
$$

The elasticity of the current account with respect to the nominal exchange rate is:

$$\varepsilon_{C,E} = [\varepsilon_T(1 - a_3) - k]$$
$$\text{If } [\varepsilon_T(1 - a_3)] > k],\ \varepsilon_{C,E} > 0.$$

A numerical example demonstrates the economic policy implication of the algebra. Consider a country with a sum of short-term trade elasticities equal to 0.5 and a marginal propensity to import of one-third, that pays 3 per cent of national income as external debt service. The trade elasticity is likely to be excessively optimistic for the short time period during which adjustment must occur. A marginal propensity to import of one-third is also modest, less than the mean value for developing countries.

With these parameters, assume that a government wishes through nominal devaluation to reduce the current account deficit from 3 to 2 per cent of GDP (by one-third). The parameters yield an elasticity of approximately 0.3, implying that the nominal devaluation required to improve the current account by one-third is over 100 per cent. From the algebra and likely parameters, I conclude that for the majority of small, open economies, there is a high probability of devaluation setting off a destabilizing price spiral before the desired adjustment in the current account could occur. This conclusion implies that external balance is not achieved by governments seeking to 'calm financial markets'. For countries with an average degree of openness, exchange rate adjustment is destabilizing in and of itself.

The algebra of this section did not include effects on exchange rate adjustment on the stock of private debt. The portion of the private sector debt that is held in foreign currency can have a substantial impact on the elasticity of exports with regard to the real exchange rate. Depending upon the share of foreign currency debt in total debt, on the one hand, and the balance between domestic and external sales on the other, depreciation could render exporting enterprises less profitable. The argument that specific countries and the global system should operate with flexible exchange rates remains an unverified hypothesis.

2.3.3 Adjustment lessons from the euro crisis

The euro crisis of the 2010s provides a clear demonstration of the problem of correcting external imbalances. It is especially instructive because it presents the challenge of correcting imbalances without use of the exchange rate tool. An adjustment process that would successfully operate in the EU context could provide guidelines for a new global system of fixed exchange rates.

Many commentators concluded that the euro-debt crisis demonstrated that the common currency system itself was fatally flawed. The frequently cited reasons were the absence of a central fiscal authority and a common euro bond rather than country-specific bonds. An analytical treatment of the source of crisis suggests otherwise, with important implications for a global system of fixed exchange rates.

The euro debt crisis was over a decade in the making. After an uneven performance in 1990s, economic growth in reunified Germany declined during the first five years of the Gerhard Schroder government (see Figure 2.10). In response to this decline, the Social Democratic government embarked on an export-led growth strategy. This strategy was based on an agreement with trade unions for real wage restraint, reduction of labour protection to allow for a lower wages in a segmented labour market, and de facto export subsidies through tax incentives linked to exports (Flassbeck, 2010a, 2010b).

The growth rate recovered, with as much as three-quarters of the recovery due to export growth (Figure 2.11). The major determinant of the export growth itself, again about three-quarters of the change, was unit labour costs, which either declined or grew slowly (Figure 2.12). As one would suspect, a large portion, about one-half, of the change

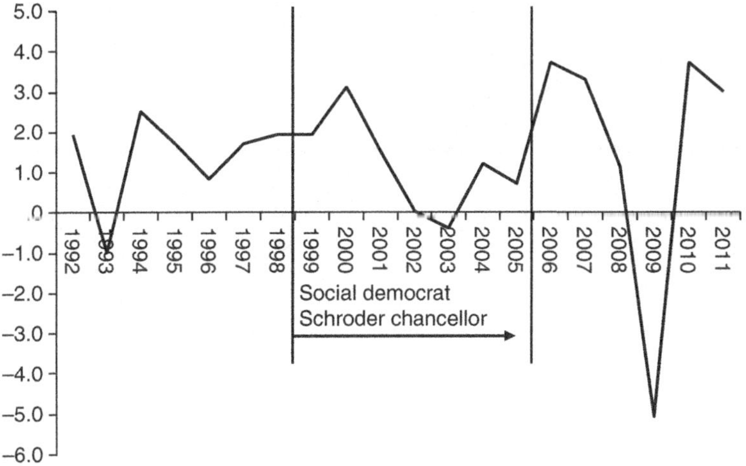

Figure 2.10 GDP growth in Germany, 1992–2011
Note: Statistics used in Figures 2.10 to 2.16 are from www.oecd.org.

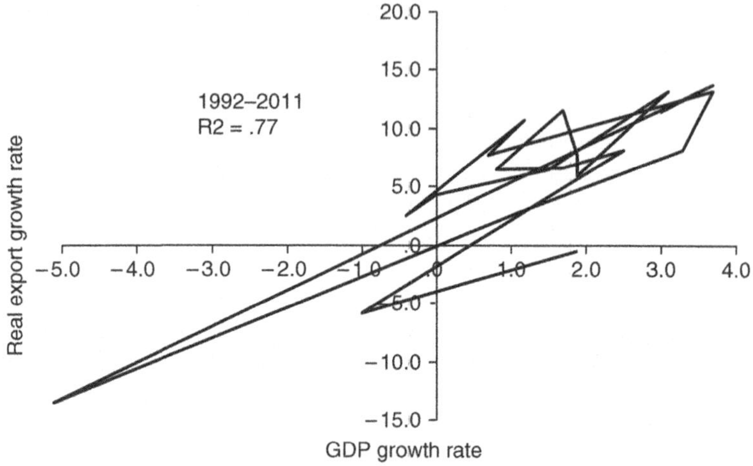

Figure 2.11 Percentage change in real export growth and GDP growth in Germany, 1992–2011

Figure 2.12 Percentage change in real export growth and nominal unit labour cost in Germany, 1992–2011

Figure 2.13 Percentage change in nominal unit labour cost and nominal wages in Germany, 1992–2011

in unit labour cost resulted from nominal wage changes (Figure 2.13). Simple multiplication suggests that we can attribute one-quarter of Germany's growth performance to the policy of real wage suppression. A predictable side effect of the wage repression was slow import growth in Germany, implying an increasing trade surplus.

Because most of Germany's exports went to other members of the European Union, an export-led growth strategy necessarily result in an import-led outcome by the other countries. In 2000 Germany had a positive trade balance of US$6 billion, and the other euro zone countries generated a combined positive balance of US$33 billion (see Figure 2.14). Two years later both balances had grown, to US$92 and US$77 billion, respectively. Then, the German government's export-led growth strategy kicked in. By the start of the financial crisis in 2008 the German balance had grown to US$227 billion, while the deficit for the others had grown to US$95 billion. The 'beggar-thy-neighbour' growth strategy had run its unnatural course. While the German trade surplus grew, the balances for the so-called PIGS (Portugal, Italy, Greece and Spain) became increasingly negative. For the first half of the 2000s Italy actually had a trade surplus, but by the end of the decade all four countries sustained large deficits (Figure 2.15).

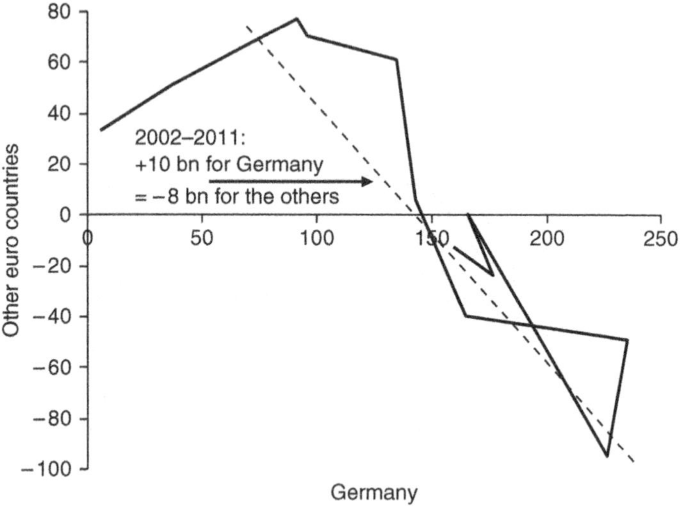

Figure 2.14 Balance on trade in goods and services, Germany and the other euro countries, 2000–2011 (US$ billion)

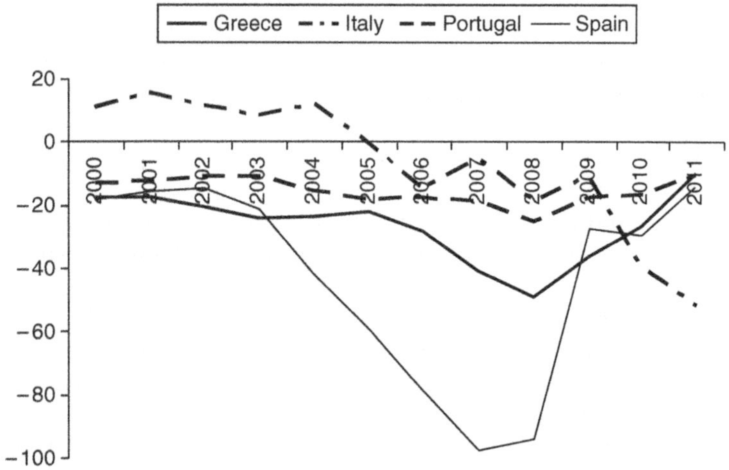

Figure 2.15 Goods and services balances of the 'PIGS', 2000–2011 (US$ billion)

The growth strategy of the Social Democratic government, continued by Angela Merkel's coalition, was the making of a crisis of the euro. The widening trade gaps went from problem to disaster when the financial crisis hit in 2007 and 2008. By the end of the decade the only question was which country would be the first to reach an unsustainable external balance. Greece approached disaster, because it was the only euro member to have both a large trade deficit and a large fiscal deficit (the latter about 7 per cent of GDP in 2007, going to 10 per cent in 2008 and 16 per cent in 2009).

When the inevitable Greece insolvency occurred in the first half of 2010, an obvious short-term solution was to suspend or amend the charter of the European Central Bank (ECB) and have the ECB purchase the entire Greek debt. This would have avoided disaster by limiting the Greek adjustment task to trade competitiveness. The triad of the German government, the European Commission and the International Monetary Fund chose instead to enforce an austerity policy that no government could implement, and, if implemented, would have made servicing the public debt impossible. Greek debt default was now a question of how soon.

Having sent financial speculators the clear signal that it would not protect Greek bonds, the triad should not have been surprised by the spread of the crisis to Italy, Spain and Portugal (engendering the acronym 'PIGS'). The external account problems of these countries paralleled the export success of German. At the beginning of the 2000s, Italy enjoyed a trade surplus, while Portugal and Spain had small deficits. Before the financial crisis only the latter had a seriously deteriorating trade account. The severe recession caused by the global financial collapse resulted in fiscal deficits in all three countries. These deficits would cause the governments to be vulnerable to speculation on their bonds. When far from prompting a reconsideration of EC and German policy, this so-called contagion brought an increasingly hard line from Berlin and Brussels (supported by secondary and minor henchmen in Austria, France, the Netherlands and Finland).

When the elected Greek government failed to implement successfully the impossible it was replaced by an unelected one, the first such event in Western Europe since the Second World War. It soon became clear that austerity was inconsistent with achieving a sustainable debt burden, as well as provoking severe economic decline (Figure 2.16). A public debt that during 2000–08 averaged 115 per cent of GDP rose to 133 per cent in 2009, 150 per cent in 2010, and 165 per cent by the end of 2011.

With the partial exception of Greece, what appeared as a public debt problem had its origin in the unbalanced trade between Germany and the other euro zone countries. The European Union lacked a direct mechanism to reduce these imbalances. In the absence of

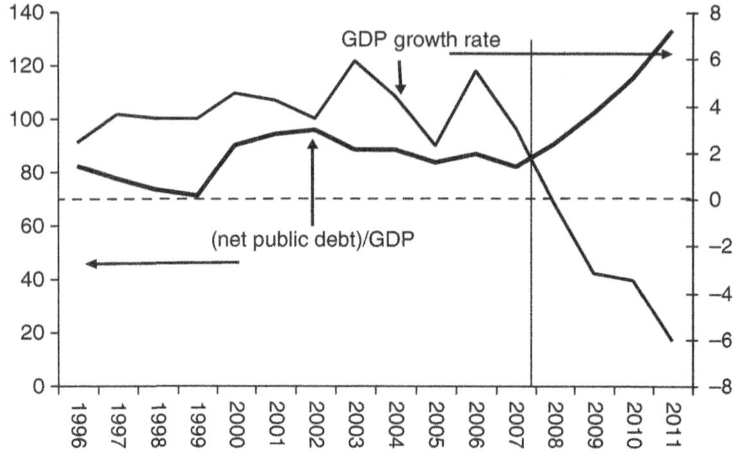

Figure 2.16 GDP growth and the public debt as percentage of GDP, Greece, 1996–2011

a direct mechanism, the triad attempted to increase Greek export competitiveness through nominal wage and price compression. Success was extremely unlikely because the recession induced by austerity depressed the private investment essential for generating productivity growth.

The triad's policy response to the gathering debt problems in the euro zone was an extreme version of the adjustment strategy pressed upon countries by the International Monetary Fund during the last six decades. The formal possibility of devaluation among IMF members obscures the essential similarity with the euro zone crisis. Because of the limited effectiveness of the exchange rate as an equilibrating mechanism as explained above, the stabilization process for governments implementing IMF programmes involved quantity adjustment. Depression of domestic demand would reduce imports to relieve current account pressures and force producers to seek external markets. The so-called PIGS could have no hope of export recovery, because the major enforcer of the austerity programme, Germany, was itself pursuing export-led growth.

This interpretation of the euro crisis rejects Krugman's argument that the central problem is the absence of the devaluation instrument,[15] and country-level trade imbalances would be more manageable with a return to national currencies. Once one recognizes the short-run ineffectiveness of the exchange rate tool, the euro lesson for global policy is quite different. An essential part of a stable international monetary system would be a mechanism to correct trade imbalances among countries to complement capital account regulation.

2.4 The new global framework

2.4.1 The problem to solve

The fundamental problem causing global monetary instability is excessive capital flows. These excessive flows reflect the dominance of finance over production that results in the circulation of money overpowering the circulation of commodities. The practical result of this dominance is that finance, not trade, rules the international economy. The solution to this problem is the strict regulation of those flows with the explicit purpose of reducing them. The purpose of the institutional arrangements for a new and progressive global monetary system is to achieve that regulation in an effective and efficient manner.

Most proposals for cross-country adjustment involve either nominal exchange rate adjustment itself, or a formal link between the nominal exchange rate and production costs. Direct nominal exchange rate adjustment was the mechanism proposed by both Harry Dexter White and J.M. Keynes (Mikesell, 1994), though in the context of radically different clearing mechanisms. The process would seem obvious: in a system of fixed exchange rates, the government of a country with an unsustainable current account deficit devalues. If one accepts the theory of comparative advantage, the devaluation should change relative price in favour of tradables. If cross-country competitiveness is determined by absolute costs, the devaluation is the international equivalent of a price cut. In both analyses exports are expected to rise and imports fall. In addition, capital should flow into the country because asset prices fall.

There are several problems with this logical sequence. The first might be called the Mundell–Fleming problem. In general, nominal changes in the exchange rate at most prompt changes in the real value discounted by the pass-through rate. The more open an economy, the less will be the real change for any nominal change. Secondly, an exchange rate-generated balance of payments adjustment requires a change in the relative price of tradables and non-tradables. Whether this occurs with sufficient rapidity to create a sustainable external balance depends upon the flexibility of domestic prices and the supply elasticity of exports and import substitutes. Finally, if private sector debt has a substantial foreign currency component, the implied valuation effect of an exchange rate adjustment would cancel the incentive created by relative price changes.

These considerations, degree of openness, price flexibility, supply response, and private debt structure, suggest that exchange rate adjustment should not be considered the appropriate mechanism for the correction of external imbalances, even in the context of an effective nominal anchor for a world currency and efficient system for clearing payments. In a more general sense, external adjustment via exchange rates would seem inconsistent with the broad theoretical approach of Keynes (1936). In the analytical framework of Keynes (op. cit.) the aggregate economy is quantity constrained, in contrast to the full employment price constrained approach of the neoclassicals.[16] I would argue that macroeconomics is quantity-constrained economics. This explains why neoclassical 'macroeconomics' is nothing more than summing across markets, micro masquerading as macro.

As is well recognized, the exponential growth of capital flow in this century is the direct result of capital account deregulation. With capital liberated from regulation, currency speculation and seizing on interest rate differentials across countries account for the great mass of cross-country financial movement. Less important quantitatively has been cross-country mergers and acquisitions, which are inappropriately defined as 'direct investment', though these are essentially speculative in nature.

Therefore, the first necessary measure for global financial stability is a system of pegged exchange rates resistant to speculative attack. The direct effect of pegged rates would be to eliminate exchange rate speculation. Pegged rates would indirectly reduce bond and equity speculation that is motivated by expectations of currency appreciation. The governments of several countries, including Argentina, Brazil and Chile in Latin America and Malaysia in Southeast Asia, have employed various mechanisms to limit financial market speculation.[17]

The objective would not be pegged rates in themselves. Rather, the pegged rates would be the mechanism by which speculative flows would be reduced from massive to a mere annoyance. Pegging requires a stable nominal anchor to which rates would be pegged. Under the post-war Bretton Woods system this anchor was the US dollar. Even were there a dominant currency, a national currency would not be satisfactory. The country (or countries) with the reserve currency enjoy advantages that approach near immunity to pressure to reduce external imbalances. In effect, the countries with reserve currencies can sustain imbalances that other countries cannot.

The fundamental difference among proposals for a global currency is the mechanism to establish its absolute value. The absolute value of the dollar was established by a link to gold during 1945–70, at US$35 an ounce. In his plan for the post-war monetary system, Keynes (1943) proposed a 'bancor' (from 'bank' and the French word for gold), which would also have a fixed gold price.[18] Keynes (op. cit.) was clear that the bancor was essential to his proposal:

> The principal object can be explained in a single sentence: to provide that money earned by selling goods to one country can be spent on purchasing the products of any other country. In jargon, a system of multilateral clearing. In English, a universal currency valid for trade transactions in all the world. Everything else in the plan is ancillary to that. (p. 1)

A multilateral institution, the International Currency Union (ICU), would oversee the 'universal currency', which would be the unit of account for cross-country trade, as well as store of value in accounts held by governments in the Union. The ICU would be a 'lender of last resort', and, as important, the currency purchaser of last resort. With the ICU able to create bancors and use them to purchase national currencies, any attempt at currency speculation would fail. Governments of member countries would use controls to reduce the necessary for the ICU to intervene in currency markets.[19] The US government, through its principal representative at the Bretton Woods conference Harry Dexter White,[20] rejected the bancor proposal in favour of a system with the dollar as the global reserve currency, a monetary institutional that would not be a bank, and the burden of adjustment would fall on the governments of deficit countries.[21]

In the 1990s Davidson proposed a 'reform of the world's money' that has many similarities to the bancor plan, but much more modest politically in that it involves an international clearing institution rather than a global central bank (Davidson, 1992–93; Arestis, 1999). The value of the unit of international account and clearing would be set through a weighted collection of major currencies. More modest still is the Stiglitz and Greenwald (2003) plan that, as with Davidson's, has no global central bank, and would use the existing Special Drawing Rights (SDRs) as the international unit of account (see, also, Stiglitz 2006 p. 245). The Davidson proposal would be a major improvement on the current disorder in international markets. Because it does not provide for an international lender and buyer of last resort, it would require further measures to limit financial speculation. Stiglitz and Greenwald (2003) do not address the speculation problem.

The problems with the mechanisms of global economic governance do not arise primarily from its formal structure,[22] but from its practice. Central to this practice is the absence of an international currency of account managed by a global bank, which is a necessary step towards meaningful reform. Almost all writers, even sympathetic ones, consider a global currency an impractical dream. For example, Bibow (2010) concludes that,

> ...[A]rrangements under which the U.S. dollar would lose its special status as other key countries mature are of course conceivable - Keynes's ideas of the early 1940s continue to offer guidance, but absent any such official agreement, a post-dollar standard may still take decades to come about by evolution. (p. 28)

While it is not possible to predict the probability of a global system with a common currency of account, it is possible to demonstrate its advantages.[23] This is necessary in the first instance to eliminate the tremendous advantage enjoyed by the country or countries whose currency serves as the international reserve.[24]

A technical issue with an international currency of account would be its underlying anchor which would determine its exchange rate to all national currencies. From 1945 to 1970 a fixed US dollar price of gold played this role. The inherently unsatisfactory nature of this arrangement was demonstrated when the US government unilaterally abandoned the fixed price guarantee. The problematical nature was twofold: that all other governments of countries with market economies had no sanction to prevent unilateral action by the United States; and that US national interest prevented timely preparations for an alternative arrangement. Several possibilities exist to provide the anchor for the global currency of account and store of value: (1) a fixed price of gold or analogous link to a basket of commodities; or (2) link to a trade-weighted group of national currencies in the manner of the Special Drawing Right (SDR). Also in the manner of the SDR, the global the commodity or currency package could be revised regularly to adjust for changes in trade patterns and relative importance of national currencies (this is done every five years for the SDR). A second technical issue would be the permissible uses and trading of the global currency. Keynes' (1943) bancor proposal limited its role to exchanges among central banks and the global currency board.

In addition to eliminating the advantages gained by nationally-based reserve currencies, a global currency of account would facilitate a more equitable and efficient system of clearing payments and rules to make adjustment fall on creditors as well as debts is also necessary and is a feature of each of the three plans. However, even under the Keynes (1943) proposal, a payments surplus position itself provides the means to escape the sanctions to eliminate it.

In addition, if the sanctions to eliminate surpluses were effective, it is likely that some countries would continue with negative and unsustainable imbalances. When a government seeks to reduce a current account surplus by a fiscal expansion that induces imports, global imbalances may decline in the aggregate, but the external account of individual countries could remain unsustainable. A possibility that goes beyond nominal exchange rate adjustment to resolve such problems would create a formal link between the exchange rate and some indicator of the cost of tradables. Perhaps the simplest version is that suggested by Heiner Flassbeck that within a fixed peg regime, changes in each country's nominal exchange rate would be tied to the rate of inflation.[25]

This mechanism would prevent unintended appreciation due to inflation above the rate of trading partners, as well as implicit depreciation through wage and price repression. Flassbeck was especially concerned by the use of the latter on the part of German governments over the last 15 years. It is not clear by what mechanism a link between inflation and nominal exchange rates would be implemented, or how this link would be enforced across countries.

2.5 Growth-enhancing, equitable adjustment

2.5.1 Adjustment analytics

Cross-country adjustment of external balances *via* exchange rates would seem to have more in common with the neoclassical approach than that of Keynes (1943) and his analytical legacy. This leads me to conclude that while the exchange rate may play a part in the correction of external imbalances, its role in the causality chain should be developed within an adjustment process that involves quantities, not relative prices. I start by assuming that the only capital flows are those to balance the trade account, and that the trade balance itself is determined by the unit costs of production in tradable sectors measured in the international currency.

International price of a composite tradable commodity =

$p_t \quad = \alpha\beta w(N_t/Q_t)$

or

$p_t \quad = \alpha\beta w q_t$

where

a = nominal exchange rate to the world currency
β = is the mark up over labour costs
w = nominal wage in national currency (equal across commodities)
Q_t = output of a composite tradable commodity
$N_t/Q_t = q_t$ = average labour–output ratio.

This simple formation states the obvious, that the international price of the composite tradable is equal to the product of the exchange rate, mark-up, wage and the inverse of labour productivity. In a quantity-adjusting system, changes in the exchange rate is price cutting, likely to provoke competitive devaluations. In a market economy, the price mark-up is beyond the control of the public authorities. Nominal wage reduction represents the 'race to the bottom' that no decent world order would allow.

Therefore, the adjustment variable appropriate for an equitable and growth-enhancing global system is labour productivity. This is not a variable suitable for short-term adjustment, because it requires investment that creates its impact over several years. Labour productivity is determined by skills, capital stock and technical change. In an integrated economy, their determinants refer to the production and distribution system as whole, not just of the tradable sectors. To take an obvious example, publicly funded improvement of a national transport system will through its indirect effects raise labour productivity.

The appropriate adjustment is labour productivity. But this is a variable that adjusts in the medium and long term. Some mediating mechanism is required to provide temporary relief for a country's external imbalance as the medium-term adjustment unfolds. This mechanism must be consistent with the negotiating weakness of governments of deficit countries relative to surplus countries. The overriding reality of international economic relations is that governments enjoying balance of payments surpluses need not adjust, while those with deficits must (except if the deficit is run by a reserve currency country). The central problem is to design an adjustment mechanism for countries with an unsustainable current account that does not reply on the goodwill of surplus countries.

2.5.2 Resolving the central problem

The theoretical support for an automatically equilibrating exchange rate mechanism is weak and contradictory, providing no compelling argument against the re-establishment of an effective fixed exchange system at the global level. On the basis of this conclusion I propose an alternative mechanism of current account adjustment with a fixed exchange rate regime, 'transitory trade interventions'. These would be in addition to the sanctions against governments of surplus countries found in other proposals, notable by Keynes (1943).

Governments of countries with persistent deficits would be allowed to impose temporary or transitional import restrictions and export subsidies. These would provide short-term correction of unsustainable external balances. The definition of an unsustainable external balance, the permissible restrictions and subsidies, and the time period allowed for adjustment would be specified by treaty. In this system would prove more effective with quantity restrictions on imports because they can be imposed and removed quickly. The principle of rapid application and removal would also apply to the export side. An example is tax rebates calculated on unit of export value. A government would be allowed to implement these interventions without retaliation if they were accompanied by an investment programme to increase trade competitiveness. A one-off devaluation might or might not be part of the combination of interventions and investment.

Adding the transitory trade interventions to the bancor plan, we obtain the following:

1. A pegged exchange rate system to minimize expectations of currency fluctuations, and, therefore, currency speculation;
2. A global bank and a common currency of account, acting as lender and currency purchaser of last resort;
3. Bancor-style sanctions on governments of countries with persistent and large surpluses; and
4. Provision for countries with persistent deficits to use quantitative trade regulation instruments for short-term adjustment if combined with an appropriate investment programme.

This proposal encourages surplus countries to expand output, while allowing deficit countries to correct imbalances without imposing contractionary fiscal and monetary policies.

2.5.3 Defence of 'protection'

The solution to global financial instability requires that governments use import and export regulations to complement capital controls. This proposal confronts a near-consensus that 'protectionism' is not only undesirable and inefficient, but also a threat to global growth.[26] Trade liberalisation is one of the few aspects of economic analysis and policy about which agreement seems to exist across the political spectrum. Almost all commentators endorse it to varying degrees. If one is an economist, with few exceptions opposition to 'protectionism' is almost a requirement of the profession.[27] This is despite the view of J. M. Keynes, who recanted from his support for free trade. In a rarely quoted passage in *The General Theory*, he wrote,

> So lately as 1923, as a faithful pupil of the classical school who did not at that time doubt what he had been taught and entertained on this matter no reserves at all, I wrote: 'If there is one thing that Protection cannot do, it is to cure Unemployment. ...' As for ... mercantilist theory ... we were brought up to believe that it was little better than nonsense. So absolutely overwhelming and complete has been the domination of the classical [free trade] school. (Keynes 1936, p. 334)

The claimed advantages of liberalising trade are well-known: it will increase welfare though a better allocation of production and consumption. It will increase domestic competition and lower prices for consumers, will stimulate exports and employment as the mirror of the cheaper imports. As demonstrated over forty years ago by a leading advocate of 'free trade', Bhagwati (1964), the assumptions required to reach the conclusion that free trade improves human welfare are extremely restrictive. These include continuous full employment of all resources, all countries could produce all traded commodities, the consumption preferences of all countries are the same, and in every country the same technology is used to produce each commodity. Even If one accepts all of these, the most that can be demonstrated is that some trade is better than no trade (autarky). It cannot be demonstrated that more liberalisation is an improvement on less.

Further, protection rarely acts to prevent competition from foreign suppliers. If effective, tariffs and non-tariff measures increase the prices at which imports sell. This does not prevent competition from being intense in the protected domestic market. As part of an industrial policy trade, protection can be designed to foster competition. It is quite common in small countries for the allegedly competing imports to be marketed by the domestic producers of the same product (who have production facilities abroad).

Specific to the principal issue of growth, there is no theoretical basis for the argument that freer trade stimulates domestic production and employment. It is quite impossible to produce such a theoretical conclusion, because trade models assume full employment. Adam Smith (reference required) made the argument that trade provided a demand outlet for a country's surplus production ('vent for surplus'). Subsequent economists rejected this argument as naïve and simplistic. If domestic demand were insufficient for full employment, increased public expenditure or domestic investment would resolve the problem as well as export demand would. The exception would be if a country requires a demand stimulus when it simultaneously suffers from an unsustainable import level. However, *via* more imports trade liberalisation would be likely to make that problem worse, not better.

What might be called a 'back entrance' argument against 'protection' alleges that developing countries would benefit from the elimination of industrial country protection, especially on agricultural products. Since the latter countries cannot expect the former to liberalise unless they do, a general liberalisation would be good for all. If this were the case, an international system allowing import and export controls might be detrimental to low-income countries. However, it is not clear that this allegation should be taken seriously. Most of the agricultural products protected by developed countries are not grown in the low-income countries. The benefiting countries are likely to be middle income, for example, Argentina and Brazil, where the benefiting agricultural population is small. For those few products that are produced by low-income countries, for example, cotton in Mauritania, the most likely beneficiary of a decline in production in the United States and the European Union would be China, not a country in Africa. The domestic consumption of these products while diversifying exports might be a considerably better outcome than mutual trade liberalisation.

Consider a counterfactual world which in 2008 responded to the global financial collapse in the manner suggested by the international monetary framework proposed in this paper. The major countries of the world would combine strong fiscal stimulus packages through deficit finance funded by monetization. This combination of fiscal and monetary expansion would be considerably more effective than so-called quantitative easing on its own. To prevent unsustainable trade imbalances some countries would implement temporary import and capital controls.

As countries approached full potential on the basis of expanding domestic demand and fixed exchange rates, it is quite possible even with the import restrictions that world trade would have grown faster than was actually the case: an anaemic 3.3 per cent in 2008, a disastrous –10 per cent in 2009, and a barely-breathing 1 per cent during the first half of 2010. A world with free trade might better come after, not before, full employment. This is all the more the case because freer trade is not an end in itself, but a vehicle to improve human welfare.

2.5.4 Capital controls

A further central element in the new global framework will be controls on cross-border capital flows. For three decades after the Second World War most governments implemented controls over capital flows as an integral part of external policy, not merely during crisis periods. The elimination of these was part of the general move towards less public intervention in markets that gathered pace in the 1980s. This deregulation was initially justified by allocative efficiency arguments, and once achieved was treated as part of the natural order, requiring no justification.

At the risk of repetition it is necessary to stress that the alleged gains in allocative efficiency associated with unregulated capital flows occur in the context of full employment general equilibrium. When an economy is demand constrained, the effect of adding or removing regulations on capital flow is an empirical issue. For example, in a depressed economy low profitability can render domestic companies vulnerable to takeovers by external investors. This vulnerability is indicated by the increase in international mergers and acquisitions from US$600 billion in 2009 to US$1,000 billion in 2011 (http://www.oecd.org/dataoecd/26/23/48946357.pdf).

Of greater immediate policy concern at the end of the 2000s was the destabilizing effect of speculative capital flows. The IMF recognized this problem even before the speculative attacks on public bonds in the euro zone. An IMF 'Staff Position Note' in 2010 concluded, 'Controls on foreign capital into emerging economies can be part of the policy options available to governments to counter the potential negative economic and financial effects of sudden surges in capital' (IMF 2010, referring to Ostry *et. al.*, 2010). Gallagher and Ocampo (2011) interpreted this document to signal a major change in the IMF's approach to capital controls,

> In February 2010 the IMF changed its stance on capital controls because IMF economists' own analyses found that, over and again, when developing countries used capital controls, they worked. Indeed, the IMF found that those nations that used capital controls were among the least hard-hit during the crisis. (Gallagher and Ocampo 2011, webpage)

From its previously negative position, the IMF 2010 position note might represent a substantial change, but a highly qualified one. For example, specifically excluded is the use of capital controls when exchange rates are 'overvalued', which refers to situations in which a country suffers from an unsustainable current account. This exclusion betrays the general equilibrium framework in which the IMF analysis arises. In demand-constrained analysis capital controls are the appropriate instrument to manage current account deficits. In the new global framework proposed in this paper capital controls would be part of the policy mix of every national government.

The specifics of the controls would vary from country to country, and their primary purpose would be to severely restrict speculation. This purpose might be achieved by so-called market-based measures, such as taxation related to the time the funds are held in the country in which the tax is levied. In extreme cases, such as the euro crisis of the early 2010s, stricter measures would be necessary. The minimum necessary measure for every country would be a requirement that all foreign exchange transactions over a specified amount be registered with the central bank. This requirement would have the advantage of facilitating management of external balance not matter what capital and current account regulations wear implemented.

2.6 The new global framework summarized

An end to the current instability of international financial markets and the associated cross-country imbalances requires a radical change in global governance. Partial measures such as an international clearing institution would be an improvement, but would not resolve the underlying difficulties which derive from the dominance of finance over production at the global level.

To reverse that dominance and return finance to its appropriate role as support for production, the governments in the United States, the European Union and Japan must act purposefully to restrict the operations of financial capital, including the effective regulation of capital flows. On the global scale, cooperation among these and other governments would create a new and progressive structure of economic governance. This structure would include a global central bank managing a global currency that circulated among central banks. The global central bank would be the lender and buyer of last resort, thereby severely restricting the scope for financial speculation. A link to commodities or a collection of major currencies would provide the stability of the global currency.

The adjustment of cross-country imbalances would be facilitated by a complementary system of sanctions on the governments of surplus countries and a 'stand-alone' mechanism for deficit countries. The former would include taxes on national accumulations of the global currency held in accounts of the global central bank. Keynes (1943) provided the details of such a mechanism over sixty years ago, which have been repeated subsequently in milder form by later writers. The intended effect of the sanctions on surpluses would be to induce expansionary fiscal policies. Deficit countries would be allowed transitory import restrictions and export subsidies, conditional upon investment programmes designed to facilitate trade competitiveness. Adjustment would not be via exchange rates, though exchange rate changes may be appropriate in some circumstances.

The overall effect of the new system would be the reduction of imbalances through economic expansion, not contraction. As a result, the global economy would achieve a growth regime rather than an austerity regime. The new global framework would be associated with a dramatic shift in macroeconomic policy at the national level. To be specific, the new fixed exchange rate system would require strict capital controls to eliminate speculation on currencies. The counter-cyclical focus of monetary and fiscal policy would end inflation targeting by central banks.

These and other basic changes would move the world economy forward by re-establishing the importance of production over finance. It is not without semantic irony that the deregulation of financial markets over the last three decades result in massive global 'capital' flows that undermined rather than facilitated the real accumulation of capital.

2.7 Summary and conclusions

The global financial system that characterized of the first decades of the twenty-first century, and the ad hoc mechanisms for clearing payments across countries, proved singularly dysfunctional. This dysfunctionalitys has resulted in the dominance of finance over trade, manifested in a rapid and massive growth of short-term capital flows among countries. These capital flows resulted in substantial external volatility, which prompted governments to accumulate excessive holdings of foreign exchange.

Notwithstanding the reserve accumulation, many if not most high- and middle-income countries experienced increasing instability in current accounts. This instability implied that nominal exchange rate 'flexibility' increased rather than facilitated the management of external accounts. This empirical outcome would be predicted by critical inspection of the main theoretical approach short-term exchange rate adjustment, the Mundell–Fleming model.

The solution to this international dysfunction would be based on a global monetary institution that managed a global currency that served as a unit of account and a store of value. Central banks would be the users of the global currency, ending the present system of nationally-based reserve currencies and the political and economic advantage associated with them. New mechanisms for adjustment of currency account imbalances would complement the global currency, most notably strict controls on portfolio capital flows. Persistent surpluses would bring financial sanctions, while governments of deficit countries would be allowed to implement temporary trade measures, including export subsidies and import restrictions. Taken together, these measures would re-establish the global predominance of trade over finance.

Notes

1. For example, Stanley Fischer, head of the central bank of Israel and formerly at the IMF, wrote, 'Flexible does not mean that a country should not intervene in the foreign exchange market, or that the capital account should be completely open. Rather it means that the country should not draw an exchange rate line in the sand and declare "thus far, and no further"; countries should not commit themselves to defending a particular exchange rate' (Fischer, 2011, p. 9).
2. That is, the nominal value for each year is deflated by the average value over the entire period. This deflator is used to reduce year-end bias.
3. Zambia in the mid-2000s provides such an example (Weeks, *et. al.,* 2006, Chapter 6).
4. The relationship is also statistically significant for first differences, which eliminates the trend in both variables.
5. A prominent neoclassical wrote, '[My] main conclusion is rather pessimistic. We have no good reason to suppose that there are forces which lead the economy to equilibrium. By that I mean we have no good theory' (Hahn, 1984, p. 13).
6. If the general equilibrium price set is unique, it is not necessary to know what it is, since by definition any price intervention prevents it from being realized.
7. 'Subjective assessment' is used in the sense that the economics profession defines 'positive' and 'normative' statements.
8. See the online dictionary 'Encarta' (http://encarta.msn.com/).
9. See Shaikh (1999), Driskall (1980) and Dooley (1979).
10. The International Monetary Fund had the task of monitoring the system of fixed exchange rates. For a historical review, see Eichengreen (1992).

11. The categories were (with number of countries in parenthesis): no independent currency (10), currency board (13), 'conventional fixed' (70), pegged in a band (5), crawling peg (6), crawling band (1), managed float (48), and independent float (23). If one eliminates the first category and takes the Euro Zone as one currency, there are 166 currencies. (IMF 2007, Appendices, page 10).
12. The independent floating category included all major trading countries except China.
13. In 2005 in the IMF journal, *Economic Issues*, a review of exchange rate policy issued the following warning about governments shifting to a flexible exchange rate regime:

    > Country experiences indicate that four ingredients are generally needed for a successful transition to exchange rate flexibility:
    >
    > - a deep and liquid foreign exchange market;
    > - a coherent policy governing central bank intervention in the foreign exchange market (the practice of buying or selling the local currency to influence its price, or exchange rate);
    > - an appropriate alternative nominal anchor to replace the fixed exchange rate; and
    > - effective systems for reviewing and managing the exposure of both the public and the private sectors to exchange rate risk. (Duttagupta et al., 2005, p. 1).

14. The equivalence to the more familiar condition of greater than unity for an increase in values is demonstrated in Weeks (2013).
15. See, for example, his discussion of 'internal devaluation' in the euro zone, at his blog, http://krugman.blogs.nytimes.com/2012/04/25/the-unbearable-slowness-of-internal-devaluation/
16. This statement of the difference between Keynes and the neoclassicals, what makes *The General Theory* 'general', is clearly explained in Leijonhufvud (1968, pp. 90ff). A summary is found in Weeks (2012 pp. 163–6).
17. The Chilean government used an unremunerated reserve requirement (URR), which required foreign investors to deposit a percentage of short-term-oriented financial transactions in an interest-free account with the central bank. The Malaysia government required that foreign funds invested in Malaysian stock cannot leave the country within one year (see discussion in http://overons.rabobank.com/content/images/Capital%20controls_tcm64-74919.pdf). A financial transactions tax of 2 per cent was introduced by the Brazilian government in 2009 (see 'Call to Ease Brazil's Capital Controls', *Financial Times*, 25 October 2011). The Argentine government introduced one of the more innovative mechanisms in 2011, the requirement that a person of company sending funds out of the country must demonstrate an income that generated those funds. This arrangement both reduces capital flight and monitors illegal money laundering.
18. Rowbotham (2000) describes the Bancor plan as follows:

    > Keynes proposed a new, neutral unit of international currency – the 'Bancor' – and a new institution – the International Clearing or Currency

> Union (ICU). All international trade would be measured in Bancors. Exporting would accrue Bancors, importing would expend Bancors. Nations were expected to maintain, within a small percentage, a zero account with the ICU. (p. 37)

See also Lucarelli (2011a and 2011b).

19. The Bancor plan did not require capital controls, but Keynes's (1943) opinion of them was clear:

> In the control of capital movements, which is quite another matter, each country is left to be its own judge whether it deems this necessary. In our own case, I do not see how we can hope to avoid it. It is not merely a question of curbing exchange speculations and movements of hot money, or even of avoiding flights of capital due to political motives; though all these it is necessary to control. The need, in my judgment, is more fundamental. Unless the aggregate of the new investments which individuals are free to make overseas is kept within the amount which our favourable trade balance is capable of looking after, we lose control over the domestic rate of interest.

See the discussion of Keynes and capital flight in Crotty (1983).

20. By chance, both John Maynard Keynes and Harry Dexter White, each chief spokesman of his country's delegation, died of heart problems, within two years of each other. White suffered a fatal heart attack in 1948, a few days after testifying before the House of Representatives Committee on Un-American Activities. White was accused of passing information to the Soviet Union. This charge is assessed and rejected by Boughton (2000).
21. The US side of the argument is found in Mikesell (1994). A more balanced view is in Parboni (1981).
22. For example, the statement of the formal objectives of the International Monetary Fund would become the preamble to a new global currency institution almost verbatim. Article I of the IMF founding document states:

> The purposes of the International Monetary Fund are:
> (i) To promote international monetary cooperation through a permanent institution which provides the machinery for consultation and collaboration on international monetary problems.
> (ii) To facilitate the expansion and balanced growth of international trade, and to contribute thereby to the promotion and maintenance of high levels of employment and real income and to the development of the productive resources of all members as primary objectives of economic policy.
> (iii) To promote exchange stability, to maintain orderly exchange arrangements among members, and to avoid competitive exchange depreciation.
> (iv) To assist in the establishment of a multilateral system of payments in respect of current transactions between members and in the elimination of foreign exchange restrictions which hamper the growth of world trade.
> (v) To give confidence to members by making the general resources of the Fund temporarily available to them under adequate safeguards, thus

> providing them with opportunity to correct maladjustments in their balance of payments without resorting to measures destructive of national or international prosperity.
> (vi) In accordance with the above, to shorten the duration and lessen the degree of disequilibrium in the international balances of payments of members.
> The Fund shall be guided in all its policies and decisions by the purposes set forth in this Article. (http://www.imf.org/external/pubs/ft/aa/#art1)

It should be noted that the words 'inflation' and 'price' do not appear in Article 1, but the instruction to aid member countries 'to correct maladjustments in their balance of payments *without resorting to measures destructive of national or international prosperity*' does appear (emphasis added).

23. An organization exists for the promotion of and research on an international currency, the single Global Currency Association, founded in 2003. This association is discussed in Riese (2008), and its website, http://www.singleglobalcurrency.org/, carries a quotation from former head of the Federal Reserve System, Paul Volcker, staying, 'a global economy requires a global currency'.
24. These advantages as analyzed by Alessandrini and Fratianni (2008), who conclude that a national reserve currency system creates vested interests in maintaining global imbalances.

> There is a convergence of interests for maintaining misaligned exchange rates and external imbalances. The equilibrium holds because the United States is keen in preserving the benefits of the key-currency and creditor countries are keen in accumulating US assets and avoiding capital losses on their rising dollar balances. This equilibrium, resulting from the convergence of interest of the two counterparties, is supported by the practice of surplus countries of sterilizing increases in the foreign component of the monetary base. (p. 1)

25. Heiner Flassbeck, Public Lecture, Globalisation Series, School of Oriental and African Studies, University of London, 1 February 2012.
26. The warning against 'protectionism' is very common. For example, in *The Daily Telegraph* (UK), Peter Mandelson was quoted as follows: 'If we start closing markets or blocking trade our prospects will be pushed down even further in a downward economic spiral we are in already' (26 January 2012).
27. A prominent exception is Ha-Joon Chang (2002).

References

Alessandrini, Pietro, and Michele Fratianni (2008) 'Resurrecting Keynes to Stabilize the International Monetary System', *MoFiR Working Paper 1*, Ancona: Money and Finance Research Group.

Arndt, H.W. (1963) *The Economic Lessons of the 1930s*, London: Frank Cass.

Arestis, P. (1999) 'The European Central Bank: Keynesian Alternatives', *Working Paper* No. 274, New York: The Jerome Levy Institute of Bard College.

Bhagwati, Jagdish (1964) 'The Pure Theory of International Trade', *Economic Journal* 74, 1–78.
Bibow, Jörg (2010) 'Bretton Woods 2 is Dead, Long Live Bretton Woods 3?', *Levi Economics Institute of Bard College*, Working Paper No. 597, New York: The Jerome Levy Institute of Bard College.
Boughton, James M. (2000) 'The Case Against Harry Dexter White: Still Not Proven', *IMF Working Paper* WP/00/149, Washington, DC: IMF.
Boughton, James M. (2002) 'Why White, not Keynes? Inventing the Post-war Monetary System', *IMF Working Paper 252*, Policy Development and Review Department, Washington, DC: IMF.
Chang, Ha-Joon (2002) *Kicking Away the Ladder: Development Strategy in Historical Perspective*, London: Anthem.
Crotty, J. (1983) 'On Keynes and Capital Flight', *Journal of Economic Literature*, 21(1): 59–65.
Davidson, P. (1992–93) 'Reforming the World's Money', *Journal of Post Keynesian Economics*, 15(2): 153–79.
Dooley, Michael P. (1979) 'The Portfolio-balance Model of Exchange Rates', *International Finance Discussion Papers* 141, Washington, DC: Federal Reserve Board.
Driskall, Robert (1980) 'Exchange Rate Dynamics, Portfolio Balance, and Relative Prices', *American Economic Review*, 70(4): 776–83.
Duttagupta, Rupa, Gilda Fernandez and Cim Karacadag (2005) 'Moving to a Flexible Exchange Rate: How, When, and How Fast?', *Economic Issues*, 38. Available at https://www.imf.org/external/pubs/ft/issues/issues38/ei38.pdf.
Fischer, Stanley (2001) 'Opening Remarks', IMF/World Bank International Reserves: Policy Issues Forum, Washington DC, 28 April. Available at http://www.imf.org/external/np/speeches/2001/042801.htm.
Fischer, Stanley (2011) 'Central Bank Lessons From the Global Crisis', Dinner lecture by Professor Stanley Fischer, at the Bank of Israel conference on "Lessons of the Global Crisis", Jerusalem, 31 March. Available at http://www.bis.org/review/r110414f.pdf.
Flassbeck, Heiner (2010a) 'Quo vadis, Germania? Das Ende des deutschen Exportmodells', *Beitrag für Zeit online*, zusammen mit Friederike Spieker, June.
Flassbeck, Heiner (2010b) 'The Greek Tragedy and the European Crisis, Made in Germany', *Monthly Review*, 13 March.
Gallagher, Kevin, and Jose Ocampo (2011) 'The IMF's Welcome Rethink on Capital Controls', *The Guardian*, 6 April. Available online at www.guardian.co.uk/commentisfree/cifamerica/2011/apr/06/imf-capital-controls.
Hahn, Frank (1984) *Equilibrium and Macroeconomics*, Oxford: Basil Blackwell.
International Monetary Fund (2007) *Annual Report*, Washington, DC: IMF.
International Monetary Fund (2010) *Controls on Capital Part of the Policy Mix*, IMF Survey. Available at http://www.imf.org/external/pubs/ft/survey/so/2010/POL021910A.htm.
Keynes, J.M. (1936) *The General Theory of Employment, Interest and Money*, London: Macmillan. Available online at http://ebooks.adelaide.edu.au/k/keynes/john_maynard/k44g/chapter18.html.
Keynes, J.M. (1943) Speech to the House of Lords, *Hansard*, HL Deb 18 May 1943 vol. 127 cc521–64.

Lane, Philip R., and Gian Maria Milesi-Ferretti 2006) 'The External Wealth of Nations Mark II: Revised and Extended Estimates of Foreign Assets and Liabilities, 1970–2004', IMF Working Paper WP/06/69, Washington, DC: IMF.
Lucarelli, B. (2011a) 'A New International Bretton Woods System?', *Real-world Economics Review*, 58: 83–8.
Lucarelli, B. (2011b) *The Economics of Financial Turbulence*, Cheltenham, UK: Edward Elgar.
Mikesell, Raymond F. (1994) *The Bretton Woods Debates: A memoir*, Essays in International Finance, Working Papers Series, Department of Economics, no 192, Princeton, NJ.
Ostry, Jonathan D., Atish R. Ghosh, Karl Habermeier, Marcos Chamon, Mahvash S. Qureshi, and Dennis B.S. Reinhardt (2010) 'Capital Inflows: The Role of Controls', *IMF Staff Position Note* SPN/10/04, Washington, DC.
Parboni, R. (1981) *The Dollar and Its Rivals*, London: New Left Books.
Riese, Martin (2008) *Reforming the Global Financial Architecture: A Comparison of Different Proposals*, Linz: Johannes Kepler Universitat.
Rodrik, Dani (2006) 'Social Cost of Foreign Exchange Reserves', National Bureau of Economic Research, Working Paper 11952, Cambridge, MA: NBER. Available at http://zunia.org/uploads/media/knowledge/Dani2.pdf.
Rowbotham, Michael (2000) *Goodbye America! Globalisation, Debt and the Dollar Empire*, Chipping Norton: Jon Carpenter Publishing.
Salvatore, Dominick (2004) *International Economics*, eighth edition, New York: John Wiley & Sons.
Shaikh, Anwar (1999) 'Real Exchange Rates and the International Mobility of Capital', Department of Economics, New School University, *Working Paper* 265. Available at http://homepage.newschool.edu/~AShaikh/Levyxrus.pdf.
Stiglitz, Joseph (2006) *Making Globalization Work*, New York: W.W. Norton.
Stiglitz, Joseph, and Bruce Greenwald (2003) 'Dealing With Debt – How to Reform the Global Financial System', *Harvard International Review*, 25(1): 54–9.
Triffin, R. (1961) *Gold and the Dollar Crisis*, New York: Yale University Press.
Weeks, John (2012) *The Irreconcilable Inconsistencies of Neoclassical Macroeconomics: A False Paradigm*, Oxford: Routledge.
Weeks, John (2013) 'Effectiveness of Monetary Policy Reconsidered', *Review of Political Economy*, 25(1): 57–67.

3
The Potential of Financial Transactions Taxes

Philip Arestis
University of Cambridge, UK, and University of Leeds, UK

Malcolm Sawyer
University of Leeds, UK

3.1 Introduction

The purpose of this paper is to examine the potentials of a range of financial transaction taxes (hereafter FTT). In the literature this term has included a wide range of different taxes: securities transaction tax, levied on transactions including equity, debt and their derivatives; currency transaction tax imposed on foreign exchange transactions, including their derivatives, currency futures, options and swaps; capital transaction tax, imposed in the form of loans and issuance of stocks and loans; bank transaction tax, which is a tax on bank accounts and withdrawals; insurance premium tax, imposed on insurance premiums; and real estate transaction tax, levied on the value of land when sold.[1] In what follows we do not discuss all of these forms of financial transactions taxes. We do, however, indicate the form that is under consideration. It is true, nonetheless, that the emphasis in what follows in this contribution is on the first two types of financial transactions taxes, namely securities including derivatives and currency (see Matheson, 2011, for a comprehensive analysis of the issues involved in terms of these two types of financial transactions taxes along with the available evidence).[2] The common feature, though, as the name suggests, is taxes on financial transactions, and hence the paper does not consider other taxes on the financial sector or part thereof such as excessive profits taxes, taxes that relate to the scale of bonuses, or taxes related to assets or liabilities of the banking system; we also do not consider here to any significant extent financial activity taxes (FAT) analogous to sales or value added tax on financial activities. We also examine the potential of financial transaction taxes, and the resistance to their introduction, which could be seen as surprising in view of the fact that at the time of writing a number of countries have implemented such a tax at the national level for some considerable time – and successfully so as we argue below. It is though much less surprising in light of the economic and political power of the financial sector, which is probably the major constraint on the introduction of such taxes. More recently, though, and in view of the 'great recession' renewed interest in such a tax has evidently re-emerged.[3]

Financial assets vary in a range of ways, including their degree of complexity and the contractual issues surrounding them (for example, loans). A financial transaction is the exchange of a financial asset for money. It can involve exchange at a fixed (nominal) price or variable price, and it can involve the exchange of either existing assets or new assets. We make those obvious distinctions as different forms of financial transactions taxes address a number of heterogeneous types of trade in different financial assets. It is also the case that the rationale for and effects of the various types of tax are different. An important distinction can be drawn between trade in existing assets for which the price is variable, and trade in assets which have a fixed (nominal) price. In the former case, there is concern over the volatility of the price (for example, of equity, of foreign exchange) and the effects that volatility may have on the rest of the economy. In the case of fixed-price assets, those concerns do not arise. The concern is rather over some combination of the nature of the financial assets (for example, derivatives) and their volume.

Although a range of arguments have been deployed in favour of financial transactions taxes, there are two sets which stand out. The first is to dampen down the volume of financial transactions. This is clearest in the case of the foreign exchange tax (hereafter FET), what is usually referred to as the Tobin tax (after Tobin 1974), often paraphrased as 'putting sand in the wheel'. In turn this is based on ideas that the volume of such financial transactions is unnecessary, unproductive or detrimental. Just as in the case of the advocacy on widely traded securities, similarly in the case of the FET, the volume is related to the degree of price volatility. In the latter case such tax reduces financial market risk and potentially preventing asset price bubbles (see, for example, Matheson, 2011). In a world of floating exchange rates, the large volume of transactions is often viewed as generating volatility in the exchange rate with consequent detrimental effects on the real economies.[4] A distinction is made between short-term and long-term transactions. Very short-term transactions are more likely to be volatile and destabilizing than long-term transactions. A much higher tax rate on short-term rather than on long-term investments should discourage the former, thereby reducing overall volatility.

John Maynard Keynes, in his *Treatise on Money* (1930) and *General Theory* (1936), suggests that a tax on foreign lending to contain speculative capital movements might be necessary (see, for example, pp. 158–61 in Keynes's *General Theory*, 1936; also Haq et al., 1996, for a later example). Keynes (op. cit.) bases his argument on the dangers of speculation; the argument is that

> As the organization of investment markets improves, the risk of the predominance of speculation does, however, increase. In one of the greatest investment markets in the world, namely, New York, the influence of speculation (in the above sense) is enormous. Even outside the field of finance, Americans are apt to be unduly interested in discovering what average opinion believes average opinion to be; and this national weakness finds its nemesis in the stock market (p. 159)

and, inevitably, in the foreign exchange market. In Keynes (1936) there is also the argument for a substantial transfer tax on securities transactions, which would reduce speculation in the financial markets (pp. 104–5). Keynes (op. cit., chapter 12) also suggested that 'The introduction of a substantial Government transfer tax on all transactions might prove the most serviceable reform available, with a view to mitigating the predominance of speculation over enterprise' (p. 160). Thus, Keynes saw such a tax as designed to influence the balance between short-term and long-term holdings of shares, with possible impacts on the volatility of share prices ('speculation'), on investment ('enterprise') and corporate governance.

The second rationale, unsurprisingly, is that such taxes are a source of tax revenue, and the advocacy of such taxes has often been associated with ideas for how such tax revenues would be spent. These tax receipts could be used for worldwide public investment. There is a sense in which FTTs have an air of hypothecation. In the case of the FET developmental or environmental purposes have been generally cited, whereas some of the current proposals in the European context envisage revenues being used in the context of the ongoing euro crisis. Proposals for some form of taxation on financial transactions have a long history, and indeed there is a long history of such taxation (for example on stock market transactions). James Tobin, in his 1972 Janeway Lecture, delivered at Princeton University and published in Tobin (1974), proposed a tax on foreign exchange transactions (usually now referred to as the 'Tobin tax') as a way of reducing short-term speculative currency flows, which should tame excessive risk-price taking, and thus exchange rate volatility and limit speculation as a result; this type of tax is what we referred to above as FET. A FET would allow greater economic policy autonomy, thereby enhancing the efficacy of macroeconomic policy, and raising tax revenues.[5] Tobin (1978) further suggests that a FET 'would apply to all purchases of financial instruments denominated in another currency – from currency and coin to equity securities. It would have to apply ... to all payments in one currency for goods, services, and real assets sold by a resident of another currency area' (p. 159).

In addition to Keynes (1936), as suggested above, more recently Tobin (1996), has also proposed a security transaction excise tax. Tobin (op. cit.) suggests that such tax 'would automatically penalize short-horizon round trips, while negligibly affecting the incentives for ... longer-term capital investments' (p. xi). Pollin et al. (2003) and Pollin (2003) strongly defend such a tax in the case of the USA, especially so in view of the repeal of the 1933 Glass–Steagall Act in 1999.

In more recent years, there have been two lines of development with regard to financial transactions taxes. The first has been the advocacy of FTTs, particularly in the form of currency or foreign exchange transactions taxes levied on a near-universal basis which could form the basis of a revenue stream from which developmental and environmental projects could be funded (see, for example, Arestis and Sawyer, 1996, for relevant references).[6] The second has been developments of broadly-based taxes on securities and derivatives, notably at the European Union. These taxes have been viewed as a tax revenue stream related to the EU budget and formulated to respond to the financial and banking crisis. A significant element here has been the thought given to the implementation of the tax (as discussed in Arestis and Sawyer, 1996).

The rest of this contribution is organized as follows. In section 3.2 we discuss more recent FTT contributions. Section 3.3 deals with the potential effects on the volume of transactions and resource use. Section 3.4 turns to the tax revenue potential. International trade effects are dealt with in section 3.5. Section 3.6 discusses issues that relate to the efficiency of markets. Section 3.7 is concerned with the effects of FTTs on the level of output. Section 3.8 deals with issues of tax avoidance and tax evasion. Finally, section 9 offers concluding comments.

3.2 Recent financial transactions tax contributions

Tobin (1996) rightly makes the point that his FET suggestion was ignored for a long time by 'the community of professional economists' and only occasionally visited by 'journalists and financial pundits'; indeed Tobin (op. cit.) suggested 'it did not make such a ripple' (p. x). However, ever since and every time there is a currency, or, more generally speaking, a financial crisis, and there have been many culminating in the 'great recession' along with the related euro crisis, renewed interest in the different forms of FTT has emerged. It is also the case that 'the fiscal difficulties created by the current crisis have led to renewed calls for the imposition of such a tax, both to boost tax revenues and as a means of extracting a larger contribution from the financial sector to fund a wide range of national and international public goods' (McCulloch and Pacillo, 2010, p. 2). It is perhaps unsurprising that a significant number of official and other relevant contributions have taken place more recently supportive of the FTT introduction with varying degrees of enthusiasm. An early relevant contribution is the United Nations Development Programme (1994), which emphasizes the potential of the FET in raising large amounts of money that could be used to finance development. Spahn (1995, 1996) proposes a two-tier transaction tax on currency lending. Low transaction taxes would be imposed and maintained during 'normal' times. A higher transaction tax would be activated wherever market activity accelerates strongly (see, also, Bencivenga, Smith and Starr, 1996, who develop a formal model to study under what conditions a FET would be justified). It must be readily admitted, though, that although governments and international fora showed approval or willingness to discuss it, not much more was in evidence at that time.

More recently, a cautiously expressed renewed interest has emerged in the context of the 'great recession'. The G20 leaders at their January 2009 Summit in Pittsburgh requested the IMF to prepare a report on the FTT by the time of their June 2010 Summit in Toronto, Canada. The IMF (2010a, 2010b) response (see, also, Cottarelli, 2010, pp. 3–4) in this context is that although the FTT idea could be considered by the IMF, and it should not be excluded, the conclusion reached, however, is that a financial stability contribution tax and a financial activity tax are thought to be more efficient ways of raising tax than a financial transactions tax.[7] Other IMF contributors recognise the value of a FTT (for recent examples, see Matheson, 2011; and, also, Brondolo, 2011). Matheson (2011) looks into the FTT as 'a means of raising revenue and regulating financial markets'. Supporting arguments for its adoption include progressivity and ease of implementation. The purpose of this paper has been to evaluate the first three of these claims; the fourth is explored in greater detail by Brondolo (2011), who concludes that while taxing exchange-traded instruments would be relatively easy and efficient, 'taxing over-the-counter transactions would prove more costly and challenging' (p. 37). Brondolo (op. cit.) also argues that 'The viability of an FTT would be enhanced by international cooperation. Countries would have greater degrees of freedom to implement an FTT – and less concern over tax arbitrage and the possible dislocation of trading – if major financial center countries were to jointly introduce the tax in a fairly uniform manner' (p. 45).

The IMF ideas have been followed by other initiatives. The Leading Group on Innovative Financing for Development (LGIFD, 2010) produced a report recommending the adoption of a global FTT. To the extent that the objective is to reduce financial transactions for the purpose of reducing negative externalities, which contribute to the systemic risk of the financial system, then a FTT is desirable. It is also argued that any financial transaction tax should be a low percentage rate; and taxing over-the-counter derivative transactions at a somewhat higher rate than exchange-based derivative transactions is desirable. The European Commission has brought forward a draft directive (European Commission Taxation and Customs Union, 2011; see, also, European Commission, 2012a) for a financial transactions tax. The European Parliament (2012) has supported the initiative of the European Commission: 'The proposed financial transaction tax should be better designed to capture more traders and make evasion unprofitable, said the European Parliament in its opinion adopted on Wednesday [23 May 2012]. The opinion also says the tax should go ahead even if only some Member States opt for it. The tax rates proposed by the Commission (0.1% for shares and bonds and 0.01% for derivatives) are considered suitable and pension funds should be the only sector exempted from the tax.' A FTT levied at 0.1 per cent on share and bond transactions, and 0.01 per cent on complex security deals such as derivative contracts, is expected to produce up to 57bn euros a year, which would be shared between the budget of the EU and participating countries' national treasuries. The EU FTT is also expected to reduce some of the more pointless transactions, which are detached from the real economy. This is minuscule relative to the impact of the austerity measures currently pursued by some EU governments. Indeed, GDP could even increase once the potential positive effects of the FTT materialize, like for example preventing crises by reducing speculative activities. Indeed, to the extent that the proceeds of the FTT are properly reinvested by the relevant governments, a positive impact on GDP could very well materialise. The strongest EU opponent of a FTT is the UK. The UK objection is based on the potential negative effect the FTT may imply for the size of the London's financial sector. Not just the UK but also Sweden, the Netherlands and Luxembourg have expressed reservations at the EU FTT proposal. Interestingly enough, if a FTT were introduced in the 17 euro area country-members, it would give a potentially significant advantage to the UK financial centre over those in the euro area, especially so in relation to those of Ireland, Luxembourg and the Netherlands. Be that as it may, and as reported in the *Financial Times*, 'EU looks at stump duty to settle tax impasse' (14 March 2012); it appears that the UK's stamp duty is emerging as a potential compromise in the EU, in view of the deadlock over the FTT plans.[8] France has proposed to implement unilaterally a FTT in the hope that this would provide a 'shock' that would persuade other countries in Europe to follow suit. This FTT was introduced in August 2012, and has been inspired by the UK's stamp duty. A levy of 0.1 per cent is contemplated, which is lower than the UK's equivalent of 0.5 per cent.[9]

There have also been significant contributions from other than official sources. The first important recent contributor in favour of the idea of a FET, which promotes the argument further, is the Eichengreen, Tobin and Wyplosz (1995) paper where it is suggested that

> The principal purpose of the tax is to expand the autonomy of national monetary policies. That does not depend upon its success in reducing volatility. The tax would not, of course, permit national macroeconomic authorities to ignore the international repercussions of their policies. In particular, it could not protect patent misvaluations in exchange parties; speculators' gain from betting on inevitable near-term realignments would far exceed the tax costs. Nor would the tax make macroeconomic policy coordination among major governments unnecessary or undesirable. (p. 165)

Further recent, relevant, and supportive contributions include, for example, Palley (2003), Westerhof (2003) and Ehrenstein et al. (2005).

A comprehensive review of the recent developments on the FTT has been undertaken by McCulloch and Pacillo (2010). The authors conclude in favour of the FTT tax in that it is both feasible and indeed could produce substantial revenue without causing serious distortions. The authors show that there is by now considerable evidence on the impact of such taxes. Indeed, McCulloch and Pacillo (op. cit.) argue that the extensive theoretical and empirical work on the FTT suggests that it is

> implementable and could make a non-trivial contribution to revenue in the major financial economies. It seems unlikely to stabilize

> financial markets, but, if appropriately designed, unlikely to destabilize them either; and, although a multilateral agreement between the key economies is clearly preferable, it would not be impossible to implement unilaterally, at least for a major economy. (p. 38)

In terms of FTT being feasible, McCulloch and Pacillo (2010) conclude that this would be the case in terms of taxes on equity, bonds and related securities. Indeed, several countries have successfully implemented such taxes. For the FET case the evidence is not so clear-cut. However, McCulloch and Pacillo (op. cit.) suggest that 'there is a clear sense that the significant shift towards centralisation in the foreign exchange market and the widespread use of common messaging and clearing systems means that a Tobin tax could be successfully implemented. Although implementation problems still remain, the literature does provide a reasonable consensus about how such a tax should be designed. There is a clear preference to coverage of a broad range of instruments, including not only spot transactions, but also outright forwards, and swaps and potentially futures, options and other derivatives. The literature is also clear on the need to differentiate the tax rate by instrument and market to ensure that it corresponds to around the same percentage of transaction costs in each market' (p. 36). Another relevant argument is that

> if the FTT is applied beyond the foreign exchange market, the question arises as to whether it should include bonds. Pollin (2003), for example, includes in all government debt (federal, state and municipal in the case of the USA), in order to minimise any distortionary effects on the tax across the markets. On the other hand, several commentators point to the common practice of excluding transactions in government bonds from taxation in order not to raise the costs of government borrowing. (McCulloch and Pacillo, 2010, p. 15)

However, the latter publication goes further to suggest that the consensus in the literature favours a broad FTT (see, also, below). A related issue is the following. A FTT is levied on a financial transaction, which is the exchange of one financial asset (for example, money denominated in one currency) for another (for example, money denominated in another currency). One question is whether there is a reduction not only in the volume of financial transactions but also in the volume of associated transactions. Such a case may arise in the FET case, where, for example, currency exchange is linked with international trade.

3.3 Effects on volume of transactions and resource use

The opponents of financial transaction taxes often point to the effects that such taxes could have on the volume of transactions. They point to the consequences for employment and for trade in goods and services, which could also be affected (notably a foreign exchange tax that inhibits currency exchange and can have implications for the costs of international trade). But, in general, the proponents of FTTs view the impact of such taxes on the volume of transactions as beneficial. In turn, this is based on the idea that the volume of financial transactions is excessive, and hence their reduction will be socially beneficial and the resources devoted to the trade in financial instruments can be better deployed.

In the context of foreign exchange dealings, the comparison has been drawn between the volume of currency exchanges and the volume of foreign trade, with the volume of currency exchange exceeding 60 times that of foreign trade. In general, financial transaction taxes have been proposed not only in the realization that the volume of relevant financial transactions would be reduced but indeed that such a reduction was part of the rationale for such taxes. In turn, the reduction in transactions is viewed to have beneficial effects – for foreign exchange and equity transactions in the volatility of prices, for others in the volume of assets and liabilities traded, and, more generally, for the resources employed in arranging such transactions.

More specifically for FET, a reduction of say half in the volume of foreign exchange transactions would also result in some significant resource savings. Frankel (1996) suggests 'a typical transaction cost for foreign exchange might be 0.1 per cent' (p. 61), though much smaller for interdealer trading. Felix and Sau (1996) use the much higher figures of 0.5 per cent and 1.0 per cent for the transaction costs in their estimates of the yield from a FET. But they also report that 'the quoted bid–ask spreads on trades of major currencies in the "wholesale" foreign exchange market (trades less [sic] than $50 million) over the electronic network are usually less than 0.1% ... The spreads are doubled for "retail" trades (less than $5 million) and can rise to more than 1.0 % for small retail transactions' (p. 231). However, other figures on the bid–ask spread are much lower (noting that transaction costs are broader than the bid–ask spread). Kenen (1996) states that 'spreads in the wholesale market are well below 10 basis points (i.e. 0.1 per cent) for the major currencies' (p. 110). Hartmann (1996, Table IV.1) reports Reuters spreads for a wide range of bilateral exchange rates. For some of the major currencies, the quoted spreads reported are around 5 basis points, although it is thought that traded spreads are smaller by a factor of two to three.

A number of arguments have been advanced in support of FET (see, Tobin's, 1974, original contribution; also, Arestis and Sawyer, 1996, 1997). The main argument is focused on reducing the volatility of financial transactions. There is a sense in which the volume of foreign and domestic exchange transactions is excessive, being many times greater than the volume required to finance trade. It is, of course, the case that an appropriate level of financial transactions would be several times the volume of trade, and also of international trade. This is necessary to allow for the financing of both direct and portfolio investment, to allow for a degree of financial mobility in pursuit of higher rates of return, which serves to bring about a degree of equalization of returns and to permit some risk-shifting and risk-spreading. This volume of transactions absorbs resources that affect transactions but, more significantly, it is seen to have an adverse effect on the domestic and world economies. In a world of floating exchange rates, this large volume of transactions is often viewed as generating volatility in the exchange rate with consequent detrimental effects on the real economies. Any attempts at fixed exchange rates are made much more difficult by the volume of transactions (see, also, Eichengreen, Tobin and Wyplosz, 1995). This rationale for the foreign exchange transaction tax requires that, under a floating exchange rate regime, there is excessive volatility of exchange rates (where excessive is taken to imply detrimental) and that reducing the volume of transactions would reduce volatility. The more usual proposition is that a thin market will tend to exhibit volatility whereas a thick market will not. The rationale for the FTT in this case, appears to be based on almost the opposite view, or at least over the range of interest, an increase in the volume of transactions of the market increases volatility.

Contributions against the FTT idea have made their views public, such as Aliber et al. (2003), who argue that volatility would increase, and Grahl and Lysandrou (2003), who argue that the introduction and implementation of FTT 'would bring about a deep disorganization of existing financial structures that would not only fail to achieve, but indeed would work against, the basic objectives of those who support it' (p. 618). However, it is the case that a reduction in financial trading volumes may not be such a negative result after all. The enormous increase in bank balance sheets prior to the 'great recession' was the result of the growth of trading between financial institutions, traditional banks and the 'shadow banking' sector, which led to the creation of the structured assets and the financial crisis of August 2007 (see, for example, Arestis and Karakitsos, 2010).

3.4 Tax revenue potential

The financial transactions taxes offer an additional stream of tax revenues. They also offer to levy taxes on the financial sector and its operations, which it can be argued have been relatively lightly taxed: specifically there are few activity-related taxes on the financial sector comparable to sales or value added taxes. There are some examples such as insurance tax in the UK and there are, as discussed further below, a range of stamp duty type taxes on equity transactions and the financial sector's wages and profits are taxed at levels comparable to the non-financial sector. Another likely feature of the tax revenue side of FTTs is that the taxes would be levied on individuals with a relatively low propensity to spend, and the levying of taxes would have a correspondingly lower impact on spending.

The United Nations Development Programme (1994) and UNCTAD (1995) have seen clearly and argued for the FTT possibilities in terms of raising large amounts of money, which could be used to finance development. UNDP (1994) agree with Tobin (1974) that 'the revenue potential is immense, over $1.5 trillion a year for the 0.5 % tax' (p. 70). It can also be noted that in the wake of the 1994 Mexican peso crisis, even the IMF endorsed, albeit cautiously, limited reliance on transactions taxes and restrictions on selected international financial transactions (Folkerts-Landau and Ito, 1995).

The United Nations Development Programme (1994) suggests that a 'logical source of funds for a global response to global threats is a set of fees on globally important transactions or polluting emissions ... One is a tax on the international movements of speculative capital suggested by James Tobin ... Tobin suggests a tax rate of 0.5 % on such transactions, but even a tax of 0.05 % during 1995–2000 could raise $150 billion a year. Such a tax would be largely invisible and totally non-discriminatory' (p. 9). These tax receipts could be used for worldwide public investment.[10] Felix and Sau (1996) provide a range of estimates with assumptions of transaction costs ranging from 0.5 per cent to 1 per cent. Their central estimates range between $205.5 billion and $267.6 billion for a 0.25 per cent tax in 1995. We may assume that revenue of the order of $200 billion could be generated through a modest transactions tax.

McCulloch and Pacillo (2010) construct a meta-analysis exercise in terms of the FTT revenue potential to conclude that their results suggest that

> the revenue potential of a Tobin Tax is still significant, albeit smaller than proponents suggest.[11] A Tobin Tax of 0.005 per cent applied only to spot, outright forward and swap foreign exchange markets could raise around $26 billion if applied globally, or US$11.1 billion (£7.7 billion) if only applied to the UK. If a financial transaction tax equivalent to 10 per cent of existing levels of transaction costs in each market was to be applied, across the board, to equity, forex and derivative markets (both on and off exchanges), the revenue potential could be as high as US$415 billion, or US$134.6 billion (£92.7 billion) if only applied in the UK. Of course, it is likely that long-run elasticities will be larger than short-run elasticities, as market actors find mechanisms to avoid the tax. Certainly the existing literature suggests considerable care needs to be taken in the design of the tax to minimise avoidance opportunities, and tax authorities would need to monitor avoidance and modify or supplement measures as appropriate (as exemplified by the UK's introduction of the Stamp Duty Reserve Tax to prevent avoidance of the UK Stamp Duty on share transactions). However, we do not find compelling evidence that these activities would be any more onerous or costly than the normal activities undertaken by tax authorities. We therefore conclude that, a Tobin Tax, could make a significant contribution to the revenues of countries that impose it. (p. 37)

The potential of tax revenues has become particularly popular recently in view of the fact that the financial sector is relatively undertaxed in the sense that financial transactions do not usually bear general sales or value added taxes and nor are they usually subject to specific taxes in the way in which these apply to, for example, tobacco and alcohol. Actually, most countries do have such taxes as Campbell and Froot (1994) show, and summarised in Frankel (1996). In fact it is shown in these publications that there are only a few industrialized countries that have no transactions taxes at all. In terms of more recent developments, and especially in view of the 'great recession', the relevant goal is to raise revenue from the financial sector to help with meeting the costs of the financial crisis associated with the 'great recession' or similar crises in future. There is, of course, the associated goal of reducing financial market risk and helping to prevent asset price bubbles.

Pollin et al. (2002) propose a similar FET case, whose tax rate varies with transaction costs: 0.2 basis points (bp) on futures (notional value), 1 bp times years to maturity on bonds; 2 bps time years to maturity on swaps (notional principle); and 50 bps on stocks and option premiums. The authors estimate that the tax would raise US$66–132 billion per annum. The low estimate assumes that trading volume contracts by 50 per cent in reaction to the STT, while the high estimate assumes that it is unchanged. Schulmeister (2009), using a similar assumption that trading volume contracts between 10 and 40 per cent in response to a one basis point STT on global stocks, bonds and derivatives (including commodity derivatives), estimate that it would raise US$202–266 billion (cited in IMF, 2010b).

Baker (2011) proposes an extended form of transaction tax that 'would tax not only stocks but also trades of options, futures, credit default swaps and other derivatives' (p. 6). It is estimated that in the case of the USA such tax 'could easily raise more than 1.0 percent of GDP (approximately $150 billion in 2011) even assuming very substantial reductions in trading volume' (Baker, 2011, p. 2; see, also, Baker, 2003).

The European Commission (2012a) provide estimates for the proposed EU-wide FTT providing revenue of 57 billion euros (around 3 per cent of EU GDP). This is composed of a 0.1 per cent tax on securities yielding 19.4 billion euros, of which 6.8 billion euros comr from trading in shares and 12.6 billion euros from trading in bonds; and a 0.01 per cent tax on derivative trading yielding 37.7 billion euros (of which equity yielded 3.3 billion euros, interest rate 29.6 billion euros and currency 4.8 billion euros).

3.5 International trade effects

A FET would tax currency transactions that finance international trade in goods and services. This is the case since such a tax cannot distinguish between speculative transactions and those to finance trade. It clearly follows that to the extent trade is negatively affected by a FET, public welfare could be reduced. A serious counterargument is that such a tax might actually increase the level of trade. To the extent that a FET reduces currency market uncertainty, foreign currency risk exposure is reduced along with the cost of trading. International trade would increase under these conditions. Still, Holtham (1995) argues that proposals for a transactions tax 'could inhibit international financial investment or trade finance' (p. 237). The imposition of a transactions tax in itself would add to the costs of conducting international trade, and the likelihood is that trade would thereby be somewhat diminished.

Goodhart (1996) argues that multiple exchanges take place through the banking sector as one bank seeks to balance its books through exchanges with other banks. The argument can then be put that a transactions tax would mean that each of the multiple transactions would be subject to tax, which in turn would in effect be passed back to the original customer. The question is that since 'no one knows' what the multiple might be, it is rather difficult to assess the extent of the implications of this argument. Be that as it may, each exchange transaction in the chain is subject to some transaction cost. Thus there is resource costs involved, which would be reduced by a transactions tax.

Assuming that the tax was passed on in full to consumers, it is clear that there could be an impact on the volume of international trade. Davidson (1997) suggests that there are five foreign exchange transactions that precede the final sale of goods (but does not cite evidence for this figure). It could be expected that in either case those involved in trade would seek to economize on exchange transactions in the face of a transactions tax. It can also be noted that much of international trade (of the order of 30 to 40 per cent) takes the form of shipment of goods (usually semi-finished) from one branch of a transnational corporation to another. Most of that trade can be financed by book-keeping entries rather than the conversion of one currency into another, and as such it would not bear a transactions tax.

In evaluating the overall balance of effects of a FET on international trade, due consideration would need to be given to the effects of reduced volume of exchange transactions, of reduced volatility, enhanced independence of national economic policies and the probable stimulus to worldwide aggregate demand. These factors would affect international trade; however, the overall net effect of a FET on international trade cannot be readily predicted. Holtham (1995) argues that 'given the existence of a J-curve in the response of the current account to exchange rate changes, any exchange rate driven wholly or largely by the current account (the situation in the absence of capital flows), is subject to unstable oscillations. Some speculative capital flows are necessary for stability' (p. 237). In the extreme case where the only foreign exchange dealings were those related to trade, then this argument may hold. At present, the general calculation is that the foreign exchange flows are of the order of 60 times those that would be necessary for financing international trade. We would infer that even after the imposition of a FET, foreign exchange flows would remain significantly in excess of those required to finance trade (perhaps of the order of 30 times).

Some 'back of the envelope' calculations suggest that the direct effect on trade of a transactions tax would be less than 1 per cent. Even if a 0.1 per cent tax was effectively a 0.5 per cent tax, as Davidson (1997) would suggest, then only part would be borne by the consumers. The proportion of the tax borne by consumers (and hence that also that is borne by producers) depends upon the relative elasticities of demand for traded goods and of the supply of those goods. Assuming the elasticities of demand and supply are roughly equal so that half of the tax is borne by consumers, and with a relatively high elasticity of demand for traded goods of, say, 4, the direct effect on international trade would be 1 per cent. A high elasticity suggests that traded and non-traded goods are readily substituted for one another, and that the welfare loss to consumers is minor.

3.6 Efficiency of markets

Financial markets are often presented as operating in an efficient manner, although it has to be stressed that the term 'efficiency' is used here in a rather specific manner; namely, that it is defined in terms of the price of financial assets incorporating all available information. In turn, this view of financial markets is closely linked with a 'rational expectations' perspective, in which market participants are well informed on how markets work and utilise fully the available information in their trading activities. But such models of rational expectations 'do not explain many of the characteristics that are observed in real financial markets such as excess liquidity (i.e. excessive trading activity due to speculative trade), excess price volatility, fat tailed distributions of returns (i.e. a much higher probability of very large positive and negative changes) and volatility clustering (i.e. switches between periods of high and low volatility)' (McCulloch and Pacillo, 2010, p. 5). This realization has led to a closer focus on the microstructure of these markets and the characteristics of traders (Frankel and Rose, 1994). Market actors in these models are assumed to have bounded rationality. Their behaviour is governed by 'rules of thumb', which are not necessarily optimal. Different types of market actors are assumed, which leads to 'heterogeneous agent models' (see Simon, 1957).

Furthermore, the more recent experience prior to the 'great recession', and the events leading to it, clearly testify to the problems that can be created as a result of belief in the extreme and wrong assumptions of rational expectations, and to the other related assumptions referred to above (see, for example, Arestis and Karakitsos, 2011). It is also recognized that financial markets suffer from asymmetric information and herd behaviour, moral hazard when participants are too big or powerful to fail, and also from the possibility of multiple equilibria. An important implication of all these problematic assumptions is persistent misalignments and unstable exchange rate regimes in the case of foreign exchange markets. Asymmetric information and herd behaviour imply that incompletely informed investors suffer bouts of optimism and pessimism. Indeed, foreign exchange market speculators watch other speculators rather than 'fundamentals'. Frankel (1996) reports the results of surveys of speculators' expectations, which clearly suggest that forecasts are dominated by 'technical models' that reflect the type of behaviour to which we have just alluded. Swings in sentiment not obviously associated with the arrival of economic or political news occur frequently and especially in the foreign exchange markets (Kindleberger, 1978; Eichengreen and Lindert, 1989; Eichengreen, 1991). It should be stressed that the assumptions just referred to lead to an analysis that is significantly closer to reality.

Moral hazard in the banking system can produce instabilities in the foreign exchange markets (Felix and Sau, 1996). This can happen when regulators are unwilling or unable to allow domestic banks to fail. Under these circumstances, domestic banks would have the incentive to borrow abroad in order to lend domestically, leading to exchange rate swings under a flexible exchange rate system, and pressures on the exchange rate in a fixed exchange rate system. Multiple equilibria become an additional source of exchange rate volatility: not only does the exchange rate exhibit wide fluctuations when the 'fundamentals' change, but it can also move from one equilibrium to another even when the 'fundamentals' remain unchanged. These arguments relate to the question of whether trade in financial assets creates undesirable externalities such as volatility. The volume of financial transactions is 'excessive' and taxing some or all of them would reduce the volume. Does volatility matter and would FTTs reduce volatility?

McCulloch and Pacillo (2010) summarize the impact of all of the above theoretical propositions, and in the process respond to the question just posed, to conclude that 'Most, if not all, studies conclude that a small Tobin tax would reduce volatility, but many models also suggest that great care should be taken in choosing the size of the tax since, if it is too large, the reductions in market trading and liquidity could result in an increase rather than a reduction in volatility' (p. 10). In terms of the empirical evidence, McCulloch and Pacillo (op. cit.) review the available evidence and conclude that despite a number of 'methodological weaknesses' in the empirical applications,

> The balance of evidence would seem to suggest that that there is a positive relationship between transaction costs and volatility, although the size of this effect varies across different studies. Whether a Tobin Tax would affect volatility in the same way as underlying market transaction costs is not clear. The Swedish experience of imposing a tax on equity transactions may have increased volatility, but the size of the tax was large; there is no evidence that UK Stamp Duty had any effect on volatility, although it clearly affected returns on equity. (p. 14)

Still, though, 'the evidence does not suggest that a Tobin Tax would be highly destabilising either, at least, not at the low rates of taxation typically proposed; volatility may increase, but only by a relatively small amount'.

The Swedish experience with a FTT is worth exploring. Introduced in January 1984 and abolished in December 1991, it was levied directly on domestic brokerage service providers, namely on domestic stock and derivative transactions. In effect, it was domestic equity and bond transactions that were taxed during this period, through Swedish brokers, thereby excluding foreign brokers; the relevant rates were doubled in 1986 and 1989. The FTT tax generated little revenue, even after the rates were doubled, and led to a massive migration to other financial centres. The result was a serious decline in trading volumes and the exodus of financial business mainly to the City of London. It should be acknowledged, though, at this stage that in the UK there is already in place a FTT in the form of stamp duty. In this form a levy of 0.5 per cent on stocks traded is levied (that is, on equities, active derivatives and fixed-income markets), and has been done so ever since 1694, being paid by both residents and non-residents. London's financial sector is truly international;[12] the London Stock Exchange is in fact the fourth largest in the world (Baker, 2011).[13] In view of this success, Baker (op. cit.) proposes an extended form of transaction tax in relation to the UK's stamp duty and in the form of a financial speculation tax as a means of government deficit reduction. This 'would tax not only stocks but also trades of options, futures, credit default swaps and other derivatives' (p. 6).[14] It should also be noted that the Swedish FTT experiment failed simply because it was so badly designed with only local brokerage services being included so that avoiding the tax only required using foreign broker services (see discussion in European Commission, 2011).

At the same time, though, it is conceivable that 'alternative designs for the Tobin Tax might have a more stabilizing effect upon markets (see McCulloch 2010 for one proposal)' (McCulloch and Pacillo, 2010, p. 36). Actually McCulloch (op. cit.) suggests a 'Panic Tax' to tackle FTT instability. This idea is based on the proposition that 'A tax that discourages manias and panics would reduce market volatility far more than a simple transaction tax' (p. 1). This suggestion intends to tax 'panics and manias' rather than the usual FTT on all trades and all the time. More concretely,

> A Panic Tax would tax transactions at a variable rate proportional to the rate of change of the *aggregate* market price – in contrast to the Tobin Tax's small fixed rate. Sales and purchases would incur virtually no tax during normal times when the aggregate market movement is very small. But during crashes and booms they would face heavy penalties. Market participants expecting heavy taxation would be discouraged from making these trades thereby lessening the mania or panic. (p. 2)

The 'Panic Tax' is thereby supposed to dampen crashes and booms, which would create the space for more orderly adjustments in the financial markets.

The main argument against the FTT relates to its possible distortionary effects, thereby distorting the efficiency of markets. The argument is that such a tax leads, in a competitive market, to an equilibrium that involves a lower quantity of transactions, and fewer resources being allocated to that particular market. There are three points to be made in connection with this argument.

First, the financial sector may at present be relatively lightly taxed, and the 'products' of the financial sector are generally not subject to either general sales or value-added taxes or to specific excise taxes and the like. This would mean that the imposition of a FTT might in effect be removing some distortions rather than imposing them. To the extent that this view is accepted, the introduction of a FTT would help to reduce the distortionary effect of the tax system.

Secondly, the distortionary nature of a tax arises from some potentially beneficial trades not taking place that would have otherwise happened. This leads to the question of whether there are gains from the current volume of transactions, which would not arise with a substantially smaller volume. Some further doubt is cast on the distortionary argument by the observation that whilst the two parties to a financial trade may believe that they will gain from the trade (through a favourable price movement), both cannot do so, that is it is a zero-sum game.

Thirdly, the analysis of distortions is based on equilibrium trades, which are discouraged. But there is a sense in which much of the trading, especially in currency markets, is disequilibrium trading in terms of seeking to take advantage of price changes. Thus, the conventional analysis of distortions does not apply to this situation, and if it is the case that the amount of 'noise trading' is excessive, then a tax is beneficial rather than distortionary.

3.7 Effects of FTTs on the level of output

The effects of FTT on the level of output is here discussed in general terms as the specific effects would depend upon the precise nature of a FTT and the rate at which it is applied in the case of different countries that would impose such a tax.

Many advocates of some form of FTT do so along the lines that the volume of transactions in financial assets, particularly those transactions that are viewed as short-term in nature and speculative (that is, undertaken in the hope that the price of the asset acquired will rise), is in some sense excessive. The buying and selling of assets on a short-term basis is largely a zero-sum game, and is often associated with the volatility of asset prices. In the same way as taxes on pollution are intended to reduce the volume of pollution, so taxes on financial transactions are designed to reduce the volume of transactions. The resources involved in the case of the financial transactions (albeit small relative to the revenues of the total of transactions) would be released. In national accounts terms, there would be a reduction in output recorded as a result of the reduction in the volume of financial transactions. This could be put in terms of resources being released from financial markets for more gainful employment (although, as indicated below, the employment of those resources will depend upon the state of demand).

The European Commission initially produced the estimate that 'the possible cumulative deviation of GDP was established at −0.53% in the long run. This means that (when assuming in the baseline an annual growth of 1.5%) in 2050, instead of GDP in Europe being 81.4% above today's level, it would be 80.9% above that level' (European Commission, 2012b). This is based on the use of a dynamic stochastic general equilibrium (DSGE) model which 'includes hypotheses in terms of relocation and market reaction and, in the absence of specific information on the speed of the process, the assumption is made that the new 'steady state' would be reached after 40 years' (European Commission, op. cit.). However in subsequent research and relevant findings, the estimates have been revised downwards, and indeed come close to estimating no adverse effect on output. The revisions first take account of the financing pattern of European enterprises, and 'in particular, the assumption that all investment has to be financed with the help of issuing new shares has been changed to take into account the fact that companies also have access to alternative sources of finance that are not subject to the tax'. Under the revised assumptions the estimation of the impact of the proposed FTT on GDP was 0.28 per cent, and European GDP would rise to 81.1 per cent above today's level with a FTT, as compared to 81.4 per cent without a FTT. In the initial estimations, the tax revenue from the FTT was returned to households on a lump-sum basis. The nature of the DSGE model (as with other neoclassical-based models) is that a tax is viewed as 'distortionary', and hence any tax reduces output and efficiency. If instead other taxes, treated as 'distortionary', are reduced as a FTT is introduced, then the estimated impact on output is reduced. A further possibility is the use of the FTT revenues to fund government expenditure and investment. The European Commission (2012b) suggests that such possibility would be effective, '[I]f the tax revenues collected were spent, be it at the European or be it at the national level, on growth-enhancing public investment. Here, model simulations show a positive impact of such spending (as compared to providing lump-sum transfers to private households) in the order of magnitude of 0.2% to 0.4% of GDP.' Under that view the impact of a FTT could have a positive impact on the level of output.

Griffiths-Jones and Persaud (2011) discuss the details of the original estimations, and argue that 'the negative long term effect of the FTT on GDP would, in this more realistic scenario developed by the Commission itself, decrease significantly to less than –0.1 per cent' (p. 5). Further, 'this number is still likely to be an over-estimate, as it does not take into account that instead of a reduction in investment, there is merely a substitution away from frequently traded sources of investment to less-frequently trade, such as bank loans, but also private equity' (p. 5). Another aspect here would be to consider the demand side with the FTT shifting taxation from high-propensity to spend groups to low-propensity groups, and hence involving a stimulation in demand (for a given tax revenue).This issue is difficult to resolve without a full investigation into the effective incidence of a FTT (that is, not who is the tax levied on but who is in effect the payer) and specification of the taxes to be reduced with the introduction of a FTT. In the case where expenditure can be increased following FTT (and environmental and development purposes have often been envisaged), then the impact of aggregate demand and thereby the level of economic activity will be positive. Griffiths-Jones and Persaud (2012) suggest that

> If the FTT replaces another tax, meaning it is fiscally neutral, and the FTT is more progressive than the other taxes, it could lead to an expansion of total aggregate demand for consumption, if – as is normally the case – lower income groups have a higher marginal propensity to consume than relatively richer groups. Such an expansion of aggregate consumption demand would have a positive effect on level of GDP, which is entirely neglected by the Commission model. (p. 2; see, also, Arestis and Karakitsos, 2011)

A further impact of a FTT introduction could be that the increase of tax revenues could be used to finance public investment, thereby increasing aggregate demand in the short run and aggregate supply in the long run. Most important, though, and in terms of the 'great recession', is the argument that to the extent FTT reduces systemic risk and, thus, the probability of future crises, it could lead to higher long-term growth. It should be carefully noted, though, that the FTT by itself is unlikely to produce the effect just discussed. Prudent macroeconomic policies, including financial stability along with effective regulation and supervision, are also important. We have dealt with issues extensively in Arestis and Sawyer (2011). When the introduction of a FTT (and indeed other taxes) is considered in a model based on supply-side equilibrium (which implies some form of market clearing and full employment) then it is highly likely that the tax will be found to reduce supply and output. But when a FTT is considered in a more demand-oriented model, and when the relative propensities to spend are taken into account, then the impact of a FTT on level of demand and on economic activity is likely to be positive.

Amongst the rationales for a FTT is the idea that through its impact on the volume of transactions an FTT would make a contribution to the reduction of volatility of asset prices and of the intensity of credit booms and to financial stability. And as Griffiths-Jones and Persaud (2012) argue,

> Indeed, possibly the most important additional positive effect on future growth is that the FTT would somewhat reduce systemic risk, and therefore the likelihood of future crises. We are clearly not

> arguing that on its own, the FTT would reduce the risk of crises, as prudent macroeconomic policies and effective financial regulation as well as supervision also have a major role to play in crisis prevention. However, by significantly reducing the level of noise trading in general and reducing (or eliminating) high frequency trading in particular, the FTT would make some contribution to the reduction of severe misalignments and hence the probability of violent adjustments. ... Should the FTT, for example, decrease the probability of crises by a mere 5%, (which is a very low assumption), and the cost of GDP lower growth in the long term due to crises were around 7% which consistent with [estimates of the losses from financial crisis], then the positive impact of the FTT on the level of GDP, due to crisis avoidance, could be a 0.35% of GDP. In that case, the net effect of the FTT on the level of GDP would be +0.25 % (if we combine the negative impact estimated by the Commission model of −0.1%, with the positive one just estimated of +0.35%). (p. 3)

Ultimately, the overall impact of the introduction of a FTT on the level of output is dependent on the nature of the FTT and inevitably is subject to much conjecture. It is, though, possible to say first that the effect on socially useful output depends upon an evaluation of the shift of resources from the financial sector to the non-financial sector and the social usefulness of the production of the financial sector. Also, and secondly, a FTT is likely to enhance rather than detract from the level of demand in the global economy, and thereby have a positive effect on the levels of employment and output.

3.8 Tax avoidance and tax evasion

Any tax faces issues of tax evasion and tax avoidance, and whilst these have often been raised as arguments against FTTs it has to be considered as whether the problems are more severe in the case of FTTs as compared with other taxes. In that context, estimates of the extent of tax evasion and avoidance may be a useful benchmark (see below for some examples).

It must be first noted that many countries have some form of financial transactions tax on share dealing (IMF, 2010b provides listing for members of G20).

> Many countries have applied financial transaction taxes in the past and a limited number of countries continue to apply financial

> transaction taxes today. These taxes are primarily levied on spot share trading, but in a few countries other types of transactions, including derivatives, are taxed as well. The best-known example is the UK's stamp duty: it is a 0.5 per cent tax on the value of spot transactions in shares of UK companies. The tax rate on share trading is 1 per cent in Ireland, 0.5 per cent in Korea, while tax rates between 0.15 and 0.3 per cent are applied in Australia, Switzerland, Greece, Hong Kong, India and Taiwan. (European Parliament, 2010, p. 8)

This document goes on to note that 'transaction taxes have not been equally successful in collecting revenues everywhere. For example, when Sweden introduced a financial transaction tax in the mid-1980s, the revenues were disappointing, not least because the tax was easily avoided as financial dealings were moved abroad' (p. 9), which indicates the importance of appropriate design of a FTT. The role of the legal position is also relevant (a point to which we return below). The same document goes on to argue that: 'The UK stamp duty, for example, essentially buys legal certainty. Only once the tax is paid has the transfer of ownership been officially stamped' (p. 9).

The distinction between tax evasion and tax avoidance is, of course, that the former involves not complying with the law on tax matters, for example, the non-payment of tax which is due, whereas the latter involves a wide range of activities (and non-activities), which avoid the payment of the tax but do so in a legal manner. Tax avoidance could at one extreme be taken to be not undertaking the activity in question because the tax has raised the price of that activity or reduced the gains from it. The estimates of tax revenue from FTT used above do allow for that as reflected in the elasticities of the activities in question. In the context of FTT (although these considerations apply to other taxes though perhaps not with the same force) the tax avoidance would likely come from two sources.

The first would come from the rearrangement of financial tradings, and the nature of the financial products, which are exchanged so that tax payable is reduced or eliminated. Thus, specifying that trading in a particular range of financial assets is to be subject to taxation would lead to a combination of development of financial assets, which are close substitutes for those that are taxed, but defined in a manner which falls outside the tax legislation and the shift from those taxed financial assets to others. It was, for example, soon realised that placing a tax on dealing in foreign currency exchange would lead to dealing in interest bearing assets denominated in the respective currencies; and the scope of a foreign exchange transactions tax would need to cover all exchanges of financial assets in one currency for those in another currency. The general lesson would be the need to cast the net of the financial transactions tax widely, and to be alive to the need to ensure that the development of new financial instruments does not fall outside the range of the tax where appropriate. These are in effect familiar issues with financial regulation.

These considerations are reflected in the proposals of the EC on a FTT. The European Commission Taxation and Customs Union (2011) clearly suggests that

> The scope of the tax is wide, because it aims at covering transactions relating to all types of financial instruments as they are often close substitutes for each other. Thus, the scope covers instruments which are negotiable on the capital market, money-market instruments (with the exception of instruments of payment), units or shares in collective investment undertakings (which include UCITS and alternative investment funds) and derivatives agreements. Furthermore, the scope of the tax is not limited to trade in organized markets, such as regulated markets, multilateral trading facilities, but also covers other types of trades including over-the-counter trade. It is also not limited to the transfer of ownership but rather represents the obligation entered into, mirroring whether or not the financial institution involved assumes the risk implied by a given financial instrument ('purchase and sale'). Also, where a derivatives agreement results in a supply of financial instruments, in addition to the taxable derivatives agreement the financial instruments supply is also subject to tax, provided that all other conditions for taxation are fulfilled. (pp. 6–7)

The second possibility would emerge from the shift of the location of the transactions of the exchange of financial assets away from a jurisdiction, which levies a financial transactions tax. This type of consideration unsurprisingly may place significant limits on the scale of any FTT-type tax. However, the significance of this argument would depend upon the nature of the financial transactions, which are being taxed and the design of the tax. For financial assets, where the trade in the asset would be accompanied by registration of the legal transfer of the financial asset, the monitoring of transactions, whether within or outside the country concerned, is feasible; but where, as in the trading of currency, there is not such registration then the scope for shifting transactions is much more significant. It is from such considerations that we would suggest that a tax on currency exchange would have to be on an internationally co-ordinated basis, whereas, as experience indicates, a securities exchange tax can be implemented within a single country.

With regard to tax evasion, the financial sector is subject to regulation and auditing, and to the payment of taxes on wages and profits. It can then be argued that the enforcement of the payment of taxes relating to transactions would be little different from the enforcement of regulation and other forms of taxation. There can be reinforcement of the payment of transactions tax through the way in which a transaction on which tax should be paid is regarded. A financial transaction is an exchange of the title of ownership of the financial instrument concerned, and as such the exchange of ownership could be regarded as incomplete and not legally enforceable if the appropriate tax has not been paid on the associated transaction. Stamp taxes are paid by anyone – residents and non-residents, corporates or individuals – on the transfer of ownership of a resident security. Where 'stamp taxes' are due, a non-taxed and therefore non-stamped financial transaction cannot be legally enforced, and there can be no registered change of ownership to local or foreign buyers until taxes are paid to, and stamped by the authorities. Non-enforceability of contract is a very high consequence of noncompliance with the stamp duty. It is particularly the case where registered owners of assets are due to receive certain benefits and rights such as voting at shareholders' meetings, dividends, interest coupons, rights issues, buy-outs and so on. These stamp taxes are collected at settlement when the change in registered ownership takes place. They are actually a levy on the transfer of legal ownership, rather than on transactions per se, and so the compliance of brokers around the world is not necessary. Griffiths-Jones and Persaud (2011) argue that

> Stamp duties are nigh impossible to avoid. A Chinese investor, using a British bank in Hong Kong, to buy a French security will still have to pay the tax because otherwise he will not receive legal title to the security and could not receive any dividends, rights and claims and his contract to buy the shares would be unenforceable in the relevant jurisdiction. This is too high a risk for investors to take – no pension fund trustee would take such a risk. Taxing by residence of issuer is therefore far more effective with very strictly limited scope for avoidance. (p. 9)

Brondolo (2011) summarizes the argument very well and suggest that:

> Facilitating factors include the expanding role of clearinghouses in settling financial transactions, the proliferation of automated trading platforms, the conversion of paper securities into electronic book entries, and the recent strengthening in the regulation of over-the-counter (OTC) derivatives in a number of countries. Complicating factors include the creation of new and complex financial instruments, the ever-growing volume of financial transactions, and the increasing globalization of financial markets. (pp. 5–6)[15]

These developments, however, enhance and support further the case of the FTT rather than weakening it. The complicating factors, referred to in the quote just above (Brondolo, 2011, pp. 5–6), were one of the main causes of the 'great recession' and need to be tackled urgently (see, for example, Arestis and Karakitsos, 2011).

The case for the approach of the European Union in proposals for financial transactions tax is well made by the European Commission Taxation and Customs Union (2011), which argues that:

> the scope of the tax is focused on financial transactions carried out by financial institutions acting as party to a financial transaction, either for their own account or for the account of other persons, or acting in the name of a party to the transaction. This approach ensures that FTT is comprehensively applied. In practical terms this is usually evident via respective entries in the books. The definition of financial institutions is broad and essentially includes investment firms, organized markets, credit institutions, insurance and reinsurance undertakings, collective investment undertakings and their managers, pension funds and their managers, holding companies, financial leasing companies, special purpose entities, and where possible refers to the definitions provided by the relevant EU legislation adopted for regulatory purposes. Additionally other persons carrying out certain financial activities on a significant basis should be considered as financial institutions. (p. 7)

The European Commission Taxation and Customs Union (2011) proceeds to elaborate on the scope of the directive, which would apply 'to all financial transactions, on condition that at least one party to the transaction is established in a Member State and that a financial institution established in the territory of a Member State is party to the transaction, acting either for its own account or for the account of another person, or is acting in the name of a party to the transaction' (p. 15).

As for the tax base for a FTT, McCulloch and Pacillo (2010), after reviewing the literature, suggest that

> the general consensus in the literature is that the tax base for a FTT should be broad, including equities, bonds, futures, options and interest rate swaps. For example, Baker et al. (2009) argue for full coverage in the traditional and non-traditional market. Schulmeister (2009) deepens the coverage to include also over the counter (OTC) derivatives, including interest rate-, foreign exchange-, equity-, commodity-, and credit- related derivatives, as well as default swaps (CDS). On the other hand, Jetin (2009) does not include exchange or OTC derivatives in his currency transaction tax's design. (p. 15)

It is clear, though, that the tax base should be broad.

The position with regard to a foreign exchange tax may be rather different, and there is a degree of agreement that a FET would have to be implemented on a coordinated international basis. It may not be necessary for there to be full agreement over the tax rate, although there would be strong pressures towards a degree of uniformity (and probably a requirement for a minimum rate to avoid competitive undercutting of the tax rate between countries). It is clear that there would be very considerable differences in the amount of tax collected in each country. Part of the international agreement could clearly be that a proportion of the tax collected be paid over to an international body and/or used for agreed development and environmental purposes. The obvious difficulty that arises here is obtaining international agreement over the introduction and the rate of the tax when the revenue from the tax would be distributed so unequally across countries (and to the extent to which countries fear that their financial centres would be reduced in size).

Most advocates of the FET recognize that it would have to be 'universal and uniform: it would have to apply to all jurisdictions, and the rate would have to be equalised across markets' (Eichengreen, Tobin and Wyplosz, 1995, p. 165). This requirement may well be the most important practical obstacle to the implementation of such a tax. It would clearly require the cooperation of all countries with significant foreign exchange dealings within their borders, although there would be incentives for countries to apply a lower tax rate within their jurisdiction.

Eichengreen, Tobin and Wyplosz (1995) argue that 'Enforcement of the universal tax would depend principally on major banks and on the jurisdictions that regulate them. The surveillance of national regulatory authorities could be the responsibility of a multilateral agency like the Bank of International Settlements or the International Monetary Fund' (p. 165). Given the IMF's considerable expertise in international financial markets, it would be in a good position to undertake such a task. Furthermore, recognition of the IMF's central objectives of the promotion of international monetary cooperation to maintain exchange rate stability, and orderly exchange arrangements amongst its members, substantially strengthens the argument that the IMF should play a central role in its implementation. Consequently, and as Tobin (1978) remarks, the FTT 'would be an internationally agreed uniform tax, administered by each government over its own jurisdiction. Britain, for example, would be responsible for taxing all inter-currency transactions in Eurocurrency banks and brokers located in London, even when sterling was not involved. The tax proceeds could appropriately be paid into the IMF or World Bank' (p. 158).

Whilst it is recognized that the tax could not be implemented in one country, the question does arise as to whether it would have to be universal in order to be effective. There may be ways of avoiding a shift of transactions to 'tax havens', and examples are evident around the world. One possibility is to consider the transfer of funds to or from such location as taxable transactions at penalty rates. Thus the movement of, say, £1 million in sterling from the UK (assumed to be applying the tax) to a 'tax haven' (not applying the tax) would be subject to tax at a multiple of the FET. Another possibility would be to tax at the site where the deal is made rather than at the site where the transaction occurs. Tobin (1996) considers both these possibilities as ways forward and maintains that the danger of transfers of funds to tax-free countries is vastly exaggerated. These are low-cost sites for financial dealing around the world which, however, do not seem to have driven activity away from the main financial centres such as London, New York and Tokyo. Similarly, the imposition of a FTT would probably not have a substantial effect either.

There are further examples of countries imposing relevant measures to avoid offshore migration to 'tax havens', as mentioned above. The best is the UK's stamp duty, which is imposed on transactions carried at either in the UK or overseas. The UK imposes a higher rate (1.5 per cent, called a 'season ticket') for shares that are listed on an overseas stock market. The Swedish experience, as explained in section 3.6 above, points to the requirements of careful design of FTT (see Brondolo, 2011, p. 17). It is also noted by Brondolo (op. cit.) that in terms of tax avoidance, FET is more likely to be avoided in view of the 'large banks maintaining worldwide networks of trading desks' (p. 32). However, in view of recent developments, namely the creation of the Continuous Linked Settlement (CLS) bank (which settles at the moment 50 per cent of the foreign exchange transactions as Brondolo, 2011, p. 36, states), transactions are settled through this single institution. Or, at a minimum, as Brondolo (op. cit.) suggests: 'this single institution reports to the tax authorities information on banks' foreign currency transactions' (p. 43). These developments and suggestions clearly imply that tax avoidance could be lessened to a large extent.

3.9 Concluding comments

A range of financial transaction taxes would be a route to addressing the relative undertaxing of the financial sector and its activities. Such taxes can be designed in a way that stimulates the economy, depending upon how the taxes are structured, how the overall tax revenue is affected, and the uses to which the funds raised by FTT are put. The existence of security exchange taxes in a number of countries is clear evidence that forms of FTTs can be implemented on a country-by-country basis, although some forms of FTT, such as currency exchange taxes, may very well have to be implemented on an international basis. It is important that a FTT is well designed, and is comprehensive with regard to the financial transactions which are to be taxed. The regulation and registration of financial institutions and the existence of clearinghouse systems provide for the monitoring of financial transactions and collection of taxes levied on such transactions. It could well be argued that the ways in which financial institutions are regulated and organized provide for the less difficult collection of tax and less ease of tax evasion as compared with many industries (compare the financial sector with, for example, the building trade). The registration of legal title of many financial assets also provides mechanisms for the enforcement of the tax.

A FTT could be expected to reduce the scale of financial transactions, and indeed many would see the rationale for a FTT to be such a reduction. A FTT on foreign exchange dealings or security trading may have some impact on price volatility in the corresponding markets, although the evidence on this is not clear-cut. But a FTT could act to reduce the resources devoted to trading in such markets, and those resources can be deployed elsewhere. It is also true what Grieve Smith (1997) suggests; namely that

> While the implementation of the tax may appear complex, it is not any more complicated, probably much less so, than the detailed provisions of many existing taxes. ... Indeed if the standards of what is feasible employed here had been used before imposing income tax or VAT they would never have been introduced! The dominant feature in the introduction of new taxation has always been the political will rather than administrative feasibility. (p. 752)

Notes

1. The list mentioned in the text is based on IMF (2010b, pp. 144–5).
2. It is actually the case that where countries have introduced and levied a financial transactions tax, it is applied to 'exchange-traded instruments'; examples on this score are: China, India, Korea, the USA and the UK (Brondolo, 2011, p. 6). There is also one example of a currency transaction tax, which is Brazil that provides a case of the practical application of this tax (Brazil also imposes a financial transaction tax on securities and lending operations; see Brondolo, op. cit., p. 38).
3. The renewed interest in financial transactions taxes may not be surprising in view of the need for more government revenues as a result of increases in public deficits and debt due to the bailouts initiated over the 'great recession' period. It is actually estimated that even a very small tax of say 0.005 per cent on foreign financial transactions would generate an estimated $30bn per year (Griffith-Jones and Persaud, 2011; see, also, Sanger, 2011).
4. The case of fixed exchange rates is made much more difficult by the volume of transactions. This is reflected in the argument that 'Modest uncertainty about whether national monetary authorities are inclined to make use of their theoretical independence can lead to significant financial market volatility. If currencies are floating, they can fluctuate widely. If the authorities attempt to peg them, the costs of doing so, measured by reserve losses or interest-rate increases, can be extremely high. Even a government otherwise prepared to maintain a pegged exchange rate may be unwilling or unable to do so when attacked by the markets and forced to raise interest rates to astronomical heights' (Eichengreen, Tobin and Wyplosz, 1995, p. 162).
5. It is true that Tobin (1978) suggested this possibility as a by-product of a transactions tax, not as the main aim of his proposal.
6. Still there is the argument that in view of the fact that currency is highly concentrated, a FTT imposition would not have to be universal. Palley (2003) summarises the argument to suggest that in view of 'the vast bulk of the world's markets' (p. 19) is within the G7, it would be possible for these countries to impose successfully a FTT.

7. The IMF's preferred way to hold this tax is to create a special fund. The special fund then 'could provide more assurance that the agency in charge of resolution has ready access to the resources it needs' (Cottarelli, 2010, p. 3).
8. The proposed EU FTT takes its inspiration from the UK Stamp Duty and Stamp Duty Reserve Tax in terms of basing the EU FTT on the issuance principle. The principle being that the origins of the party in the transactions would not matter. Transactions would be taxed even when there was no EU party involved.
9. Another interesting suggestion, put forward by the German Social Democratic Party, is for a euro area Marshall Plan, financed by FTT revenues. The euro area austerity measures have clearly failed to produce growth in the area, so that a new 'pro-growth' Marshall-type plan should be set up. The proceeds of the FTT should be sufficient to support such a plan, it is argued.
10. A relevant advantage in relation to the discussion in the text is that the FTT can potentially tackle the problems it is designed to cure more flexibly than the introduction of financial controls. This is particularly so in terms of the quantitative exchange controls, which are usually viewed as rigid.
11. Meta-analysis refers to methods that combine and contrast results from different studies, in an attempt to identify patterns among study results, but also sources of disagreement among those results. It is also focused on establishing related and interesting relationships that may arise in the context of the multiple studies employed.
12. New research by the think-tank Z/Yen Group, and reported in the *Financial Times*, 'London Stays Top of Finance League' (19 March 2012), clearly shows that London is the leading 'global financial centre', followed by New York and Hong Kong.
13. It is estimated that 40 per cent of the UK stamp duty on equities is paid by non-UK residents and that the administrative cost of collecting this tax is lower than any other tax (Bond et al., 2004, p. 4). Interestingly enough, almost half of the $23bn of the revenue raised annually by seven countries in the world that impose this tax (Hong Kong, India, South Korea, South Africa, Switzerland, Taiwan, UK), is raised by the UK and South Korea (Griffith-Jones and Persaud, 2011).
14. It is estimated that in the case of the US such tax 'could easily raise more than 1.0 per cent of GDP (approximately $150 billion in 2011) even assuming very substantial reductions in trading volume' (Baker, 2011, p. 2).
15. It is important to explain the notion of 'clearinghouses' referred to in the quote in the text; it is a relatively new term in the context used here. Clearinghouses, often referred to as central counterparty (CCP), is the name of broker-dealers, whose duty is to clear and settle transactions of their security depositors, both for themselves and other broker-dealers. The members of the clearinghouses are required to hold a 'settlement account' with a central bank acceptable to the clearinghouse with which they operate closely in their clearing of the security depositors; it is also the case that the number of settlement banks is small. The countries involved have one or very few clearinghouses; clearly, clearinghouse arrangements would facilitate the administration of the FTT arrangements. A further clear advantage of the clearinghouse arrangements is the fact that that the tax is automatically withheld; as such the system of clearinghouses avoids underreporting of

taxable transactions (see Bardolo, 2011, pp. 7–8, p. 15 and footnote 12, for more details on the clearinghouse arrangements).

References

Aliber, R.Z., Chowdhry, B. and Yan, S. (2003) 'Some Evidence that a Tobin Tax on Foreign Exchange Transactions May Increase Volatility', *European Finance Review*, 7: 481–510.

Arestis, P. and Karakitsos, E. (2010) 'Subprime Mortgage Market and Current Financial Crisis', in P. Arestis, P. Mooslechner and K. Wagner (eds), *Housing Market Challenges in Europe and the United States*, Basingstoke: Palgrave Macmillan, pp. 40–59.

Arestis, P. and Karakitsos, E. (2011) 'An Analysis of the Causes of the "Great Recession" and Some Policy Implications', in T. Niechoj, Ö. Onaran, E. Stockhammer, A. Truger and T. van Treeck (eds), *Stabilising an Unequal Economy? Public Debt, Financial Regulation, and Income Distribution*, Marburg: Metropolis-Verlag, pp. 63–80.

Arestis, P. and Sawyer, M. (1996) 'The Tobin Financial Transactions Tax: Its Potential and Feasibility', *International Papers in Political Economy*, 3(3): 1–37.

Arestis, P. and Sawyer, M. (1997) 'How Many Cheers for the Tobin Financial Transaction Tax?', *Cambridge Journal of Economics*, 21(6): 753–68.

Arestis, P. and Sawyer, M. (2011) 'Economic Theory and Policies: New Directions Neoliberalism', in P. Arestis and M. Sawyer (eds), *New Economics as Mainstream Economics*, Basingstoke: Palgrave Macmillan, pp. 1–38.

Baker, D. (2003) 'Tobin Taxes: Are They Enforeable?', in New Rules for Global Finance Coalition (ed.), *Debating the Tobin Tax: New Rules for Global Finance*, Washington DC: Automated Graphics Systems, INC, November.

Baker, D. (2011) 'The Deficit-Reducing Potential of a Financial Speculation Tax', *Issue Brief*, January, Washington, DC: Center for Economic and Policy Research (CEPR), University of Massachusetts.

Baker, D., Pollin, R., McCarthur, T. and Sherman, M. (2011) 'The Potential Revenue from Financial Transaction Taxes', memorandum, Washington, DC: Center for Economic and Policy Research (CEPR) and Political Economic Research Institute, University of Massachusetts.

Bencivenga, V.R., Smith, B.D. and Starr, R.M. (1996) 'Equity Markets, Transactions Costs and Capital Accumulation: An Illustration', *World Bank Economic Review*, 4(2): 241–65.

Bond, S., Hawkins, M. and Klemn, A. (2004) 'Stamp Duty on Shares and its Effect on Share Prices', London: The Institute of Fiscal Studies, WP04 no. 11. Available at: http://www.ifs.org.uk/wps/wp0411.pdf.

Brondolo, J. (2011) 'Taxing Financial Transactions: An Assessment of Administrative Feasibility', *IMF Working Paper, WP/11/185*, Washington, DC: International Monetary Fund.

Campbell, J.Y. and Froot, K. (1994) 'International Experiences with Security Transaction Taxes', in J. Frankel (ed.), *The Internationalization of Equity Markets*, Chicago: University of Chicago Press.

Cottarelli, C. (2010) 'Fair and Substantial – Taxing the Financial Sector', *IMF Direct*. Available at: http://blog-imfdirect.imf.org/2010/04/25/fair-and-substantial%E2%80%94taxing-the-financial-sector.

Davidson, P. (1997) 'Are Grains of Sand in the Wheels of International Finance Sufficient to do the Job when Boulders are often Required?', *Economic Journal*, 107(442): 671–86.

Ehrenstein, G., Westerholf, F. and Stauffer, D. (2005) 'Tobin Tax and Market Depth', *Quantitative Finance*, 5(2): 213–18.

Eichengreen, B. (1991) 'Trends and Cycles in Foreign Lending', in H. Siebert (ed.), *Capital Flows in the World Economy*, Tübingen: Mohr.

Eichengreen, B. and Lindert, P. (eds) (1989) *The International Debt Crisis in Historical Perspective*, Cambridge, MA: MIT Press.

Eichengreen, B., Tobin, J. and Wyplosz, G. (1995) 'Two Cases for Sand in the Wheels of International Finance', *Economic Journal*, 105(1): 162–72.

European Commission (2011) Commission Staff Working Paper Impact Assessment Accompanying the Document Proposal for a Council Directive on a Common System of Financial Transaction Tax and amending Directive 2008/7/EC SEC(2011) 1102 final, vol. 9. Available at http://www.parlament.gv.at/cgi-bin/eukp.pdf?P_EU=XXIV.pdf/EU/05/98/059894.pdf.

European Commission (2012a) 'Technical Fiche: Revenue Estimations'. Available at: http://ec.europa.eu/taxation_customs/resources/documents/taxation/other_taxes/financial_sector/fact_sheet/revenue-estimates.pdf (downloaded May 2012).

European Commission (2012b) 'Technical Fiche: Macroeconomic Impacts'. Available at: http://ec.europa.eu/taxation_customs/resources/documents/taxation/other_taxes/financial_sector/fact_sheet/macroeconomic-effects.pdf (downloaded May 2012).

European Commission Taxation and Customs Union (2011) *The Commission Proposal for a Council Directive on a Common System of FTT*, COM 594, 28 September.

European Parliament (2010) 'Financial Transaction Tax: Small is Beautiful', *Policy Department A: Economic and Scientific Policies Economic and Monetary Affairs, Directorate General for Internal Policies*, Brussels: European Parliament. Available at: http://www.europarl.europa.eu/activities/committees/studies.do?language=EN.

European Parliament (2012) 'Parliament Adopts Ambitious Approach on Financial Transaction Tax', Press Release Reference No:20120523IPR45627.

Felix, D. and Sau, R. (1996) 'On the Revenue Potential and Phasing in of the Tobin Tax', in M.U. Haq, I. Kaul, and I. Grunberg (eds), *The Tobin Tax: Coping with Financial Volatility*, Oxford: Oxford University Press.

Folkerts-Landau, D. and Ito, T. (1995) *International Capital Markets: Developments, Prospects and Policy Issues*, Washington, DC: International Monetary Fund.

Frankel, J.A. (1996) 'How Well do Foreign Exchange Markets Work: Might a Tobin Tax Help?', in Haq et al. (1996).

Frankel, J.A. and Rose, A.K. (1994) 'A Survey of Empirical Research on Nominal Exchange Rates', *NBER Working Paper Series No. 4865*, Cambridge MA: National Bureau of Economic Research.

Goodhart, C.A. (1996) 'Discussant to Professor J. Tobin', *Economic Systems with Journal of International and Comparative Economics*, 20(1): 91–5.

Grahl, J. and Lysandrou, P. (2003) 'Sand in the Wheels or Spanner in the Works? The Tobin Tax and Global Finance', *Cambridge Journal of Economics*, 27(4): 597–621.

Grieve Smith, J. (1997) 'Exchange Rate Instability and the Tobin Tax: Review Article', *Cambridge Journal of Economics*, 26(6): 745–52.

Griffith-Jones, S. and Persaud, A. (2011) 'Financial Transaction Taxes', mimeo, Columbia University.

Haq, M., Kaul, I. and Grunberg, I. (eds) (1996) *The Tobin Tax: Coping with Financial Volatility*, Oxford: Oxford University Press.

Hartmann, P. (1996) 'Do Reuters Spreads Reflect Currencies' Differences in Global Trading Volumes?', mimeo, London School of Economics.

Holtham, G. (1995) 'Managing the Exchange Rate System', in J. Michie and J. Grieve Smith (eds), *Managing the Global Economy*. Oxford: Oxford University Press.

IMF (2010a) 'A Fair and Substantial Contribution by the Financial Sector: Final Report for the G20', June, Washington, DC: International Monetary Fund. Available at: http://www.imf.org/external/np/g20/pdf/062710b.pdf.

IMF (2010b) 'Financial Sector Taxation: The IMF's Report to the G-20 and Background Materials', in S. Claessens, M. Keen, and C. Pazarbasioglu (eds), Financial Sector Taxation: the IMF's Report to the G-20 and Background Material, Washington, DC: International Monetary Fund.

Jetin, B. (2009) 'Financing Development with Global Taxes: Fiscal Revenues of a Currency Transaction Tax', mimeo, Paris: Université Paris-Nord.

Keynes, J.M. (1930) *A Treatise on Money: The Pure Theory of Money*, London: Macmillan.

Keynes, J.M. (1936) *The General Theory of Employment, Interest and Money*, London: Macmillan.

Kenen, P.B. (1996) 'The Feasibility of Taxing Foreign Exchange Transactions' in Haq et al. (1996).

Kindleberger, C. (1978) *Manias, Panics and Crashes*, New York; Norton.

Leading Group on Innovating Financing in Development (LGIFD) (2010) 'Globalizing Solidarity: The Case for Financial Levies', *Report to the Task Force on International Financial Transactions and Development*, French Ministry of Foreign and European Affairs, Paris: Leading Group on Innovating Financing in Development.

Matheson, T. (2011) 'Taxing Financial Transactions: Issues and Evidence', *IMF Working Paper, WP/11/54*, Washington, DC: International Monetary Fund.

McCulloch, N. (2010) 'Tackling Instability in Financial Markets with a Panic Tax', *IDS In Focus Policy Briefing, Issue 14*, March, Brighton: Institute of Development Studies (IDS).

McCulloch, N. and Pacillo, G. (2010) 'The Tobin Tax: A Review of the Evidence', Economics Department Working Paper Series No. 16-2010, Department of Economics: University of Sussex.

Palley, I.T. (2003) 'The Economic Case for the Tobin Tax', in New Rules for Global Finance Coalition (ed.), *Debating the Tobin Tax: New Rules for Global Finance*, Washington DC: Automated Graphics Systems, Inc, November.

Pollin, R. (2003) 'Applying a Securities Transactions Tax to the US: Design Issues, Market Impact, Revenue Estimates', in New Rules for Global Finance Coalition (ed.), *Debating the Tobin Tax: New Rules for Global Finance*. Washington, DC: Automated Graphics Systems, Inc, November.

Pollin, R., Baker, D. and Schaberg, M. (2003) 'Security Transaction Taxes for U.S. Financial Market', *Eastern Economic Journal*, 29(4): 527–59.

Sanger, T. (2011) 'Taxing Finance', *Global Labour Column (GLU), Global Labour University*, No. 66 (July), University of the Witwatersrand, South Africa: Corporate Strategy and Industrial Development. Available at: http://column.global-labour-university.org/.

Schulmeister, S. (2009) 'A General Financial Transaction Tax: A Short Cut of the Pros, the Cons and a Proposal', *WIFO Working Paper 344/2009*, Vienna: Osterreichisches Institut Für Wirtschaftsforschung.

Simon, H.A. (1957) *Models of Man*, New York: John Wiley & Sons.

Spahn, P.B. (1995) 'International Financial Flows and Transaction Taxes', *IMF Working Paper No. 60, June*, Fiscal Affairs Department, Washington, DC: International Monetary Fund.

Spahn, P.B. (1996) 'The Tobin Tax and Exchange Rate Stability', Finance and Development, June.

Tobin, J. (1974) *The New Economics One Decade Older*, Princeton: Princeton University Press.

Tobin, J. (1978) 'A Proposal for International Monetary Reform', *Eastern Economic Journal*, 4(3–4): 153–9. Reprinted in J. Tobin, *Essays in Economics: Theory and Policy*, Cambridge, Mass.: The MIT Press, 1996.

Tobin, J. (1996) 'Prologue', in Haq et al. (1996).

United Nations Conference on Trade and Development (UNCTAD) (1995) *Trade and Development Report, 1995*, New York and Geneva: United Nations.

United Nations Development Programme (UNDP) (1994) *Human Development Report 1994*, New York and Oxford: Oxford University Press.

Westerhof, F. (2003) 'Heterogeneous Traders and the Tobin Tax', *Journal of Evolutionary Economics*, 13(1): 53–70.

4
Global Imbalances as Constraints to the Economic Activity in the World Economy

Jesús Ferreiro
Department of Applied Economics V, University of the Basque Country UPV-EHU, Spain

Patricia Peinado
Department of Applied Economics V, University of the Basque Country UPV-EHU, Spain

Felipe Serrano
Department of Applied Economics V, University of the Basque Country UPV-EHU, Spain

4.1 Introduction[1]

Since the beginning of the 2000s, the phenomenon of the global imbalances has been the object of special attention by economists and the international institutions. As we will see later, before the crisis there was a clear division between those that interpreted these imbalances as a disequilibrium and those that argued that they were a new kind of world equilibrium (the so-called 'Bretton Woods II' hypothesis), where the countries with current account surpluses were financing the countries with current account deficits.

Both analyses focused on the financial implications of the balance of payments imbalances. Attention was paid to the international financial flows which resulted from those imbalances. It was argued that global imbalances, namely, the current account surpluses mainly generated in some emerging economies and oil-exporting countries, were fuelling the massive capital inflows into the US economy. Consequently, many papers pointed to the global imbalances as the main cause of the excessive international liquidity that gave rise in 2007–08 to the burst of the current financial and economic crisis. However, recent studies argue that the global imbalances are not the main cause of the crisis, since the latter is due to the high levels of gross capital international flows, and not to the net capital flows directly related to the existence of the balance of payments imbalances (Bernanke et al., 2011). This, however, does not mean that the global imbalances are not a source of problems. In the chapter, we defend the need to analyze these imbalances not only from a financial perspective but also from a real one, focusing on the negative consequences of the existence of high and persistent current account imbalances, which can have a direct negative impact on the economic activity and the welfare of the economies involved, thus leading to a necessary adjustment of these imbalances.

The objective of this chapter is twofold. The first is to analyse whether the current account imbalances registered in many developed and emerging and developing economies are a problem for the countries that suffer these imbalances, mainly for those economies that register high and permanent deficits in their current accounts, but also for the whole global economy. The second is to study the reasons why these imbalances can be a source of economic and financial problems at the national and global levels.

We argue that the existence of the current account imbalances and its size is explained by structural factors, related to the change registered since the 2000s in the global value-added chain that has led to a recomposition of the world aggregate supply and of the pattern of world trade. To the extent that current account imbalances are not a short-term cyclical phenomenon, they cannot be solved with the implementation of macroeconomic policies or changes in the exchange rates of the involved economies, but with the combination of policies in the surplus countries focused on the expansion of the domestic demand and the implementation of supply-side policies in the deficit countries that help to match the domestic demand and the domestic supply.

The paper is structured as follows. In the first section, we survey the pre-'great recession' contributions to the theme of global imbalances. In the second section, we focus on the role played by the existence of global imbalances in the burst of the financial crisis. In the third and fourth sections we analyze, respectively, why current account imbalances can be a source of financial and economic problems for the individual economies affected and also for the world economy as a whole. The fifth section studies the relationship between current account imbalances and the foreign direct investments (FDI), since we argue that the current account imbalances is directly related to a geographical change in the global value added chain fuelled by the FDI. The sixth section analyzes the measures required to correct the current account imbalances. The final section concludes.

4.2 The 'global saving glut' approach

In 2005 the International Monetary Fund (IMF) warned of the risks for the international economic and financial stability coming from rising balance of payments imbalances, which were rapidly rising since the end of the 1990s (International Monetary Fund, 2005). The main countries involved with these imbalances were the USA and the Asian emerging economies (mainly China) and the oil exporting countries. The US economy generated the demand for the export goods of the emerging economies, which, in turn, financed the US trade deficit through the purchase of US public debt.

In the years preceding the burst of the financial crisis there was two lines of research of the global imbalances. The first line saw global imbalances as the result of an imbalance that had to be corrected with a depreciation of the US dollar (Cline, 2005; Ahearne et al., 2007). The second line analyzed the global imbalances as an equilibrium outcome that could be maintained without leading to a crisis. We will focus on this second line, because the 'global saving glut' has often be identified as a cause of the current financial and economic crisis (Porter, 2009) or, at least, as a necessary, but not sufficient, condition of the crisis (Obstfeld and Rogoff, 2009).

The two main features of the identification of the global imbalances with an equilibrium situation (Servén and Nguyen, 2010) are, first, that the origin of the problem is not in the US economy but, mainly, in the emerging market economies. The US current account deficit is not the result of the excessive fiscal deficit or a highly expansionary monetary policy developed by the Federal Reserve, but rather the results of the excessive world savings existing before the crisis. Second, the focus is moved away from the current account balance to the capital account balance, and, thus, the real depreciation of the US dollar is no longer the main solution to re-balance the current account.

The identification of the phenomenon of the global imbalances as an equilibrium situation demanded an explanation of the causes of the rising savings in the emerging market economies, mainly in China. Moreover, it also demanded an explanation of the preference of these economies to invest their excess savings in the US financial market. And, finally, it also demanded an understanding of the mechanism through which the foreign capital inflows arriving in the US economy contributed to a fuelling of the credit boom and the speculative bubble. In the years before the crisis some of these questions, mainly the first two, had been solved, but the third question had not yet been clearly answered.

The first version of the global imbalances as an equilibrium outcome was presented by Dooley, Folkerts-Landau and Garber (2003, 2005). For these authors, the world economy was in the presence of a 'Bretton Woods II', with the emerging economies adopting the same strategy that Europe had used after the Second World War to accelerate their economic growth: that is, a policy of export-led growth. This strategy calls for an undervalued real exchange rate to preserve the export competitiveness. The best way to achieve this is by restraining domestic spending, particularly private consumption, which inevitably leads to persistent current accounts surpluses and foreign reserve accumulation. These foreign reserves, in turn, were invested in the developed economies, mainly in the United States of America, financing in this way the demand of goods produced in the emerging economies.

In the Sandridge Lecture, Bernanke (2005), following the equilibrium argument developed by Dooley, Folkerts-Landau and Garbe (op. cit.), reformulated some of the ideas initially posed by the latter authors to set the hypothesis of the 'global saving glut'. Bernanke (op. cit.) argued that the excess of world savings (over world investment) was the result of some changes that were not only taking place in the developed economies but also, and mainly, in the emerging economies. Regarding the changes taking place in the developed economies, Bernanke (op. cit.) argued that the ageing process in these economies was leading to an increase in the retirement motive for savings. However, Bernanke (2005) argued that 'although strong saving motives on the part of many industrial economies contribute to the global saving glut, the saving behavior of these countries does not explain much of the *increase* in desired global saving in the past decade (...) a possibly more important source of the rise in the global supply of saving is the recent metamorphosis of the developing world from a net user to a net supplier of funds to international capital markets'.

How can the metamorphosis mentioned by Bernanke (2005) be explained? Bernanke (op. cit.) related the reserve accumulation with the experiences suffered by the emerging economies during the financial crises that took place in the 1990s. Bernanke (op. cit.) set the hypothesis that these economies accumulated foreign reserves as a buffer against potential capital outflows. This hypothesis is not in contradiction with the former one, because both hypotheses reach a similar conclusion about the domestic effects resulting from the reserve accumulation: a loss of welfare in the emerging economies. However, Bernanke (2005), in opposition to the hypothesis of the Bretton Woods II, shows the potentially destabilizing role of the capital inflows in the host economies of these capitals.

Bernanke (2005) warned about the potential negative impact on the US economy of the capital inflows from the emerging economies. He identified, on the one hand, the effects on the real economy, arguing that the resource allocation (increasing the real estate investments) generated by the capital inflows was in contradiction to the required allocation (in export industries) to balance the balance of payments. On the other hand, he also pointed out 'the risk of a disorderly adjustment in financial markets always exists, and the appropriately conservative approach for policymakers is to be on guard for any such developments'. Nonetheless, the strategy defended by Bernanke (2005) to correct the balance of payments imbalances was

> to help and encourage developing countries to re-enter international capital markets in their more natural role as borrowers, rather than as lenders. For example, developing countries could improve their investment climates by continuing to increase macroeconomic stability, strengthen property rights, reduce corruption, and remove barriers to the free flow of financial capital. Providing assistance to developing countries in strengthening their financial institutions – for example, by improving bank regulation and supervision and by increasing financial transparency – could lessen the risk of financial crises and thus increase both the willingness of those countries to accept capital inflows and the willingness of foreigners to invest there.

The inefficiency of the financial markets in the emerging economies pointed out by Bernanke (2005) was the focus of other papers that explained the accumulation of foreign assets by the emerging economies. Thus, Caballero et al. (2008a, 2008b) argue that the accumulation of foreign assets is directly related to the financial underdevelopment of emerging countries, which prevents them from generating financial instruments that are attractive to their savers. The result is that international savers tilt their portfolios towards the assets of countries with more advanced financial markets. However, these authors do not explain the origin of the individual savings invested in foreign assets. The reform of the financial systems in the emerging economies is the cornerstone in the attempt to reach the equilibrium of the balance of payments.

The explanation of this last aspect is the objective of the second generation of analyses of the global saving glut. The increase of savings in the emerging economies, mainly in China, is related to reforms in the social protection systems (Mendoza et al., 2009; Carrol and Jeanne,

2009; Prasad, 2009). These reforms would generate a fall in the protection in the areas of health and retirement pensions, leading to an increase in the precautionary motive for savings. Therefore, the accumulation of foreign reserves is not the result of the strategy selected of economic growth or of the lessons obtained during the past financial crises. The fall in the savings rates would depend upon the setting of a minimum network of social protection that, by diminishing the retirement motive for savings, help to foster the domestic demand and to rebalance the balances of payments of the emerging economies and the developed countries.

The second element of the equilibrium hypothesis is related to the preference of the emerging economies to place their savings in the US financial market. The most representative work of this line of research developed before the crisis about the preferences of foreign investors was Forbes (2008):

> Although foreigners investing in US equity and bond markets have earned lower returns over the past five years than if they had invested in the same asset classes in their own countries, there are still several reasons why they might choose to continue investing in the United States and financing the large US current account deficit. More specifically, foreign investors may choose to purchase US portfolio investments in order to benefit from the highly developed, liquid, and efficient US financial markets, from the strong corporate governance and institutions in the United States, and/or to diversify risk (especially if returns in US financial markets have a low correlation with returns in their own country's domestic financial markets). (p. 32)

The hypothesis of the equilibrium approach was based on a strong belief about the ability of the US financial system to recycle the foreign capital inflows. As Bernanke (2005) points out, this recycling could generate inefficient resource allocations, making the adjustment of the balance of payments difficult in the long run. But, what is more surprising, at least from the current perspective, is the confidence existing, both in the USA and abroad, in the institutional quality of the US financial system.

The crisis has proved that such a belief is wrong. But it is difficult to understand, even with the information available before the crisis, the reasons that justify this belief. The financial crises of the decade of the 1990s, mainly the South East Asian financial crisis, showed the risks resulting from an excessive short-term borrowing to finance long-term lending. Although in the US financial system that risk was not amplified by the exchange rate risk, as happened in the financial crises in the emerging and developing economies, it could not be ignored. Only when the financial crisis had burst was it accepted that those risks had been ignored. In the Economic Report of the President 2009 this problem is explicitly accepted: 'those institutions (financial) were vulnerable ... because they were highly leveraged and, in particular, were highly dependent on short-term funding. In other words, those institutions had borrowed extensively against their long-term assets, and a large part of their debt was short-term, so that their existing debt needed to be paid off and replaced with new short-term debt with some frequency' (US Government, 2009, p. 61).

It is possible that the reluctance to accept the existence of this problem before the crisis was to the result of another belief, although the latter could have an empirical basis: the financial crises in the emerging economies were due to the financial underdevelopment of these countries. Consequently, it was believed that a financial crisis could not take place in a highly efficient financial system.

The link between the foreign capital inflows and the credit boom remains as the weakest element of the global saving glut approach. Although we will develop this point later when we deal with the different financial inflows in the US financial market, we wish to point out here that the main difficulties appear when we want to know the precise moment when the foreign capital inflows led to the fall in the long-term interest rates in the USA (which is assumed to have triggered the credit boom).

During the last decade, several factors combined to generate the observed fall in the long-term interest rates. One of these elements was the reduction of the official interest rates to fight the effects of the crisis of the early 2000s. In addition to these low short-term interest rates, which increased the liquidity levels in the developed economies, another element was the liquidity fuelled by the reserves accumulation in the emerging economies and the oil-exporting countries. The final result was an unparalleled increase in world liquidity (Bank of England, 2007). The placing of these capitals in the American financial market could influence the fall of the long-term interest rates. Actually, these interest rates showed a declining trend from the beginning of the decade as a result of the monetary strategy implemented by the US Federal Reserve (Obstfeld and Rogoff, 2009). Moreover, the credit expansion and the beginning of the housing boom, fuelled by financial innovations, had already been detected before the inflow of the foreign capital. In sum, the massive inward flows might have influenced the reduction of the long-term interest rates since, around the first half of the decade, when the Fed and the rest of the central banks in the developed economies increased their short-term interest rates. However, this capital inflow is very likely only to have helped to maintain a credit expansion that had begun some years before.

In the years preceding the burst of the financial crisis the hypothesis that the global imbalances could be understood as an equilibrium situation, that, although it could generate risks, at least for Bernanke, could be sustainable in the long term, had become dominant. It was believed that the US financial system was strong enough to recycle the huge capital inflows. The adjustment of the balance of payments, which was considered to be necessary in the long term, did not involve changing the macroeconomic policies implemented in the developed countries. The focus was placed instead on the emerging economies. These economies should reform their financial systems and their social protection schemes. Such reforms would help to reduce the savings rates and to increase the consumption, both directly and indirectly, because of the stimulus to the credit that would be generated with a more efficient financial system.

4.3 The economic crisis and the global imbalances

The explanations of the origins of the current financial crisis have been divided in two main groups (Eichengreen, 2009). Some authors (for example, Porter, 2009) argue that the origin of the crisis can be found in the current account imbalances. However, other authors trace the roots of the crisis in the shortcomings of the financial regulation (Barth et al., 2012).

According to the first group of explanations, the global imbalances helped to trigger the financial crisis because they put financial intermediation under stress. This is the diagnosis of the Economic Report of the US President in 2009:

> The roots of the current global financial crisis began in the late 1990s. A rapid increase in saving by developing countries (sometimes called the 'global saving glut') resulted in a large influx of capital to the United States and other industrialized countries, driving down the return on safe assets. The relatively low yield on safe assets likely encouraged investors to look for higher yields from riskier assets, whose yields also went down. What turned out to be an underpricing

> of risk across a number of markets (housing, commercial real estate, and leveraged buyouts, among others) in the United States and abroad, and an uncertainty about how this risk was distributed throughout the global financial system, set the stage for subsequent financial distress. (US Government, 2009, p. 22)

However, as Servén and Nguyen (2010) argue, this argument has some weaknesses:

> It is not obvious why the stress on the financial intermediation system should relate to *net* capital flows, which are the counterpart of current account deficits. It seems more logical to think that such pressures depend, if anything, on the volume of *gross* resources intermediates, which bears no systematic relation with net flows. In this regard, it is important to note that the order of magnitude of the US current account deficit (around of 5–6% of GDP at its peak) is very modest in relation to the size of its financial system. (p. 12)

Bernanke et al. (2011) defend a similar view. They complement the hypothesis of the global saving glut adding to the net capital inflows coming from the emerging economies other financial flows, mainly the capital flows fuelled by the European banks in the US financial market. Before we discuss the conclusions reached by Bernanke et al. (op. cit.) we wish to note that their paper is a significant deviation from the dominant thesis held prior to the crisis about the nature of the balance of payments imbalances. The past dominant thesis concluded that the ultimate cause of the US current account imbalance was the excess of savings generated in the emerging economies. Moreover, the North American financial system was solid enough to recycle the huge inward capital flows. However, for Bernanke et al. (2011) there is a shared responsibility for these imbalances: 'domestic factors (including problems with the originate-to-distribute model for mortgages loans, deteriorating lending standards, deficiencies in risk management and shortcomings of supervision and regulation) were the primary sources of the boom and bust and the associated financial crisis. However, an examination of how changes in the pattern of international capital affected yields on US assets is important for understanding the origins and dynamics of the crisis' (p. 3).

The analysis made by these authors about the changes in the pattern of international capital flows shows two interesting results that question the former dominant view that the origin of the crisis was the excess of savings in the emerging economies. The first result is that the capital inflows coming from the emerging economies were mainly directed to the purchase of assets issued by US Treasuries and Agencies. The second result is that the private assets, such as the structured financial assets or the mortgage-backed credits, were the main destination for the investors from the developed economies, principally the European banks and the US investors. Although both capital inflows pushed interest rates downwards, the capital inflows that really fuelled the credit bubble were the financial inflows coming from a region (Europe) that did not participate in the problem of the global imbalances. Moreover, many European financial institutions were funding their purchases of US assets with short-term dollar-denominated liabilities like commercial paper or bank deposits, much of which attracted US investors (McGuire and Von Peter, 2009).

This kind of financial loop created in the years preceding the financial crisis leads to a reconsideration of the relative weight that the net capital inflows coming from the emerging markets had in the credit expansion process. Borio and Disyat (2010, 2011) argue that the relevant capital flows are not the net flows resulting from the existence of a global saving glut, but the gross capital flows generated by the process of financial globalization. We need to consider these gross capital flows to realize the key role played by the European banking system in the process of financial intermediation and in the allocation capitals in the US financial market. By doing these, Borio and Disyat (ops. cit.) divert the focus of attention that the global saving glut had placed in the emerging economies to the international monetary and financial system: 'the main macroeconomic cause of the financial crisis was not the excess saving but the excess elasticity of the monetary and financial regimes in place' (p. 2). The authors identify the excess elasticity with the lack of anchors sufficiently strong to prevent the build-up of unsustainable booms in credit and asset prices (financial imbalances); these can eventually lead to serious financial strains and derail the world economy. The roots of the financial crisis are to be found where Minsky (1982) had already concluded: in the financial innovations developed during the expansion phases that escape from the control of the regulators.

4.4 Do current account imbalances matter for affected countries?

As mentioned in the previous sections, since the mid-2000s the economists and the international institutions have begun to pay particular attention to the current account imbalances in some developed and emerging market economies. These analyses shared the general conclusion that these imbalances could be a source of problems and risks, not only for the economies with the current account imbalances but also for the whole economy, thus making current account imbalances a systemic risk.

We can group the potential problems arising from the existence of current account imbalances into four different, although interrelated categories. The first problem is related to the fact that a current account imbalance involves the existence of net financial flows. Consequently, the higher the size of the current account imbalance, the higher the size on the net financial flow will be. The corresponding financial flows can be a source of potential problems for the economy involved, affecting the domestic interest rate, the exchange rates (for instance, leading to exchange rates departing from the fundamental real exchange rate that balances the balance of payment),[2] the accumulation of foreign reserves, affecting the capacity of monetary policy to fulfil domestic objectives, and so on.

Starting from the usual Keynesian income equation, where (Savings – Investment) + (Tax revenue – Government expenditure) = Current account deficit, if the private sector is balanced (private investment being equal to private savings), an imbalance in the current account comes necessarily with a fiscal imbalance: countries with surpluses (deficits) in the current account have surpluses (deficits) in their public finances. In the specific case of deficit countries, these economies have twin deficits. This raises the possibility for these economies to suffer twin crises (balance of payments and fiscal crisis), a situation that can be even worse in these problems moves to the banking-financial domestic sector.

Third, if current account imbalances are permanent, they can also generate further problems. Assuming that the exchange rate remains unchanged, countries with permanent surpluses in the current account will accumulate foreign reserves. This accumulation can lead to losses in the welfare of the domestic agents and, also, to problems in the management of the domestic policy, reducing its effectiveness as a tool of macroeconomic policy to correct domestic problems. In countries have deficits in the current account, they will have to finance that deficit with a net capital inflow, increasing their external debt. The accumulation of external debt and the continuous deficit in the current account involve increasing needs for capital to finance the new deficit in the current account but also to refinance the outstanding external debt. This can have potentially highly devastating problems in case of a sudden stop and a consequent debt crisis (Catão and Milesi-Ferretti, 2011), mainly in the case of emerging economies (Reinhart and Reinhart, 2009).

It is important to note that the three arguments above involve the idea that the existence of a current account imbalance, regardless of its sign and size, is not a problem in itself. The problems are the financial flows related to that imbalance. This is the thesis defended, among others by Obstfeld (2012), who argues that current account imbalances are a financial problem, but not a real problem for economies with these imbalances.

However, there also exists a fourth source of problems directly related to the existence of current account imbalances, and this is the line of reasoning that will be further explored in this contribution. Current account imbalances matter because these imbalances involves either a current account deficit that constrains the economic activity or a current account surplus that involves an export-led growth strategy, whose long-term sustainability depends upon the economic activity in foreign partners.

In this line of reasoning, current account imbalances are important because they influence the economic activity and the economic growth through their impact on aggregate demand. In countries with current account deficits, these deficits make that the domestic absorption (the domestic demand) higher than the aggregate demand, thus putting a brake on the economic activity and the rate of economic growth. Moreover, if these deficits are unsustainable, in the absence of an increase in the exports, the external adjustment will involve a decline in the level of domestic demand, either through a decline in the private spending (consumption and/or investment) or through a fiscal adjustment, again having a negative effecting on the level of economic activity. For surplus countries, the surplus can have two origins: a decline in the domestic demand or an acceleration in the foreign demand of domestic goods and services. In both cases, foreign demand becomes the engine of domestic growth, thus making the economy dependent on the economic situation and the aggregate demand abroad.

This line of reasoning, and the consequent transmission channel of the impact of current account imbalances, is missed in mainstream analyses. The reason is twofold. First, for mainstream economics the flexibility of exchange rates removes the possibility that balance of payment imbalances exist in the long run (Herr, 2011; Liang, 2012). Second, in the mainstream economics, the aggregate demand is not a determinant of the economic activity and the economic growth in the long run (Arestis, 2009 and 2011), what leads to a neglecting of the relevance of issues related to the aggregate demand and the macroeconomic policies as determinants of the economic activity (Ferreiro and Serrano, 2009).

4.5 Can current account imbalances be a problem for the world economy?

Obstfeld (2012) argues that temporary current account imbalances are not a bad thing per se – along similar lines to the arguments used in Weber (2010). For Weber (2010) these imbalances would be a problem if they were persistent and if they were unsustainable (as, for instance, in the case of the US deficits due to its low savings) and if they were generated by wrong exchange rate policies leading to exchange rate misalignments and an excessive accumulation of foreign reserves (as in the case of the Chinese surpluses). Again, it is important to highlight that for both authors the problems of the current account imbalances are generated by their financial counterpart – that is, by the capital flows required to finance that imbalance.

In any case, regardless of the source of the problems resulting from the existence of current account imbalances, if we analyze the relevance of these imbalances from a worldwide perspective, we cannot forget that, at a global level, the world current account is always in balance, since the deficits of one or more countries are offset by the equivalent surpluses of the rest of countries. Consequently, the finance of individual current account imbalances merely involves a geographical redistribution of capitals, with capital flows going from surpluses to deficit countries. However, this does mean that the existence of current account imbalances cannot be global imbalances, something that can happen as far as the problems that one economy suffers as a result of its imbalance can be transferred to third parties. In this sense, the current account imbalances can be a source of systemic risks for the whole economy depending upon the size of the imbalances, the nature of their trend and evolution, the concentration of the current account imbalances in a low/high number of countries, and, finally, the extension of the phenomenon, that is, the number of countries with high current account imbalances. In this section we will focus on these four elements.

4.5.1 The size of the current account imbalances

As mentioned above, the first determinant of the potential problems on the world economy arisen from the existence of current account imbalances is the size of these imbalances. Two elements are here relevant: the size and the trend of these imbalances.

Figure 4.1 shows the evolution of current account imbalances in the world economy since the year 1980. As mentioned above, at a worldwide level the global balance of payments must (should) be in equilibrium, and, thus, the global current account balance should be zero. However, this analysis lacks of sense and economic meaning, since what actually matters is the imbalances that individual economies suffer and the sum of the individual imbalances taking into account their corresponding sign.

Consequently, we have summed in Figure 4.1, the current account imbalances of those countries with deficits in their current accounts, and the imbalances of those countries with surpluses in their current account. Although these figures should be the same, due to discrepancies in the statistics on the balance of payments, the two sums are different, as is easily seen in Figure 4.1.

Figure 4.1 shows the rising size of the current account imbalances, measured in billions of US dollars. Furthermore, the increase in the absolute size of the imbalances accelerates since 2001. The imbalances peaked in 2008, when the sum of total current account deficits amounted to US$1,575 billion and the total current account surpluses amounted to US$1,763 billion. Although the burst of the crisis led to a correction of these imbalances this adjustment was temporary and short-term in

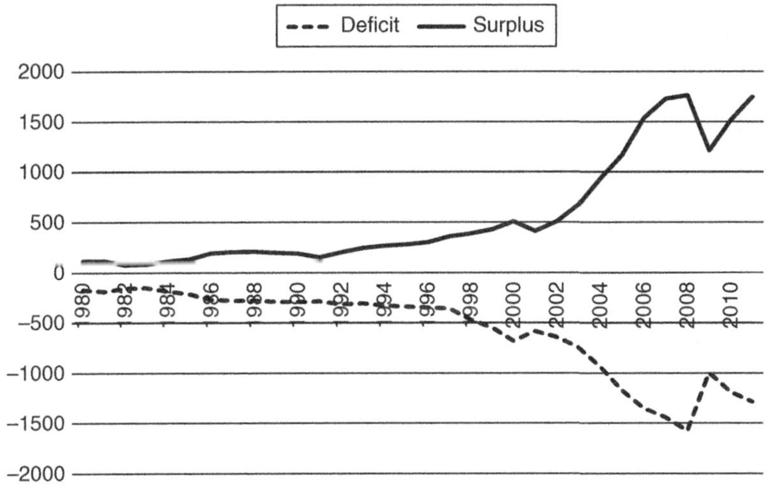

Figure 4.1 Current account balances in the period 1980–2011 (US$ billion)
Source: Authors' own elaboration based on International Monetary Fund, World Economic Outlook Database.

nature, and in 2011 the size of current account imbalances reached a similar size to that registered before the crisis. Thus, in 2011 the sum of total current account deficits amounted to US$1,285 billion and the total current account surpluses amounted to US$1,748 billion.

In order to reach a correct valuation of the relevance for the world economy of the size of the current account imbalances, we have calculated the size of these imbalances as a percentage of the world gross domestic product (GDP). Since, as explained above, the total amounts of the current account deficits and surpluses do not match up, we have calculated the size of the world current account imbalances as the mean of the sum of the absolute values of the current account deficits and surpluses (as shown in Figure 4.1), calculating the percentage of these average in terms of the world GDP.[3]

The results are shown in Figure 4.2. The size of the current account imbalances increases since the end of the 1990s in absolute terms and also as a percentage of the world GDP. In 1996 the current account imbalance, according to our valuation, reached 0.98 per cent of the world GDP. In 2006, this percentage peaked at 2.93 per cent. And although in 2009, it had fallen to 1.91 per cent, since 2010 it has been rising again, and, thus, in the year 2011 the size of the world current account imbalance amounted to 2.17 percentage points of the world gross domestic product.

The visual inspection of the evolution of the size of the current account imbalances displays a clear rising trend. Since the beginning

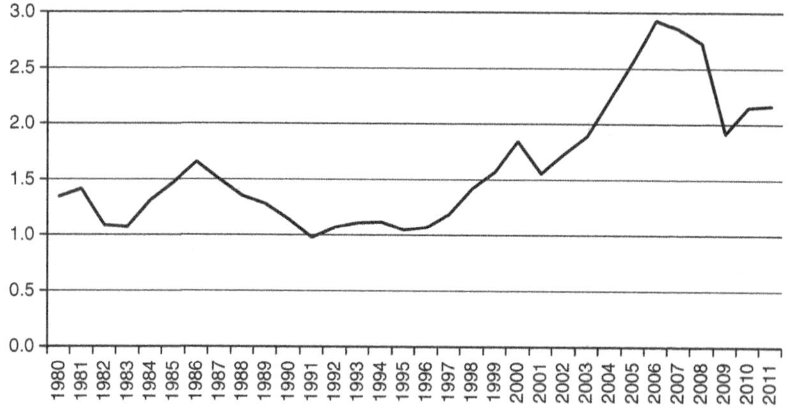

Figure 4.2 Current account balances in the period 1980–2011 as percentage of world gross domestic product

Source: Authors' own elaboration based on International Monetary Fund, World Economic Outlook Database.

of the new century, the size of these imbalances (as a percentage of world GDP) has nearly doubled. Thus, during the period 1980–89, the world current account imbalances would have amounted, according to our calculations, to 1.26 percentage points of world GDP. However, in the period 2000–11 that figure would have climbed to 2.21 per cent of world GDP.

The conclusion that we can reach from these data is that the current size of the current account imbalances is not a short-term situation or the result of a cyclical pattern of behavior of the balance of payments, but rather the result of a structural change and transformation in the world economy, that has led to a significant, and permanent, increase in the size of these imbalances.

4.5.2 The concentration of world imbalances in current accounts

As mentioned above, the global imbalances can be a source of problems for the world economy. This is the case not only because of the size of the current account imbalances but also because the concentration of the imbalances in a small number of countries means that the imbalances in these economies become a systemic risk for the global economy.

It is clear that the size of the current account imbalances have increased over the last four decades. But an equally important fact is that during that period the imbalances have been concentrated in a small number of countries. Table 4.1 shows the countries where the current account imbalances, both deficits and surpluses, have concentrated since 1980. Thus we have analysed, on the one hand, the countries that in each year have registered surpluses or deficits in their respective current account balances. As we have done in Figure 4.1, we have summed all of the current account deficits and the current account surpluses. For each total sum, we show the countries whose imbalances represent, respectively, the 25 per cent, the 50 per cent, and the 75 per cent of the accumulated surpluses and deficits.[4]

It is important to notice that the current account imbalances are increasingly concentrating in a smaller number of countries. This trend is even more evident in the case of the current accounts deficits. Thus, in 2007, the current account deficit of the USA was equivalent to 49.3 per cent of the world current account deficit, the deficit of Spain amounted to 10 per cent, the deficit of the United Kingdom 5.1 per cent, the deficit of Australia 4.1 per cent, the deficit of Italy 3.6 per cent, and the deficit of Greece amounted to 3.1 per cent of the world current account deficit.

Table 4.1 Concentration by countries of world current account imbalances

Year	Accumulated % of the world current account imbalances	Countries with surplus on the current account	Countries with deficit on the current account
1980	25	Saudi Arabia	Italy, Germany, Brazil
	50	Saudi Arabia, Kuwait	Italy, Germany, Brazil, Japan, Mexico, Poland, Canada, Korea, Spain
	75	Saudi Arabia, Kuwait, United Arab Emirates, Qatar, Libya, Nigeria	Italy, Germany, Brazil, Japan, Mexico, Poland, Canada, Korea, Spain, Belgium, Australia, Sweden, France, Austria, Iran, Turkey, Ivory Coast, Argentina, Philippines, Romania, Ireland
1990	25	Germany, Japan	USA
	50	Germany, Japan, China	USA, United Kingdom, Italy, Canada
	75	Germany, Japan, China, Taiwan, Switzerland, Venezuela, Netherlands, United Arab Emirates	USA, United Kingdom, Italy, Canada, Spain, Australia, France, India, Mexico, Thailand
1995	25	Japan	USA
	50	Japan, Netherlands, Italy	USA, Germany, Australia, Brazil
	75	Japan, Netherlands, Italy, Switzerland, Belgium, Singapore, France	USA, Germany, Australia, Brazil, United Kingdom, Thailand, Hong Kong, Korea, Malaysia, Austria, Indonesia, India, Turkey
2000	25	Japan, Russia	USA
	50	Japan, Russia, Switzerland, Norway, France, China	USA
	75	Japan, Russia, Switzerland, Norway, France, China, Canada, Kuwait, Saudi Arabia, Iran, Korea, United Arab Emirates, Venezuela, Libya, Singapore	USA, United Kingdom, Germany, Brazil

(*continued*)

Table 4.1 Continued

Year	Accumulated % of the world current account imbalances	Countries with surplus on the current account	Countries with deficit on the current account
2007	25	China, Germany	USA
	50	China, Germany, Japan, Saudi Arabia	USA, Spain
	75	China, Germany, Japan, Saudi Arabia, Norway, Netherlands, Singapore, Sweden, Kuwait, Switzerland, Taiwan	USA, Spain, United Kingdom, Australia, Italy, Greece
2011	25	China, Germany	USA
	50	China, Germany, Japan, Saudi Arabia, Russia	USA, Turkey, Italy, France
	75	China, Germany, Japan, Saudi Arabia, Russia, Switzerland, Norway, Netherlands, Kuwait, Qatar, Taiwan, Singapore, Sweden	USA, Turkey, Italy, France, United Kingdom, Canada, Brazil, Spain, India

Source: Authors' own elaboration based on International Monetary Fund, World Economic Outlook Database.

The high concentration of the current account imbalances in a small number of countries can be easily observed from the behaviour of the countries with the highest current account imbalances. Figure 4.3 shows the size of the total surpluses and deficits in the current account and accumulated values of the imbalances of the three countries with the highest current account deficits and surpluses, respectively.

The increase in the size of global imbalances have run in parallel with the increase of the highest current account imbalances, mainly, as we will see later, in the case of the deficit countries. Thus, whilst in the year 1980, the three highest deficits and surpluses in the current account amounted, respectively, to \$44 and \$68 billion, in 2007 these imbalances had reached, respectively, \$928 and \$813 billion.

The concentration of the world current account imbalances is more evident when we consider the share of the three highest imbalances in the world current account imbalances (see Figure 4.4). Besides the high share that the three highest imbalances represent in respect of the total world

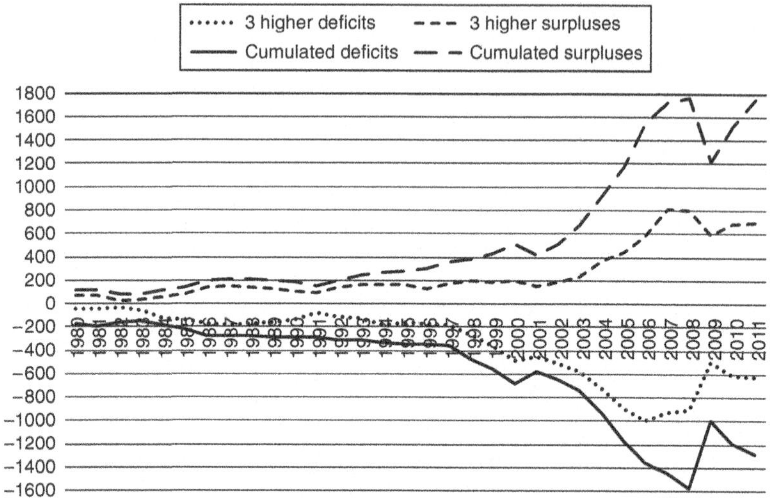

Figure 4.3 Current account imbalances, 1980–2011 (US$ billion)
Source: Authors' own elaboration based on International Monetary Fund, World Economic Outlook Database.

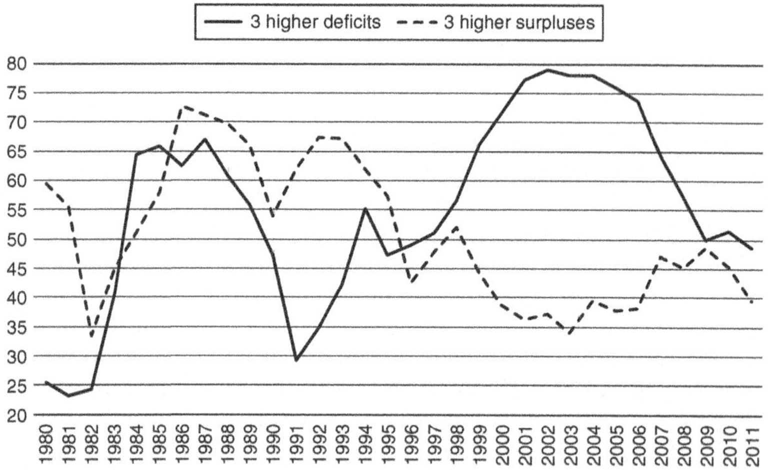

Figure 4.4 Three highest current account imbalances as a percentage of total current account imbalances (%)
Source: Authors' own elaboration based on International Monetary Fund, World Economic Outlook Database.

current account imbalances, we can reach two additional relevant conclusions. The first is that the concentration of current account imbalances is higher for deficits than for surpluses. Thus, in the 2000s, the share of the three highest deficits is double that of the three highest surpluses. The second is that whilst the share of the three highest surpluses shows a clear declining trend, the share of the three highest deficits has a rising trend.[5]

This concentration of imbalances, mainly in the case of deficit countries, implies that current account imbalances are a problem. This is the case not only because these countries have these imbalances, but also because they are a source of systemic risks for the world economy, given the size of these economies – most of them, if not all, developed economies.

However, this does not mean that the current account imbalances are a problem simply because they are concentrated in a small group of countries like China or the United States of America, whose large size makes these economies a potential source of systemic risks for the global economy. Current account imbalances are a relevant problem not only because of the large imbalances in some economies, but also because of the enormous figure of economies with imbalances in their current accounts, regardless of the size of these economies.

A first way to consider the spread of the current account imbalances is to analyse the evolution of current account regions by regions. Here we have used the regional classification used by the International Monetary Fund in hits World Economic Outlook Database. That information is shown in Figures 4.5 and 4.6, which show, respectively, the current account balances of developed and developing economies.

As we have mentioned earlier, most existing studies focus their analyses of the global imbalances and the current account imbalances as a problem exclusively on one big developed economy (the USA) and one big developing economy (China) or, at most, a small group of developing and emerging market economies (China plus a few number of Asian economies).[6] However, this analysis has nothing to do with the reality.

As Figure 4.5 shows, the imbalances in the current account of the European Union, the euro area, and the G7 countries are small. However, the Central and Eastern Europe economies[7] register very high current account deficits, whilst the group of Other Advanced Economies register high current account surpluses.[8]

The situation repeats when we analyse the developing and emerging market economies (see Figure 4.6). Only the regions of Latin America and the Caribbean and Sub-Saharan Africa register small imbalances in their current accounts. On the contrary, the rest of developing and emerging economies, register very high current account surpluses.

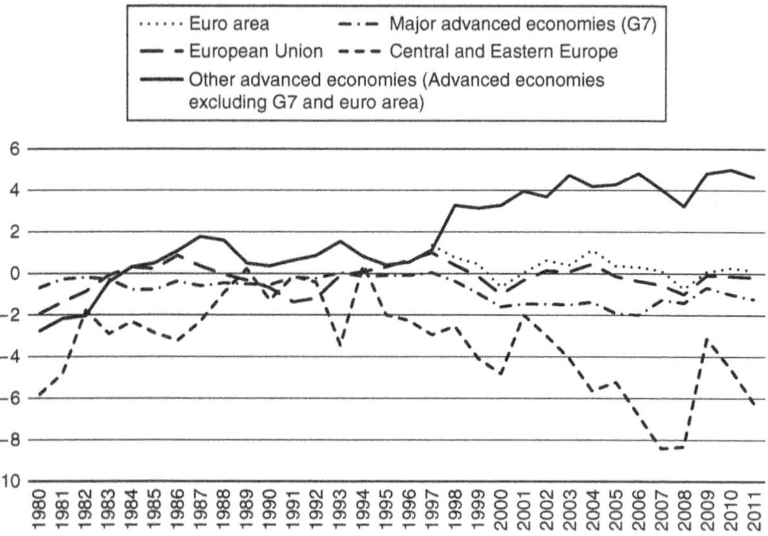

Figure 4.5 Current account imbalances as a percentage of the GDP: developed economies
Source: Authors' own elaboration based on International Monetary Fund, World Economic Outlook Database.

The second way to analyze the spread of the current account imbalances is looking at individual countries. Figure 4.7 shows the number of countries with significant current account imbalances in their respective balance of payments. We have classified all the economies for which the World Economic Outlook Database of the International Monetary Fund provides data about their current account balance and their gross domestic product into three groups of countries according to the sign and size of their current account balances. One group collects those countries whose current account surpluses are higher than 4 per cent of their GDP. The second group collects those countries whose current account deficits are above 4 per cent of their GDP. Finally, the third group if formed by the rest of countries, that is, countries whose current account imbalances are in the range (+4 per cent GDP, −4 per cent GDP). This grouping has been made for all the years of the period 1980–2011.

The use of the threshold of 4 per cent of the gross domestic product to define a current account imbalance as significant is an arbitrary and subjective decision. Narrower thresholds reduce the number of

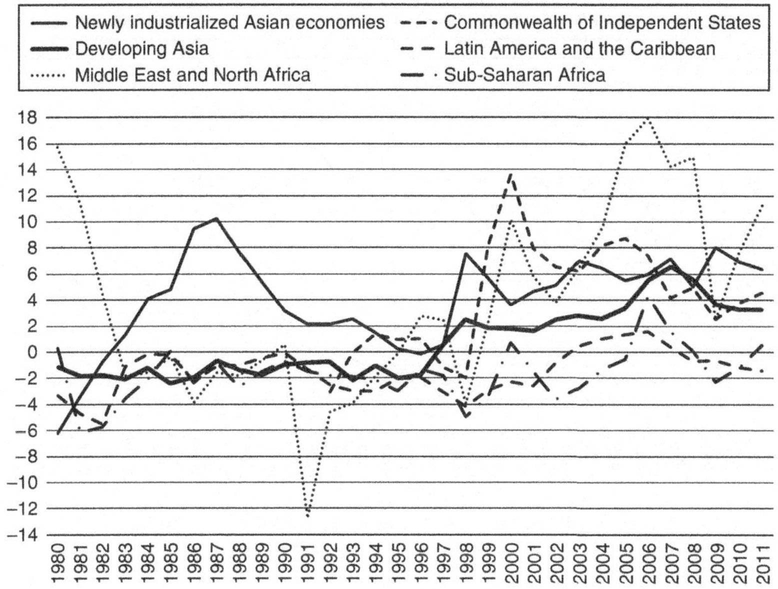

Figure 4.6 Current account imbalances as a percentage of the GDP: developing economies
Source: Authors' own elaboration based on International Monetary Fund, World Economic Outlook Database.

countries with significant external imbalances, whilst wider thresholds increase that number.[9]

Figure 4.7 shows for the period 1980–2011 the number of countries that form each of the groups of countries. Since 2000, the number of countries with high deficits and high surpluses has increased, although the high increase takes place in the group of deficit countries. Furthermore, the number of countries without significant current account imbalances falls dramatically. Thus, in the year 2008 out of a total of 184 countries, 107 countries registered a current account deficit above 4 per cent of GDP, 40 countries registered surpluses above 4 per cent of GDP, and only in 37 economies was the current account balance in the range (−4 per cent GDP; +4 per cent GDP).

We could be tempted to think that the high number of countries involved can be explained by the choice of too low a threshold. But this is not the case. If instead of choosing the threshold of ±4 per cent GDP, we used a threshold of ±10 per cent GDP, the outcomes are also surprising:, in 2008 61 countries had deficits in the current account

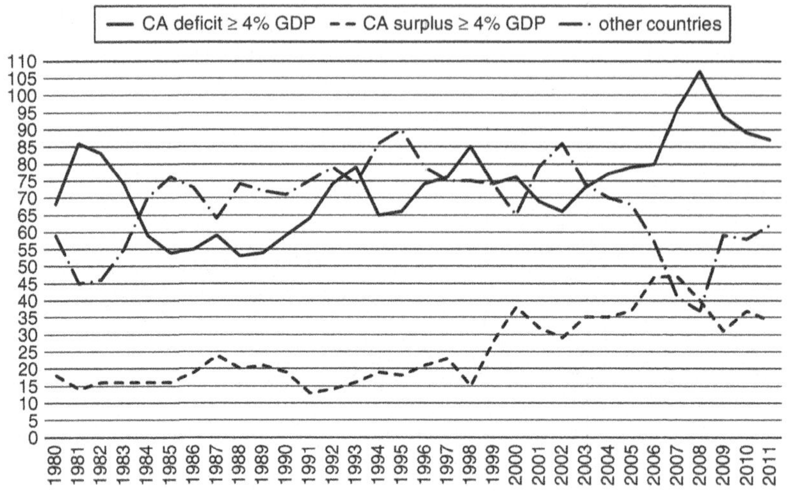

Figure 4.7 Number of countries with high current account imbalances
Source: Authors' own elaboration based on International Monetary Fund, World Economic Outlook Database.

above 10 per cent of GDP, and 21 economies registered current account surpluses above this new limit.

The above result is even clearer when we look at the percentages that the countries with significant current account deficits or surpluses represent in terms of the total number of countries. The results are shown in Figure 4.8.

Since the year 2000 the percentage of countries with significant deficits and surpluses in their current account (above 4 per cent of GDP) has increased dramatically. In 1995, 90 countries, representing 52 per cent of all the countries, had current account balances in the range of ±4 per cent GDP. However, in 2007, 96 countries (52.2 per cent of total countries) had deficits above 4 per cent GDP, and 47 countries registered surpluses above 4 per cent GDP (25.5 per cent of total countries). Only 41 countries (22.3 per cent of total countries) registered 'small' imbalances in their current accounts. The current crisis has reduced the figures and shares of highly imbalanced countries, but figures are still very high. In 2011, 87 countries (47.5 per cent of all the countries in the world) had deficits above 4 per cent of GDP, and 34 countries registered surpluses above 4 per cent of GDP (18.6 per cent of the countries). Only 62 countries (33.9 per cent of total countries) registered 'small' imbalances in their current accounts.

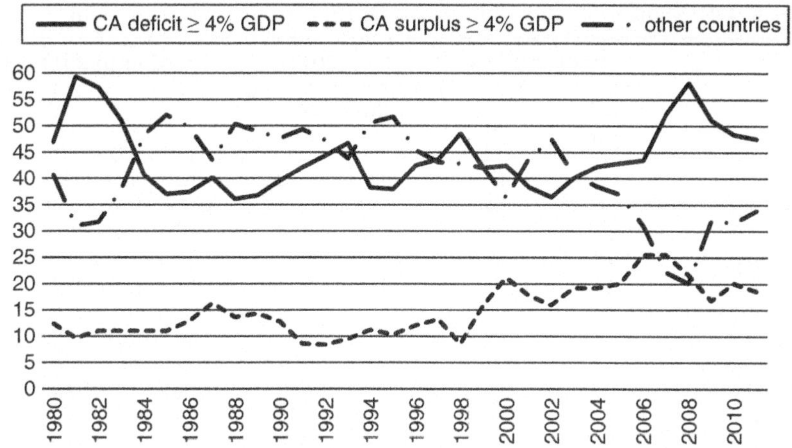

Figure 4.8 Countries with high current account imbalances as percentage of the total number of countries (%)

Source: Authors' own elaboration based on International Monetary Fund, World Economic Outlook Database.

4.5.3 Persistence of current account imbalances

The relevance of the current account imbalances is determined not only by the size (and the sign) of the imbalances but also by their persistence. If the current account imbalances were a temporary phenomenon, related to (domestic or foreign) cyclical situations, in the long run, the current account imbalances would be fully offset by imbalances with the opposite sign. That is, in the long run the current account balance would be in equilibrium. On the contrary, if current account imbalances are permanent, having a structural nature, these disequilibria may accumulate, becoming a source of macroeconomic imbalances that could gain the category of systemic risks.

To test the persistence of the current account imbalances we have analyzed the behaviour since the year 1980 of the current account balances of the biggest countries, those that we could consider as systemic. In this sense, we have included in this analysis those economies whose gross domestic products amount more than 1 per cent of the world GDP. These economies are those shown in Table 4.2. According to the data from the World Economic Outlook Database of the IMF, these 18 economies amount 78.5 per cent of the world GDP.

Table 4.2 Number of years with surplus or deficit in the current account

	1980–2011		2000–2011		Situation in 2011 (5)
	Surplus (1)	Deficit (2)	Surplus (3)	Deficit (4)	
Australia	0	32	0	12	deficit since 1980
Brazil	8	24	5	7	deficit since 2008
Canada	12	20	9	3	deficit since 2009
China	27	5	12	0	surplus since 1994
France	14	18	5	7	deficit since 2005
Germany	20	12	11	1	surplus since 2001
India	4	28	4	8	deficit since 2005
Indonesia	13	19	10	2	surplus since 1998
Italy	9	23	0	12	deficit since 2000
Japan	1	31	12	0	surplus since 1981
Korea	20	12	12	0	surplus since 1998
Mexico	4	28	0	12	deficit since 1988
Netherlands	31	1	12	0	surplus since 1981
Russia	18	2	12	0	surplus since 1993
Spain	3	29	0	12	deficit since 1987
Turkey	5	27	0	12	deficit since 1999
United Kingdom	4	28	0	12	deficit since 1994
USA	3	29	0	12	deficit since 1992

Source: Authors' own elaboration based on International Monetary Fund, World Economic Outlook Database.

Table 4.2 shows the number of years that these 18 economies have registered current account surpluses or deficits. Columns 2 and 3 show the results corresponding to the whole period analyzed, 1980–2011. In all the countries, with the sole exception of France, there is a sign that dominates the whole period. Actually, as mentioned with the exception of France, the imbalances of a certain sign (surplus or deficit) takes place in at least 60 per cent of the years studied.

This persistence is even higher if we focus in the recent past, that is, since 2000 (columns 3 and 4). The same result takes place again. Only France has a balanced current account in terms of the years with imbalances of different sign. In 12 out of the 18 countries the sign of the current account imbalances is the same for the whole period.

The hypothesis of persistence of the current account imbalances is reinforced by the data in column 5. This column shows the sign of the current account balance registered in each country in the year 2011 and the time period over which such an imbalance is taking place. In our study 13 economies are registering the same current imbalance since 2000 or even before. This outcome is another indication of the persistence of the current account imbalances.

4.6 Current account imbalances and foreign direct investments

As previously argued, our hypothesis is that the evolution of the current account imbalances is explained by a process of the worldwide relocation of the production of tradable goods and services, that is, of those goods and services that form the current account; in sum, by a change in the global value added chain. This change in the global value added chain has been fuelled by the huge increase in the foreign direct investment (FDI) flows from developed economies to emerging economies, mainly to Asian economies.

Figure 4.9 shows the evolution since 1980 of three variables: the FDI flows, the FDI stocks and the current account imbalances. As in the case of the current account balances, the statistics about the FDI flows

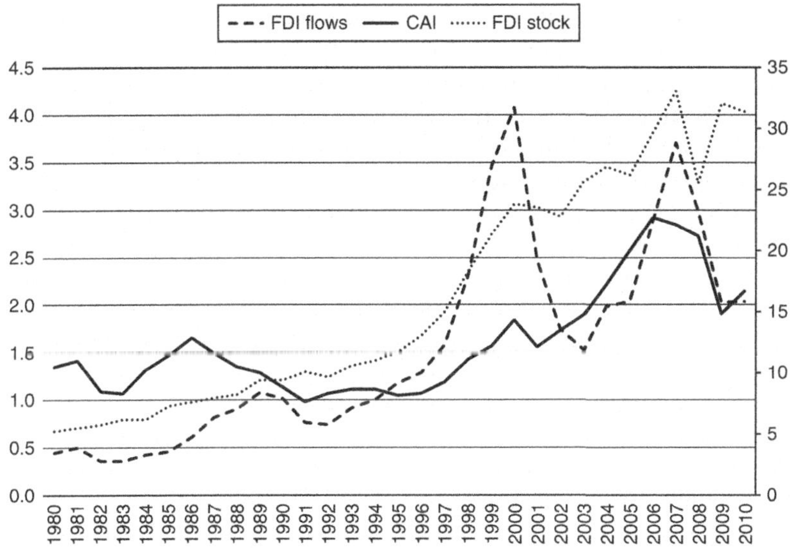

Figure 4.9 Foreign direct investment flows and stocks and current account imbalances (percentage of world GDP)

Source: Authors' own elaboration based on International Monetary Fund, World Economic Outlook Database, and UNCTAD, UNCTADstat.

and stocks show large discrepancies between the values of the foreign direct investment inflows and outflows, and between the values of the FDI inward and outward stocks. To solve this problem, we have opted to apply the same solution than in the case of the current account imbalances, that is, to use as the representative value of the FDI flows and stocks for each year the average of the sum of the foreign direct investment inflows and outflows, on the one hand, and the average of the sum of the foreign direct investment inward and outward stocks, on the other hand.

On the left axis of Figure 4.9, we show the size of the current account imbalances and the size of the foreign direct investment flows as a percentage of the world gross domestic product. On the right axis of Figure 4.9, we show the size of the FDI stocks again measured as a percentage of the world gross domestic product.

What can be seen in Figure 4.9 is that since the end of the 1990s there is an acceleration in the sizes of the FDI flows and stocks that a few years later is translated in the form of an increase in the world current account imbalances.

In 1980, the foreign direct investment flows amounted to 0.44 percentage points of the world gross domestic product. Sixteen years later, the size of these flows had risen but even then they only amounted to 1.28 percentage points of the world GDP. As a result of the higher foreign direct investment flows, the size of the FDI stocks increased from 5.25 percentage points of the world GDP to 13.01 percentage points of the world GDP. During this period, the size of the current account imbalances remained quite stable. Actually, they had fallen: in 1980, the current account imbalances amounted to 1.35 percentage points of the world gross domestic product, but in 1996, these imbalances only represented 1.07 percentage points of the world gross domestic product.

Since then, the size of foreign direct investment has accelerated. Thus, FDI flows peaked 4.08 percentage points of world GDP, and although they fell, in 2004 they started to increase again, reaching 3.71 percentage points of the world gross domestic product in 2007. With the current financial and economic crisis, the size of the FDI flows diminished, but even now, the size of these flows (above 2 per cent of world GDP) is higher than those registered before 1997.

As a result of these higher FDI flows, the size of the foreign direct investment stocks have reached unparalleled levels, climbing from 5.25 percentage points of the world GDP to 33.04 percentage points of the world gross domestic product. The crisis led to a large fall in the size of the world foreign direct investment stocks, but they recovered in 2009, and in 2009 and 2010 that size has been above 31 percentage points of the world GDP.

The worldwide reallocation of productive resources and the consequent change in the world global value-added chain can be observed clearly when we look at the distribution of the foreign direct investments across the planet. Figure 4.10 shows the distribution of the foreign direct investment inflows during the period 1970–2010. The growth in the size of these flows of FDI that began at the beginning of the decade of the 1990s took place mainly in the developed economies. However, since 2003 the inward foreign direct investments in developing economies, in the Latin American economies, and, mainly, in Asian countries, started a boom (and also in the transition economies, though at a smaller scale). The current economic crisis has had a dramatic effect on the inward FDI inflows in developed economies, but the impact of these flows directed to developing and transition economies has been very small. As a result, in 2010, the size of the FDI inflows in developing

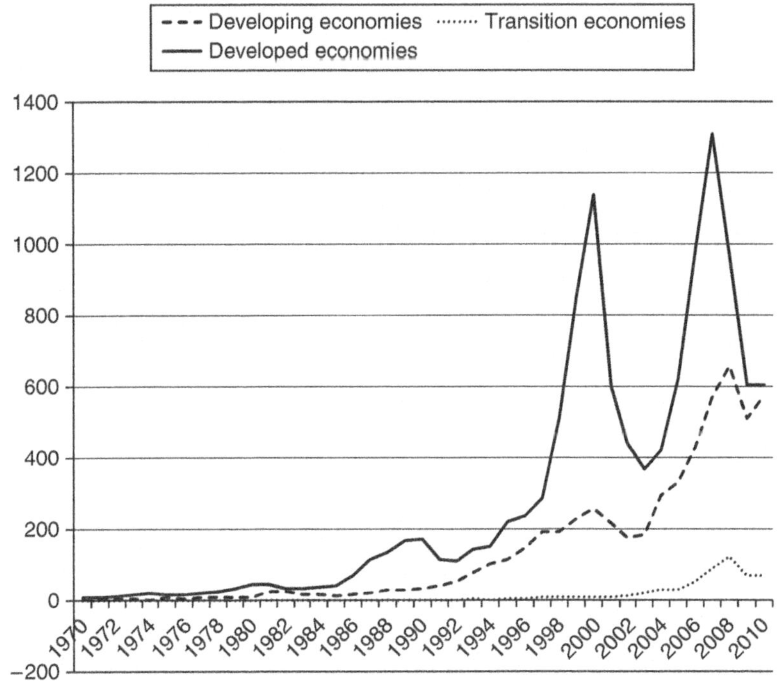

Figure 4.10 Inward foreign direct investment flows (US$ billion)
Source: Authors' own elaboration based on UNCTAD, UNCTADstat.

and transition economies is higher than those registered in developed economies.

The recomposition of the distribution of inward FDI flows has changed the worldwide distribution of the inward FDI stocks, as can be seen in Figure 4.11. In the year 2003, developed economies concentrated 77.1 per cent of the world stock on inward FDI, whilst developing economies only represented 21.3 per cent, and transition economies 1.6 per cent of this stock. However, in 2010, the inward FDI stock in developing economies accounted for 31.1 per cent of the world inward FDI stock, transition economies represented 3.6 per cent, and the share of developed economies was 65.3 per cent.

As a result of the change in the distribution of the inward foreign direct investments flows and stocks, the ranking of the economies with the highest flows and stocks of inward FDI has changed, mainly in the last twenty years. As Tables 4.3 and 4.4 show, the 15 countries with the highest inward FDI flows and stocks, and since 1995, some traditional host economies of foreign investments, mainly developed economies, have lost positions in the rank. Mostly new host economies, some of them developed countries such as Spain, but most of them being developing

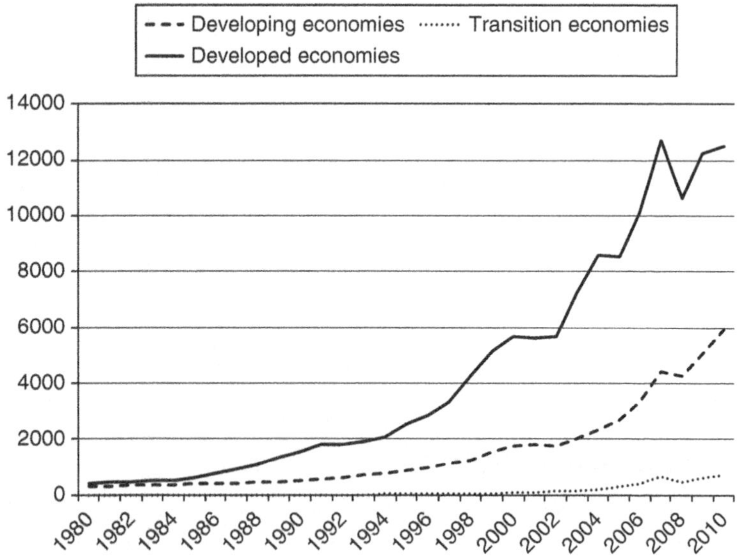

Figure 4.11 Inward foreign direct investment stocks (US$ billion)
Source: Authors' own elaboration based on UNCTAD, UNCTADstat.

Table 4.3 Ranking of the countries by the size of the inward foreign direct investment flows

Rank	1970	1975	1980	1985	1990	1995	2000	2005	2010
1	Canada	Canada	United States	United States	United States	United States	United States	United Kingdom	United States
2	United Kingdom	United Kingdom	United Kingdom	United Kingdom	United Kingdom	China	Germany	United States	China
3	United States	United States	Canada	France	France	France	United Kingdom	France	China, Hong Kong SAR
4	Australia	Saudi Arabia	France	Australia	Spain	United Kingdom	Belgium	China	Belgium
5	Germany	France	Mexico	Mexico	Netherlands	Sweden	Canada	Germany	Brazil
6	Netherlands	Indonesia	Netherlands	Spain	Australia	Australia	Netherlands	Netherlands	Germany
7	Italy	Netherlands	Brazil	China	Belgium	Netherlands	China, Hong Kong SAR	Belgium	United Kingdom
8	France	Brazil	Australia	Brazil	Canada	Germany	France	China, Hong Kong SAR	Russian Federation
9	Brazil	Belgium	Belgium	Netherlands	Italy	Singapore	China	Canada	Singapore
10	South Africa	Spain	Spain	Canada	Singapore	Belgium	Spain	Spain	France
11	Libya	Germany	Singapore	Egypt	Switzerland	Mexico	Denmark	Mexico	Australia
12	Belgium	Italy	Malaysia	Italy	China	Canada	Brazil	Italy	British Virgin Islands
13	Mexico	Iran	China, Hong Kong SAR	Belgium	China, Hong Kong SAR	Spain	Ireland	Singapore	Saudi Arabia
14	Spain	Nigeria	Argentina	Switzerland	Germany	China, Hong Kong SAR	Sweden	Brazil	Ireland
15	Nigeria	Mexico	Greece	Singapore	Portugal	Malaysia	Switzerland	Russian Federation	India

Source: Authors' own elaboration based on UNCTAD, UNCTADstat.

Table 4.4 Ranking of the countries by the size of the inward foreign direct investment stocks

Rank	1980	1985	1990	1995	2000	2005	2010
1	China, Hong Kong SAR	United States	United States	United States	United States	United States	United States
2	United States	China, Hong Kong SAR	United Kingdom	China, Hong Kong SAR	China, Hong Kong SAR	France	China, Hong Kong SAR
3	United Kingdom	Canada	China, Hong Kong SAR	United Kingdom	United Kingdom	United Kingdom	United Kingdom
4	Canada	United Kingdom	Canada	France	France	China, Hong Kong SAR	France
5	Germany	France	Germany	Germany	Germany	Netherlands	Germany
6	Ireland	Germany	France	Canada	Netherlands	Germany	Belgium
7	France	Ireland	Australia	Netherlands	Canada	Spain	Spain
8	Australia	Australia	Netherlands	Belgium	Belgium	Belgium	Netherlands
9	Netherlands	Brazil	Spain	Australia	China	Canada	China
10	Brazil	Netherlands	Italy	Spain	Spain	China	Canada
11	South Africa	Italy	Belgium	China	Ireland	Australia	Switzerland
12	Chile	Belgium	Ireland	Singapore	Brazil	Mexico	Australia
13	Italy	Saudi Arabia	Brazil	Italy	Italy	Italy	Brazil
14	Turkey	Chile	Switzerland	Switzerland	Australia	Singapore	Singapore
15	Belgium	Singapore	Singapore	Brazil	Singapore	Brazil	Russian Federation

Source: Authors' own elaboration based on UNCTAD, UNCTADstat.

and emerging economies, like China, climbing up positions in the ranking of the countries with the highest foreign direct investments.

Therefore, there is a close connection between the evolution of the size of the FDI flows and stocks and the size of the current account imbalances. Consequently, as we will analyse later, the behaviour of the current account imbalances is a structural-nature process that cannot be solved with the implementation of short-term measures, like the exchange rate adjustments or the implementation of macroeconomic (fiscal and/or monetary) policies.

4.7 Should current account imbalances be adjusted? If so, how?

To argue that the financial dimension of the global imbalances has a weak relationship with the economic crisis does not mean, however, that we neglect that these imbalances are a problem, and, therefore, that measures to correct them must be implemented. What we mean is that the analysis of the relevance for the world economy of the existence of the global imbalances must be moved from the financial dimension of these imbalances to the real dimension of the current account imbalances. The persistence of the current account imbalances is the result of the existence of internal imbalances in these economies, and the result also of the lack of mechanisms that help to correct them. Furthermore, these imbalances have negative real effects both in the surplus and the deficit countries.

In the surplus emerging economies, the accumulation of foreign reserves, at least the accumulation that is above certain thresholds, means a loss of welfare for the population of these countries. The export-led growth strategies have succeeded as instruments to increase the stock of capital in these economies. Actually, they have performed much better than the models based on the imports substitution implemented by Latin American economies in the second half of the last century. However, this growth model, at least in some emerging economies, like, for instance China, can be nowadays generating higher costs than benefits (Adams and Park, 2009). This can be contributing to accelerate the need to implement in these countries reforms focused on the stimulus of the domestic demand. Moreover, the model may be facing external limits arising of the impossibility to increase the current foreign markets shares (Guo and N'Diaye, 2009).

In the case of those developed economies that in recent years have shown a clear tendency to generate persistent current account deficits, the costs of these imbalances have adopted different forms. First, these economies have seen how the structural unemployment rates are higher than those registered in the 1980s and 1990s. Secondly, major changes in the income distribution and in the reallocation of productive resources towards sectors less open to the international competition have been observed, with the consequent negative impact on the productivity. These changes have put pressure on the public finances, which have entered into high deficits to maintain their compromise with the welfare state (Boyer, 2012). As far as the funding of the public deficits could be done at low interest rates, the need to correct the external imbalances was less present than nowadays.

The economic crisis is helping to correct the balance account deficits, mainly in some European countries, like Spain or Italy, which are experiencing strong deflationary policies. However, this cannot be the way to solve the problem, since the implementation of those policies is a non-cooperative game where all the countries lose. The Chinese economy (and even the German economy) is starting to show some symptoms of weakness in her economic growth as a result of the lower growth of her exports. Therefore, the crisis is showing the limits that face the export-led growth model implemented by the emerging economies and some developed countries.

Therefore, in our opinion, the current account imbalances must be adjusted and corrected, both the surpluses and the deficits, not only because the financial implications of these imbalances, but also, and mainly, because their real impact on the economic activity and the welfare of the affected economies. But, how can this adjustment take place?

The current account is the sum of the balance of trade (net earnings on exports minus payments for imports), factor income (earnings on foreign investments minus payments made to foreign investors) and cash transfers. The adjustment of the current account involves the reduction of the absolute value of the current account balance, making it closer to zero. To achieve this adjustment, the balances of trade, factor income and cash transfer must be adjusted. Traditionally, the strategy to adjust the current account imbalances has focused on the adjustment in the trade balance of goods and services. Two reasons explain this focus. The first reason is that the flows of exports and imports of goods and services are the main component of the current account. The second reason is that it is much easier to modify, through the accurate policies, the value of the exports and imports of goods and services. The reason is that, on the one hand, it is much more difficult to influence the value and the sign of the balance of cash transfer, and, on the other, that the amount of the flows of factor income depends upon the profitability but also, and mainly, of the stock of foreign inward and outward investments.

Thus, in this section, we will identify the adjustment of the current account with the adjustment of the trade balance. Consequently, the policies to achieve the adjustment of the current account balance that we will analyze are those policies that try to adjust the trade balance, changing the value of the flows of exports and imports of goods and services.

Traditional solutions to solve a current account imbalance can be grouped in two categories: demand-side policies (fiscal and monetary policies) and the exchange rate policy.[10] In both cases the objective of these policies is to approximate absorption to output (domestic production being equal to domestic absorption). The demand-side policies are based on the Keynesian income equation:

$$(T - G) + (S - I) = (X - Q)$$

where the symbols have their usual meaning: T stands for taxes, G for government expenditure, S for savings, I for investment, X for exports and Q for imports.

This equation means that current account imbalances are explained by an excess of savings (the surpluses in the current account) or by an excess of spending (the deficits). In order to adjust a deficit in the current account, the economic authorities must implement measures to reduce the public and/or private spending (to increase public and/or private savings). This involves the implementation of a restrictive fiscal policy or a restrictive monetary policy (or a mix of both policies). In the case of the existence of a current account surplus, the adjustment of this imbalance involves measures to reduce the public and/or private savings (to increase public and/or private spending). This involves the implementation of an expansionary fiscal policy or an expansionary monetary policy (or a mix of both policies).[11]

The second option is to use the exchange rate as tool to reach the desired current account imbalance. Current account deficits would be corrected with a depreciation of the currency of the deficit country, whilst a current account surplus would involve an appreciation of the currency of the surplus country.

However, these strategies to adjust the current account imbalances are not without problems. Thus, first, in the case of demand-side policies, the reduction of the current account deficits involves the implementation of restrictive monetary and/or fiscal policies. These policies may have a negative impact on economic activity, in terms of output and employment, an impact that will be higher the higher current account deficit. Moreover, to improve the current account deficit, domestic producers must move that part of their output that formerly was directed to satisfy the domestic demand to exports. This involves that there is a foreign demand for the domestic goods and services. In a similar way, the lower domestic demand must involve a lower demand of imported goods and services. This means that domestic producers can supply the foreign goods that were previously imported, and that domestic consumer can effectively reduce the necessity to consume goods and services produced abroad.

Similarly, the measures implemented to reduce a current account surplus also are based on a set of assumptions, mainly: that surplus country will increase the demand of goods and services produced abroad; that domestic agents absorb some of the production formerly exported; that foreign partners will be able to generate the (higher) supply of these goods; and, finally, that there is a foreign supply of these goods.

It is important to notice that to reduce the current account surplus domestic agents must effectively generate a demand of foreign goods and services in order to generate the required higher imports. Moreover, the surplus country must reduce the value of its exports, something that involves not only a fall in the number of units of goods and services sold abroad but also a fall in the price of exports. Thus, if the lower supply of exports of domestic goods does not come with an increase in the supply of the same goods made by third parties, export prices of the goods produced in the surplus country may rise, thus contributing to maintain, or increase the current account surplus.

Like in the case of macroeconomic policies, the management of the exchange rate as a tool to adjust the current account imbalances is not without problems. Thus, the impact of changes in the exchange rate on the current account depends upon the elasticity of the demands of imports and exports. The Marshall–Lerner condition shows that for a change in the exchange rate has the desired impact on the current account the sum of the elasticities of the demands of imports and exports must be higher than 1. If this condition is not fulfilled, the change in the exchange rate will have the opposite result, with depreciations generating a worsening in the current account deficit if the domestic demand of imported goods is highly inelastic, and appreciations of the currency leading to higher current account surpluses. In this sense, empirical analyses (see, for instance, Altuzarra et al.,

2010), using cointegration and vector correction model analyses, show that a depreciation of the euro improves the trade balance with China, but a depreciation of the dollar deteriorates the US trade balance with China.

In this sense, a low elasticity of the demand of imports, which involves a low substitutability between domestic goods and imported goods, means that a significant reduction in a current account deficits a very large depreciation of the domestic currency must take place. If we think that an abrupt and sudden depreciation of the exchange rate can be considered as a currency crisis, something to be avoided, then there must be a soft landing of the exchange rate to the levels compatible with the desired target of the current account. Consequently, the exchange rate cannot reach a short-term adjustment of the current account imbalance.

Furthermore, the impact on trade balances of changes in the real exchange rate depends on the level of intra-industrial trade. Thus, in countries with low intra-industrial trade (like is the case of countries exporting raw materials or natural resources, or countries specialized in certain industries, the depreciation of the real exchange rate can deteriorate the trade balance (Kharroubi, 2011).

A change in the exchange rate of a single currency might not affect the current account balance of a third partner, if the exports of the first country compete with other countries whose currencies do not change. In this sense, the appreciation of the currency of the surplus country may well reduce this surplus, but it will not improve the current account of the deficit country if the imports from the surplus country are substituted by imports from other countries whose currencies have not changed. Based on this argument an increasing number of papers focusing on the trade balance between the USA and China argue that an appreciation of the Chinese renminbi is not a sufficient condition to reduce the US trade deficit. The reason is that although the trade deficit of the US economy with China can be reduced with the renminbi appreciation, however, it may come with rising trade deficits with other Asian economies. Thus, for instance, Mattoo et al. (2012), argue that an appreciation of the Chinese real exchange rate with the US dollar leads to higher exports to the USA from competitor countries (other emerging economies, mainly Asian). The final results is that the appreciation of the renminbi leads to a lower Chinese trade surplus but to higher trade surpluses of Asian economies.

These results show that in order to make an adjustment of the current account deficit, even in the case where there is one deficit country and one surplus country, the change in the exchange rate of both currencies is not a sufficient condition to correct that imbalance, being necessary that third currencies be also adjusted. Thus, Méjean et al. (2011) estimate that to reduce the US current account deficit by 1 percentage point of the US gross domestic product is required an appreciation of the Asian exchange rate of 23 per cent, that is, the US dollar must depreciate 23 per cent against the whole basket of Asian currencies. That depreciation would be much higher if the adjustment of the exchange rate of the US dollar would take place with respect to only one currency or with a group of Asian economies. However, if the adjustment of the exchange rate were not generalized, the required depreciation of the US dollar should be much higher: if the US dollar only depreciated against the Chinese renminbi, the US dollar would need to depreciate by 45 per cent; if the depreciation would be with the rest of Asian economies, leaving the exchange rate with the renminbi unchanged, the dollar should depreciate by 42 per cent.

In any case, the strategy implemented in one country to adjust its current account imbalance will be effective if and only if the other economy (or economies) also adjust its corresponding imbalance. Thus, in a two-country world, a current account deficit in country A will only be adjusted if country B reduces its surplus. Consequently, the implementation of the tight macroeconomic policies or the depreciation of the exchange rate in the deficit country will only be effective as far as the partner country does not adopt the same kind of measures, which will offset the measures adopted in the deficit country. This opens a new debate: how to discipline surplus countries. In other words, which incentive should be generated for surplus countries to reduce their current account surpluses (Williamson, 2012).

Consequently, the correction of these imbalances cannot be the result of measures adopted at a national level. On the contrary, it must be the result of internationally arranged actions. These actions require a deep knowledge of the factors behind the balance of payments imbalances. As we have argued, the exchange rate policy followed by many emerging economies, based on maintaining the currencies undervalued to foster the exports, only explain partially the origin of these imbalances. Therefore, the adjustments in the real exchange rates would not be useful to adjust the global imbalances unless they come with another measures.

These other measures are related to structural changes shown by the analyses of the global imbalances made before the crisis. The high savings rate of the emerging economies is a constraint on the expansion of the domestic demand in these economies. Another constraint is the lack of a developed financial system. The latter lack creates relevant restrictions in the credit access, which, in the case of corporations, lead to downwards wage pressures to increase the corporations' capacity to self-finance their investments (Aziz and Cui, 2007).

The impulses to the domestic demand in the emerging economies do not mean the adjustment of the individual current account imbalances. If the world supply does not increase in response to the higher demand of the emerging economies, the result can be an increase in the price of tradable goods. This is a problem that can affect mainly developed economies, highly dependent on the imports of certain goods from the emerging economies, mainly, from Asian emerging economies. Unless these economies develop a new productive capacity of goods currently produced in the emerging economies, the higher domestic demand of these goods in the latter economies will involve a fall in the supply available for developed economies, which may well lead to higher prices in the world markets, something that can lead to a higher value of the imports and, consequently, to higher current account deficits.

4.8 Summary and conclusions

The global imbalances have been considered, in some cases, to be the ultimate and direct cause of the current crisis, and, in other cases, as a necessary but not sufficient cause of the crisis. The relationship between the financial crisis and the balance of payments imbalances has been mainly focused on the financial effects generated in the net capital flows arising from these imbalances. It is argued that the arrival of these capitals in the US financial system led to a fall in the long-term interest rates, which, in turn, fuelled a boom in the domestic credit and a bubble in the real estate sector.

However, the size of the net capital flows is not sufficiently high to justify the dominant thesis about the relationship between the financial crisis and the global imbalances. Moreover, that explanation forgets the role played by the gross capital flows before the crisis. When we include in the analysis the gross capital flows, it is easy to see that the capital inflows in the US financial system coming from the European banks were as high as the capital inflows from the emerging economies. This fact, first, questions the relationship between the crisis and the balance of payments imbalances; and, secondly, places into the correct perspective the weaknesses of the international financial and monetary system as the ultimate cause of the financial crisis.

Questioning the financial dimension of the global imbalances as a cause of the financial and economic crisis does not mean that these imbalances are not a problem. The current account imbalances are proof of the existence of real imbalances at a worldwide level that show the deep structural changes that have taken place in the world economy during the recent period of economic globalization. These imbalances are generating high costs in the emerging and in the developed economies. In the former economies, these costs adopt the form of welfare losses generated by the accumulation of foreign reserves. In the latter, the consequences are the existence of chronic current account deficits that have a negative effect on economic growth and that need to be financed with external debt.

The current crisis is helping to reduce, at least partially, most current account deficits, although the external adjustment is coming with economic stagnation. Moreover, the adjustment of the current account imbalances cannot be generated with adjustments in the exchange rates, because the elasticities of the import and export functions have changed. Although it can be accepted that some currency realignments can be necessary, the adjustment of the current account imbalances involves another kind of measures. In the emerging economies, mainly in China, domestic demand must be impulse, what requires the reform of their financial systems and a fall in the domestic savings rates. In the developed economies, there must be a re-industrialization that will increase the international supply of tradable goods and satisfy not only the demand coming from the developed economies, but also the higher demand coming from the emerging economies.

Notes

1. Previous versions of the paper were presented at the Conference International Economic Policies, Governance and New Economics (Cambridge, 12 April 2012), and at the 9th International Conference Developments in Economic Theory and Policy (Bilbao, 28–9 June 2012). Comments from participants at these conferences and the editors of this volume are acknowledged. We also thank the support of the Basque Government (Consolidated Research Group GIC10/153).
2. For an analysis of the problems of the argument that current account imbalances are explained by a misalignment of the fundamental real exchange rates, see Ferreiro and Serrano (2011) and Liang (2012).
3. This means that, for instance, the world current account imbalance in 2008 amounted US$1,669 billion, whilst in 2011 the imbalance reached US$1,516 billion.

4. Thus, for instance, in 1990 the current account surpluses of Germany and Japan amounted above 25 per cent of the world current account surplus, whilst the current account deficit of the USA by itself amounted more than 25 per cent of the world current account deficit. If we sum the surpluses of Germany, Japan and China, that sum was higher than 50 per cent of the world current account surplus. In the case of deficit countries, the sum of the USA, United Kingdom, Italy and Canada amounted to more than 50 per cent of the world current account deficit.
5. Since the bursts of the financial and economic crisis, the gap between the highest deficits and surpluses has fallen dramatically. Nonetheless, it is important to notice that since 2007 the share of the highest deficits has fallen but the share of the highest surpluses has increased.
6. See, for instance, Bracke et al. (2010).
7. A group formed by Albania, Bosnia and Herzegovina, Bulgaria, Croatia, Hungary, Kosovo, Latvia, Lithuania, the Former Yugoslav Republic of Macedonia, Montenegro, Poland, Romania, Serbia, and Turkey.
8. Formed by Australia, the Czech Republic, Denmark, Hong Kong SAR, Iceland, Israel, South Korea, New Zealand, Norway, Singapore, Sweden, Switzerland, and Taiwan Province of China.
9. The figure of ±4 per cent GDP was the threshold set for current account deficits by Treasury Secretary Geithner in the G20 summit in November in 2010 in Seoul (Hallet and Martinez Oliva, 2012). Nonetheless, other authors and institutions, however, have suggested different thresholds. Williamson (2012) suggests a lower threshold: ±3 per cent GDP. For the US economy, Mussa (2004) suggested a limit for the US current account deficit of −5 per cent GDP, although Cline (2005) suggested a lower limit: −3 per cent GDP. In the case of the European Union, within the recent framework for the surveillance of macroeconomic imbalances, adopted different thresholds for surpluses and surpluses in the current account balances: +6 per cent GDP and −4 per cent GDP (European Commission, 2012).
10. An alternative to the use of macroeconomic policies and the exchange rate policies is the use of an incomes/wages policy. An acceleration in the growth of wages (with real wages growing faster than productivity) would be an effective tool to adjust a surplus in the current account. The higher wages would involve an increase in the labour costs and a lower competitiveness of domestic goods and services, thus reducing exports and increasing imports. Moreover, the higher labour incomes would expand the domestic demand, increasing imports and deteriorating the current account balance. On the contrary, wage moderation (with real wages growing below productivity) would help to improve the current account deficits. Lower wages would reduce labour costs and would increase competitiveness. Moreover, the lower labour incomes would have a negative impact on domestic demand, reducing imports, and reducing the current account deficit.
11. We are implicitly assuming that public authorities can effectively implement the kind of macroeconomic policies required and that these policies have the desired impact on the aggregate demand. This means that in deficit countries, demand-side policies can effectively reduce fiscal deficits, and/or increase private savings and/or reduce private investments; in surplus countries, these policies are able to worsen public finances, foster investment and reduce private savings.

References

Adams, Ch. and Park, D. (2009) 'Causes and Consequences of Global Imbalances: Perspective from Developing Asia', *Asian Development Bank Working Paper Series*, No. 157, Manila: ADB.

Ahearne, A., Cline, W.R., Tae Lee, K., Chul Park, Y., Pisani-Ferry, J., and Williamson, J. (2007) 'Global Imbalances: Time for Action', *Peterson Institute Policy Brief*, March.

Altuzarra, A., Ferreiro, J. and Serrano, F. (2010) 'The Role of Global Imbalances as a Cause of the Current Crisis', *Journal of Innovation Economics*, 6: 25–48.

Arestis, P. (2009) 'The New Consensus in Macroeconomics: a Critical Appraisal', in G. Fontana and M. Setterfield (eds), *Macroeconomic Theory and Macroeconomic Pedagogy*, Basingstoke: Palgrave Macmillan, pp. 100–17.

Arestis, P. (2011) 'Keynesian Economics and the New Consensus in Macroeconomics', in E. Hein and E. Stockhammer (eds), *A Modern Guide to Keynesian Macroeconomics and Economic Policies*, Cheltenham: Edward Elgar, pp. 88–111.

Aziz, J. and Cui, L. (2007) 'Explaining China's Low Consumption: the Neglected Role of Household Income', IMF Working Paper, No. 181, Washington, DC: IMF.

Bank of England (2007) *Financial Stability Report*, April, London: Bank of England.

Barth, J.R., Caprio, G., and Levine, R. (2012) *Guardians of Finance: Making Regulators Work for Us*, Cambridge MA: MIT Press.

Bernanke, B. (2005) 'The Global Saving Glut and the US Current Account Deficit', Remarks delivered before the Federal Reserve Board, 10 March. Available at www.federalreserve.gov/boarddocs/speeches/2005/200503102/default.htm.

Bernanke, B., Bertaut, C., Punder DeMarco, L., and Kamin, S. (2011) 'International Capital Flows and the Returns to Safe Assets in the United States, 2003–2007', *FED International Finance Discussion Papers*, No. 1014, Washington DC.

Borio, C. and Disyat, P. (2010) 'Global Imbalances and the Financial Crisis: Reassessing the Role of International Finance', *Asian Economic Policy Review*, 5(2): 198–216.

Borio, C. and Disyat, P. (2011) 'Global Imbalances and the Financial Crisis: Link or No Link', *BIS Working Papers*, No. 346, Basel: BIS.

Boyer, R. (2012) 'The Four Fallacies of Contemporary Austerity Policies: the Lost Keynesian Legacy', *Cambridge Journal of Economics*, 36: 283–312.

Bracke, T., Bussière, M., Fidora, M., and Straub, R. (2010) 'A Framework for Assessing Global Imbalances', *The World Economy*, 33(9): 1140–74.

Caballero, R., Farhi, E. and Gourinchas, P. (2008a) 'An Equilibrium Model of "Global Imbalances" and Low Interest Rates', *American Economic Review*, 98(1): 358–93.

Caballero, R., Farhi, E. and Gourinchas, P. (2008b) 'Financial Crash, Commodity Process and Global Imbalances', *NBER Working Paper*, No. 14521, Cambridge, MA: NBER.

Carrol, C. and Jeanne, O. (2009) 'A Tractable Model of Precautionary Reserves, Net Foreign Assets, or Sovereign Wealth Funds', *NBER Working Paper*, No. 15228, Cambridge, MA: NBER.

Catão, L. and Milesi-Ferretti, G.M. (2011) 'External Liabilities and Crises', mimeo, Washington, DC: International Monetary Fund.

Cline, W.R. (2005) *The United States as a Debtor Nation*, Washington, DC: Institute for International Economics.

Dooley, M., Folkerts-Landau, D. and Garber, P. (2003) 'An Essay on the Revived Bretton Woods System', *NBER Working Paper*, 9971, Cambridge, MA: NBER.

Dooley, M., Folkerts-Landau, D. and Garber, P. (2005) *International Financial Stability. Asia, Interest Rates, and the Dollar*, Deutsche Bank.

Eichengreen, B. (2009) 'The Financial Crisis and Global Policy Reforms', Federal Reserve Bank of San Francisco, Asia Economic Policy Conference, 18–20 October.

European Commission (2012) 'Scoreboard for the Surveillance of Macroeconomic Imbalances', *European Economy. Occasional Papers*, 92.

Ferreiro, J. and Serrano, F. (2011) 'The Impact of the Current Crisis on Emerging Market and Developing Countries', in P. Arestis, R. Sobreira and J.L. Oreiro (eds), *An Assessment of the Global Impact of the Financial Crisis*, Basingstoke: Palgrave Macmillan, pp. 108–34.

Ferreiro, J. and Serrano, F. (2009) 'Institutions, Expectations and Aggregate Demand', in G. Fontana and M. Setterfield (eds), *Macroeconomic Theory and Macroeconomic Pedagogy*, Basingstoke: Palgrave Macmillan, pp. 309–22.

Forbes, K.J. (2008) 'Why Do Foreigners Invest in the United States?', *NBER Working Paper*, No. 13098, Cambridge, MA: NBER.

Guo, K. and N'Diaye, P. (2009) 'Is China's Export-oriented Growth Sustainable?', *IMF Working Paper*, No. 172, Washington, DC: IMF.

Hallet, A.H. and Martinez Oliva, J.C. (2012) 'Reducing Global Imbalances: Can Fixed Exchange Rates and Current Account Limits Help?', *Open Economies Review*, 23: 163–92.

Herr, H. (2011) 'International Monetary and Financial Architecture', in E. Hein and E. Stockhammer (eds), *A Modern Guide to Keynesian Macroeconomics and Economic Policies*, Cheltenham: Edward Elgar, pp. 267–93.

International Monetary Fund (2005) *International Monetary Fund Annual Report 2005: Making the Global Economy Work for All*, Washington, DC: International Monetary Fund.

Kharroubi, E. (2011) 'The Trade Balance and the Real Exchange Rate', *BIS Quarterly Review*, September: 33–42.

Liang, Y. (2012) 'Global Imbalances as Root Cause of Global Financial Crisis? A Critical Analysis', *Journal of Economic Issues*, 46(1): 101–17.

Mattoo, A., Mishra, P. and Subramanian, A. (2012) 'Spillover Effects of Exchange Rates: a Study of the Renminbi', *Peterson Institute for International Economics Working Paper*, No. 12-4, Washington, DC.

McGuire, P. and Von Peter, G. (2009) 'The US Dollar Shortage in Global Banking', *BIS Quarterly Review*, March: 47–60.

Méjean, I., Rabanal, P., and Sandri, D. (2011) 'Current Account Rebalancing and Real Exchange Rate Adjustment between the US and Emerging Asia', *IMF Working Paper*, 11/46, Washington, DC: IMF.

Mendoza, E., Quadrini, V. and Rios-Rull, J. (2009) 'Financial Integration, Financial Deepness and Global Imbalances', *Journal of Political Economy*, 117: 371–416.

Minsky, H. (1982) *Can 'It' Happen Again?*, Armonk, NY: M.E. Sharpe.

Mussa, M. (2004) 'Exchange Rate Adjustments Needed to Reduce Global Payments Imbalances', in F. Bergsten and J. Williamson (eds), *Dollar Adjustment: How Far? Against What?*, Washington, DC: Institute for International Economics.

Obstfeld, M. (2012) 'Does the Current Account Still Matter?', *American Economic Review: Papers and Proceedings*, 102(3): 1–23.

Obstfeld, M. and Rogoff, K. (2009) 'Global Imbalances and the Financial Crisis: Products of Common Causes', CEPR *Discussion Paper*, No. 7606, London: Centre for Economic Policy Research.

Porter, R. (2009) 'Global Imbalances', in X. Freixas and R. Porter (eds), *Macroeconomic Stability and Financial Regulation: Key Issues for the G20*, London: Centre for Economic Policy Research, pp. 19–26.

Prasad, E.S. (2009) 'Rebalancing Growth in Asia', *IZA Discussion Papers Series*, No. 4298.

Reinhart, C.M. and Reinhart, V.R. (2009) 'Capital Flow Bonanzas: an Encompassing View of the Past and Present', in J.A. Frankel, and C. Pissarides (eds), *International Seminar on Macroeconomics 2008*, Chicago: University of Chicago Press.

Servén, L. and Nguyen, H. (2010) 'Global Imbalances Before and After the Global Crisis', *World Bank Policy Research Working Paper*, No. 5354, Washington, DC: World Bank.

US Government (2009) *Economic Report of the President*, Washington, DC: US Government Printing Office.

Weber, A. (2010) 'Global Imbalances. Causes and Challenges', Introductory remarks at the international conference '20 Years of Technical Central Bank Cooperation', Eltville, Hesse, 28 October.

Williamson, J. (2012) 'Rules for Correcting External Imbalances', *Open Economies Review*, 23: 151–61.

5
Africa and the Perversities of International Capital Flows

Howard Stein
University of Michigan, USA

5.1 Introduction[1]

During the 1980s and 1990s, neoclassical economists inside and outside of the International Financial Institutions (IFIs) heavily supported the unfettered movement of capital flows to developing countries. They argued that once impediments to free capital mobility were removed funds would flow from low marginal product of capital-rich countries to high marginal product of capital-poor countries as the capital market worked to equalize risk-adjusted marginal products of capital across borders. On the promise of significant *net* gains for productive investment and economic growth, many African countries embraced financial globalization. They removed restrictions on capital accounts, opened up to FDI, privatized state assets which frequently included selling off banks to foreign owners, built significant international reserves and built stock markets often under the encouragement and supervision of the International Financial Institutions (IFI).

The promised gains of these policies have not only been unrealized; they have had a number of perverse effects. Capital flows have moved in the opposite direction with funds flowing to the rich countries from some of the poorest African countries. While orthodox economists like Lucas (1990) have tried to provide explanations, most are aimed at rescuing their flawed axioms and few would admit to the basic cause of this perversion, the asymmetries of power inherent in the structures of international finance.

Worldwide we have witnessed a three-decade-long project, which has been aimed at what one could call the global financialization imperative.[2] It has a number of key components. First are movements to commodify all products or services that have any utility or use value.

Second is to try to capture all commodities with financial instruments or related derivatives. Third is to allow the unfettered movement of private financial institutions and their products into every corner of the globe by demobilizing the capacity of nation-states to impede or restrict their activities while building institutions that provide a common platform of accessibility. Domestic financial flows everywhere become part of global flows and are tapped as component parts of the accumulation strategies of large financial corporate organizations and their wealthy clients. Increasingly, official and private flows are blurred and closely interconnected. Financial liberalization and its associated legitimizing theories have been embedded into the dictums and practices of the international aid community for decades. They have used their power and resources to alter the terrain for global capital.

5.2 Mainstream literature and the globalization of finance: paradoxes and perversities

The key function of financial systems in the saving–investment–growth relationships is to act as an effective conduit for the mobilization and allocation of loanable funds; and the transformation and distribution of risks and maturities. Thus, if the system operates efficiently, financial institutions should, first of all, be able to channel funds from surplus to deficit units by mobilizing resources and ensuring efficient transformation of these funds into real productive capital. In addition, through the diversification of investment and greater flows of information, financial institutions and markets together have the potential to efficiently transform maturity between savers and investors, while providing sufficient liquidity to the system as the need arises. They are also assumed to reduce risks from the system through diversification and techniques of risk-sharing and risk-pooling.

In the mainstream literature, the role of capital markets in providing efficient and transparent price signals and liquidity in the secondary market for equities and bonds is emphasized as mechanisms for vigorous portfolio arbitrage of bond- and shareholders. Here, capital markets are, above all, seen as a mechanism of enabling the public an easy asset and portfolio allocation and diversification. With a liquid developed secondary market, savers/investors with strong preference for holding short-term liquid assets could participate in markets of long-term securities and bonds issued for illiquid productive investment, with knowledge that these long-term assets can be easily disposed on the secondary markets. Capital markets are further to provide a medium, whereby banks and other financial institutions such as pension fund and life insurance companies could take on long-term investment through the sale of long-term financial assets to the surplus units of the economies, either directly to households or via pension funds or insurance companies which mobilizes contractual savings. Hence, an active and broad-based capital market is thought to mitigate the acute shortage of term loans and equity financing, and transform and lengthen credit maturities as well as reduce the credit risks inherent in transactions among individuals.

Extending these lines of arguments across borders, financial globalization is seen as to improve economic development and global welfare through the same saving–investment–growth relationship while ensuring efficient intermediation on a global scale (Rousseau and Sylla 2003). With opening up to international borrowing, a capital-poor developing country is able to: (a) divert resources to more future production by undertaking extra investment at a lower world interest rate; and (b) enjoy higher current consumption, as its saving–investment resource gap (and hence, the emerging current account deficit) is being filled by foreign saving (Obstfeld and Rogoff 1996). In short, the intertemporal model of capital trade is used to show benefits from financial globalization in allowing capital to seek out its highest returns permitting consumption smoothing and insurance against shocks in developing countries.

In the extreme version of the neoclassical world with perfect information and no transaction costs, the removal of barriers to free capital mobility leads to a flow to high marginal product of capital-poor countries from low marginal product of capital-rich countries as the capital market equalizes cross-border risk-adjusted marginal products of capital. In particular, as the interest rate parity condition dictates, financial globalization ensures that asset markets gravitate towards equilibrium in response to risk-adjusted relative returns, even if instantaneous price adjustments are often prevented because international traded assets are imperfect substitutes in their risk characteristics under real world conditions. Consequently, it is claimed that as financial globalization proceeds, there is an increase in the efficiency of global resource allocation, while developing countries emerge as a winner, benefiting from higher investment and consumption with lower interest rates as well as from an opportunity of global risk-sharing.

This is precisely the perspective embedded in arguments by Stanley Fischer and other senior IMF officials as they pushed for an amendment to the Articles of Agreement to make capital account liberalization a prerequisite for IMF membership even in the wake of the Asian crisis:

> ... free capital movements facilitate a more efficient global allocation of savings, and help channel resources into their most productive uses, thus increasing economic growth and welfare. From the individual country's perspective, the benefits take the form of increases in both the potential pool of investable funds, and the access of domestic residents to foreign capital markets. And just as current account liberalization promotes growth by increasing access to sophisticated technology, and export competition has improved domestic technology, so capital account liberalization can increase the efficiency of the domestic financial system. ... an amendment of the Fund's Articles of Agreement is the best way of ensuring that capital account liberalization is carried out in an orderly, non-disruptive way, that minimizes the risks that premature liberalization could pose for an economy and its policymakers (Fischer, 1997, p. 3).

The IMF has been a big player in many aspects of financial liberalization. However, contrary to the predictions of the IMF and of many mainstream economists, capital in the era of neoliberal globalization has tended to flow from the emerging economies to the rich countries. Starting with Lucas (1990), mainstream economists have tried to rescue the neoclassical economic perspective with explanations of the 'Lucas paradox'. Alfaro, Kalemli-Ozcam and Volosovych (2006) classify the literature into two groups. The first focuses on differences in fundamentals that affect the structure of production, including technological gaps, missing factors of production, policies of governments and the structure of institutions (King and Rebelo, 1993; Razin and Yuen, 1994; Gomme, 1993; and Tornell and Velasco, 1992). The second focuses on market imperfections embedded in capital flows including asymmetric information and perceptions of sovereign risk. Though high returns are known, market imperfections prevent capital from flowing to developing countries (Gertler and Rogoff, 1990; Gordon and Bovenberg, 1996; Lane, 2004; and Portes and Rey, 2005).

Others like Alfaro, Kalemli-Ozcam and Volosovych (2006) focus on 'institutional' dimensions as a source of explanation for the Lucas Paradox using data from the International Country Risk Guide (ICRG). The ICRG composite index includes assessments of things such as government stability of investment, internal conflict non-militarized politics, law and order, property right assessment, democratic accountability and so on. In their sample the Lucas Paradox is measured by the log of PPP-adjusted GDP/capita. They introduce institutional variables, restrictions to capital mobility, 'distantness' between capital cities (to capture information asymmetries) and years of schooling/capita into the equation to see if the log GDP per capita becomes insignificant covering the period 1970–1998/2000. Both the variable for institutions and capital restrictions are significant but only the former also makes the GDP variable insignificant and hence they conclude that the paradox can only be explained by institutional quality.

However, the exercise is less than cogent. First, there is no attempt to disaggregate by institution type, by time or by region. It is hard to know what institutions are important or if there are any regional fixed effects. Secondly, these kinds of measures are little better than opinion polls even if they are generated by employees of PRS group assigning a number from 1 to 10 or 12. What does it mean to have a score of 7 for one country vs 6 in another? How does anyone avoid subjectivity or arbitrary selection? Thirdly, the data sample they use is focused only on FDI and portfolio equity rather than any other debt flows. Yet, in the context of Africa, capital flows from official sources have tended to dominate. Fourthly, they use three different empirical sources, which only include a very small sample of African countries. None of them incorporate Angola or Nigeria, which have been, over many decades, the two biggest recipients of FDI in Africa. Yet, by most measures, both have very low institutional quality. Fifthly, there is a very high correlation between the variables. Correlations are as high as .84 between log GDP/capita and institutional quality, which raises red flags about the direction of causation not just that the results might be spurious (which they test for using Monte Carlo simulations). As Khan (2007) argues, there is strong evidence that higher income and growth leads to improved governance indicators (along the lines specified in the ICRG). Thus if higher income is both a good predictor of net capital flows and generates good institutions how can one anoint 'institutions' as the penultimate causal variable.

Lucas (1990) himself proposes three explanations for the paradox. First large differences of labour productivity could counter the differences in the marginal productivity of capital. Secondly, he tries introducing human capital into total capital measures (often used by neoclassical economists to try to rescue Heckscher–Ohlin–Samuelson theorem (HOS) on international trade) and introduces differences in sovereign risk which was expanded by Reinhart and Rogoff (2004).

Ju and Wei (2006) show that all three cannot hold in the neoclassical HOS world. In the first case, higher labour productivity would lead to higher wages, which would counter the effect of higher labour productivity. In the second case, returns to capital, human capital and labour would be all equalized through free trade and therefore could not account for the opposite flows. In the third case, in the model with two factors and two sectors, free trade in goods has already led to an equal return to capital across countries and therefore there is no room for sovereign risk to further affect the return to capital. In their model they introduce property right and financial development to explain the paradox.

Like most work in this area, there is an underlying belief in the naturalism of the system which suggests that once some impediment such as improper property rights is removed, then all will behave as is predicted by neoclassical economics. Overall, these kind of studies abstract from the real world systemic relationships, which are imbued with asymmetric power and real world actors that gain from the types and directions of international capital flows. The idea of perversion in international finance is very different than a paradox, which assumes that flows are contradictory to what we would expect. In fact, the result is unsurprising given the underlying asymmetries of power. The idea of a perversion here is ethical; one where the global system is deliberately deviating from what is good or proper.

As we will document below, neoliberalism and international capital flows have generated grotesque perversities in Africa. Among other things the poorest in the world are financially supporting the wealthiest. The system of debt generation and servicing has helped fuel massive capital flight. Capital flows have pushed African economies into perverse economic structures aimed at unfettered resource extraction that can be readily financialized. Everywhere human needs become subservient to the whim of the accumulation strategies of hedge funds servicing wealth and power.

5.3 Globalization and global flows: inequality, financialization and neoliberalism

Globalization in an era of financialization has pushed in three main directions. First it has been the drive to commodify all products that have any utility or, in classical economic terms, use value. For finance capital to expand its reach goods and services must become tradable on private markets. This has multiple dimensions and not only incorporates pressures to move subsistence labour into market-producing activities,[3] but also means commodifying resources like water and privatizing public goods like health care and education.[4] The second is to transform all value that is exchanged (whether tangible, intangible, future or present promises, and so on) into either a financial instrument or a derivative of a financial instrument. Third is to allow the unfettered movement of private financial institutions and their products into every corner of the globe by demobilizing the capacity of nation-states to impede or restrict their activities while building institutions that provide a common platform of accessibility. Growing income inequality and neoliberalism have been central drivers behind financial globalization. A recent OECD study illustrates the trends in rising inequality. In 27 OECD countries the ratio of the annual growth of the top quintile's income to the bottom quintile's income was 1.9/1.3 from the mid-1980s to the late 2000s. The Gini coefficient rose or showed no improvement in 20 out of 22 countries with long-term data available (OECD, 2011a).

Increasingly, managing the wealth of the rich has been an important source of profitability for finance. Take the example of hedge funds which are typically only available to large investors. In 1995, there were an estimated 2,800 hedge funds managing $2.8 billion in assets. By the end of 2006 the number had jumped to 8,500 with over $1.4 trillion in assets (Ubide, 2006; IMF, 2007). Prior to the crisis, the number continued to grow perceptibly. By the second quarter of 2008, assets in the funds reached $1.93 trillion. After falling during the crisis, the hedge fund levels fully recovered to pre-crisis levels, hitting $1.92 trillion in the 4th quarter of 2010 (Financial Times, 2011). By September, 2012 they had soared to $2.8 trillion (McIntosh, 2012) Their influence on markets has increased appreciably. In 2005, 174 hedge funds reported trading volumes which accounted for 15 per cent of the US fixed income market, 25 per cent of the high yield market, 58 per cent of credit derivatives, 47 per cent of distressed debt, 45 per cent of emerging market bonds and 32 per cent of leverage loans (IMF, 2007). Pressures for returns for the wealthy have pushed speculation into new areas such as the purchase of commodities (more on this below) as part of a broad push toward financialization of the global economy.

On the simplest level, financialization is understood as the growing domination of the financial sector over all other economic activity. One striking indicator is the massive growth of the world's financial assets compared to GDP. In 1980, global financial assets (equities and private debt securities, government debt securities and deposits) were around $12 trillion and slightly above a one-to-one ratio to GDP. By 2007, financial assets had reached $196 trillion or nearly 360 per cent of GDP (McKinsey Global Institute, 2008). Global financial stock fell in 2008 and 2009 compared to 2007 but by 2010 it had recovered and surpassed the 2007 levels (McKinsey Global Institute, 2011). While the statistics illustrate the general trend toward the dominance of finance, the meaning and consequence of these trends have been explored by a number of authors.

Epstein (2002) sees financialization as 'the increasing importance of financial markets, financial motives, financial institutions, and financial elites in the operations of the economy and its governing institutions, both at the national and international levels' (p. 3). The impact goes beyond the realm of banking and finance to affect the operation of non-financial institutions including those that govern the economy. As Watson (2009) puts it, financialization can mean 'the attempt by government to subject the entire process of macroeconomic management to the needs of the finance-led growth regime' (p. 258). Increasingly, companies have become the 'playthings of the capital markets' with firms no more than 'an accidental bundle of liabilities and assets that is there to be reorganized to maximize shareholder value' (Blackburn, 2006, p. 43).

In the period of financialization, companies were seen no longer as a single entity but rather as a bundle of financial assets, which could be taken over, repackaged and sold off for a value that would exceed the original price. Once grabbed, cash on hand could be seized along with a new capacity to raise debt. Companies would have stock value not only due to its current capacity to generate income but also as a potential target for hostile or friendly takeovers.

To align the interest of corporate management with maximizing stockholder returns, stock options became the predominant source of executive earnings. Increasingly, the effort was to undertake any measure that would maximize the value of stocks – often at the expense of the long-term growth prospects of companies including stock buybacks. From 1997 to 2008, 438 S&P companies spent $2.4 trillion on stock buybacks. Many of the leading high-tech companies spent more on stock purchases than on research and development.

In the era of financialization, investment was dominated by speculation and limited time horizons. In the past, shares were seen as a part of the ownership of a company where individuals could literally share in the growth and prosperity of companies over an extended period. However, this began to change. In 1960 only 12 per cent of listed company shares on the New York Stock Exchange changed hands. The turnover increased to 46 per cent by 1990, 88 per cent in 2000 and 100 per cent in 2008. Overall, one source estimated that in 2009, stocks changed hands 250 per cent compared with just 20 per cent three decades before. In the NASDAQ traders can see orders for thirty milliseconds before they are available to others, allowing hedge funds and investment banks to place millions of orders to garner tiny profits on each share but huge gains overall.

While the growing income concentration has provided the fuel for the vehicle of financialization, neoliberalism has paved the roads and removed any barriers. At the core of neoliberalism is a commitment to deregulation aimed at retracting state intervention in markets in order to reverse price distortions. At every turn, financialization has been able to speed up with deregulation or a failure to regulate new financial instruments. In the case of stock options, in 1992, the rules under section 16(b) of the Securities and Exchange Act were relaxed and permitted officers and directors to exercises stock options and to sell the shares without the formerly required six months. Options were not treated as expenses and while they needed to be legally reported they were frequently placed in tiny print in footnotes in annual reports (Tabb, 2012). As specified above, the result was an increasing focus on short-term strategies to raise stock prices. Deregulation also played a key role in encouraging financialization in new markets.

Increasingly, hedge and other wealth funds have moved into commodities speculation with implications for the food security of billions of people. Limits from the Commodities Exchange Act of 1936 on the speculative holdings of commodities were lifted following the passing of the 2000 Commodities Future Modernization Act which deregulated over the counter trading. Deregulation of commodity markets has attracted hedge fund speculation and lead to a massive increase in the financialization of commodities including food and with it tremendous volatility in prices. The number of commodity futures and options contracts increased dramatically and reached nearly 70 million contracts by 2010 – up from roughly 10 million contracts in 2003. By 2008, the value of outstanding derivative contracts in commodities hit nearly $14 trillion compared to around $1 trillion in 2003 (UNCTAD, 2011b).

Commodity markets are being driven not by fundamentals of producers and end users but by other factors. Among other things, commodities are seen as a good hedge when the value of the dollar falls which lowers the value of global commodities in non-dollar terms. Strategies now include speculation on food which has become a bio-substitute for fuels with frightening implications for the welfare of millions of net food buyers in poor developing countries. In 2011, for example, it is estimated that 61 per cent of the wheat futures market was held by speculators compared to only 12 per cent in the mid-1990s prior to deregulation. The amount of money flowing to speculation in food markets futures continues to grow appreciably and roughly doubled between 2006 and 2011 (to around $126 billion) (Worthy, 2011). The result was a steep rise in food prices which more than doubled between July 2003 and June, 2008.[5] After declining following the financial crisis they started rising and peaked in April 2011 at more than 2½ times the pre-deregulation level in June, 1999 (Index Mundi, 2012).

The impact on food consumers in poor African countries is well documented. IMF (2011) estimates that, on average, the internal price of food rises by 0.33 per cent for every 1 per cent in global food prices. In a survey of 58 developing countries, food prices had risen by 56 per cent between 2007 and 2010, putting millions more at risk of undernourishment and malnutrition (Worthy, 2011).

The perversity of these results seems to escape the participants in these markets. CBOT traders were interviewed for a recent article in the German magazine *Spiegel* entitled 'How Global Investors Make Money Out of Hunger':

> For Alan Knuckman, there is hardly a nicer place than the CBOT trading floor. 'This is capitalism in its purest form,' the commodities expert raves. 'This is where millionaires are made.' How he makes money doesn't make any difference to Knuckman. He draws no distinctions among commodities like petroleum, silver or food products. 'I don't believe in politics,' he says. 'I believe in the market, and the market is always right.' How does he feel about exploding food prices? The age of cheap food is over,' predicts Knuckman, noting that this can't be such a bad thing for US citizens. 'Most Americans eat too much, anyway'. (Knaup et al. 2011, p. 1)

Perversities embedded in global capital flows have other dimensions.

5.4 Liberalization in Africa

In line with Fischer's remarks above, the IMF and other donors pursued an active agenda to build stock markets while removing capital account restrictions. Joyce and Noy (2005) find a correlation between IMF programmes and capital account liberalization between 1982 and 1998.[6] The largest coefficient is in countries receiving concessional IMF loans reflecting the embedded asymmetries of power. In all, 26 of 53 countries deregulating capital accounts during IMF loans were in Sub-Saharan Africa (SSA).[7]

In 1980, prior to the start of era of structural adjustment, there were only three stock exchanges in Sub-Saharan Africa (in Kenya, Nigeria and

South Africa). In 2011 there were 22 exchanges covering 31 countries in SSA. Most have been organized after the beginning of the Asian Crisis when the logic of capital account liberalization came into question even within the IMF. In all, exchanges covering 21 countries in Africa were established in 1997 and after, many with the support of foreign assistance.[8] Few have any restrictions on the foreign purchase and sale of stocks. For example, T. Rowe Price's Africa and Middle East Fund lists investments in stocks in a dozen SSA countries.[9] Other funds expand the list.[10]

The World Bank's FDI project in Africa has deliberately pushed countries into privatization and a minimalist and uniform regulatory and legal framework aimed at encouraging countries to follow their comparative advantage in resource extraction. A particular emphasis in the effort over the past two decades or more was on reforms aimed at attracting FDI to the mining sector in Africa (Campbell, 2008).

World Bank (1992) lays out a clear strategy. Emphasis is on 'market based foreign exchange and trade policies', 'mining sector policy that emphasizes the role of the private sector as owner and operator', 'legislation that ensures access to land and that permits secure and tradeable exploration and mining rights', 'provision of private incentive marketing systems to reduce illegal and artisan exports' and finally 'total or partial privatization of state mining' (p. 53). The document is adamant in pointing to Chile as the international standard where there are no laws governing mining which is covered by property right laws, no restrictions on foreign exchange and where taxation rates are the lowest of all countries studied (p. 70).

In Africa, the Bank points to Ghana in providing a positive climate for foreign investment following their Minerals and Mining Laws of 1986, which was introduced as part of the World Bank and IMF's structural adjustment program. Among other things the law guarantees the mineral rights of FDI with a very liberal foreign exchange policy that permitted them to retain up to 80 per cent of their foreign exchange earnings in foreign accounts. Subsequently, the Minerals and Mining Act, 2006, was written with the technical support of the World Bank and goes further to improve conditions for FDI in mining by removing a windfall profit tax of 25 per cent on mining revenues and reducing royalties ceiling to 6 per cent from 12 per cent. It also lowered the maximum state ownership to 10 per cent from 30 per cent (Rutherford and Ofori-Mensah, 2011).

In African countries resource industries have a heavy representation on local stock exchanges, which both opens up the resources to investment funds from the developed world while also providing a mechanism for FDI to liquidate their assets. Ghana is no exception. There are 37 stocks listed on the exchange. Two completely dominate the exchange AngloGold Ashanti Limited[11] and Tullow Oil PLC. Their combined market capitalization is 42.8 billion cedis and completely dwarfs the rest of the market. All other stocks together have a capitalization which is less than 15 per cent of the total of the two stocks (Ghana Stock Exchange, 2012).

Table 5.1 provides examples of the variation of controls on investment in a selection of African countries. The combination of the lack of restraint both on FDI and portfolio capital has become increasingly common throughout Africa. Both are central to the strategy of global financialization. The table also provides information that illustrates a lack of constraints on access to all forms of debt including government treasuries. This opens the economies to the full force of debt related capital inflows and outflows, which again leaves these countries open to the whim of investment strategies of wealth management funds in the financial centers of the developed world.

Table 5.2 provides examples of a process of capital account liberalization in a selection of African countries. It illustrates the push toward greater capital account liberalization across the board, although the strategy has varied. The table illustrates the variation in the speed and sequencing of capital account liberalization. Uganda selected a 'big bang' approach in 1997, while Ghana, Nigeria and Zambia have adopted a gradualist strategy. In Ghana, Nigeria and Zambia, capital account liberalization has been part of a comprehensive liberalization of the financial sector.

Other sources confirm the push toward capital account liberalization in SSA. Schindler (2009) generates a data set from a number of countries on capital account restrictions over time, which includes 11 SSA countries, four of which are in in the table above covering the period from 1995 to 2005. All but one of them indicated a decline in the index of restrictions.[12]

5.5 FDI and the structure of African economies

FDI has responded to the relaxation of regulations in SSA and has focused overwhelmingly on resource-exploiting countries, particularly oil exporters. This has increasingly pushed African economies into somewhat perverse structures; one which emphasizes pure resource extraction with all of its problematic consequences. Table 5.3 summarizes FDI flows to SSA over a thirty-year period.

Table 5.1 Controls on debt, equity and FDI in a selection of African countries

Control type / Country	Debt		Equity and FDI	
	Inflows	**Outflows**	**E&FDI Inflows**	**E&FDI Outflows**
No controls				
Uganda	Bonds: ***no controls***	Bonds: ***no controls***	Shares: ***no controls***	Shares: ***no controls***
	Money market securities: ***no controls***	Money market securities: ***no controls***	FDI: ***no controls***	FDI: ***no controls***
	Derivatives: ***no controls***	Derivatives: ***no controls***		
Zambia	Bonds: ***no controls***	Bonds: ***no controls***	Shares: ***no controls***	Shares: ***no controls***
	Money market securities: ***no controls***	Money market securities: ***no controls***	FDI: ***no controls***	FDI: ***no controls***
	Derivatives: ***no controls***	Derivatives: ***no controls***		
Minimal controls				
Nigeria	Bonds: ***no controls***	Bonds: ***no controls***	Shares: ***no controls***	Shares: ***no controls***

(*continued*)

Table 5.1 Continued

Control type / Country	Debt		Equity and FDI	
	Inflows	**Outflows**	**E&FDI Inflows**	**E&FDI Outflows**
	Money market securities: ***controls***	Money market securities: ***controls on resident purchases abroad***	FDI: ***no controls, only registration***	FDI: ***no controls***
	Derivatives: ***no controls***	Derivatives: ***no controls***		
South Africa	Bonds: ***controls on resident sale or issue abroad***	Bonds: ***controls***	Shares: ***controls on resident sale or issue abroad***	Shares: ***limits on resident purchases abroad***
	Money market securities: ***controls on resident sale or issue abroad***	Money market securities: ***controls***	FDI: ***no controls***	FDI: ***controls***
	Derivatives: ***controls on resident sale or issue abroad***	Derivatives: ***controls***		

Controls				
Cameroon	Bonds ***controls***	Bonds: ***controls***	Shares: ***controls on issuing, advertising, and sale of foreign securities of more than CFAF 10 million***	Shares: ***no controls***
	Money market securities: ***controls***	Money market securities: ***controls***	FDI: ***no controls if below CFAF 100 million***	FDI: ***no controls if below CFAF 100 million***
	Derivatives: ***Not applicable***	Derivatives: ***Not applicable***		

Source: Murinde (2009).

Table 5.2 Examples of capital account liberalization

Status/ sequencing	Fully open	Partially open	Fairly open
One-step opening	**Uganda** (1997) Liberalization part of a broad package of market-oriented reforms, privatization and trade liberalization		
Sequenced opening	**Zambia** (1990–95) 1993–94: liberalization of capital transactions 1995: banks allowed to accept foreign currency deposits Liberalization part of broad reforms focused on economic stabilization, competitiveness, and debt restructuring, accompanied by financial market reforms	**Ghana** (1995–2006) Mid-1990s: partial liberalization of portfolio and direct investment 2006: Foreign Exchange Act, allowing non-residents to buy government securities with maturities of three years or longer, minimum holding period of one year Liberalization following economic stabilization and debt restructuring: parallel reforms in the primary government debt and stock markets; efforts to develop interbank money and foreign exchange markets and to strengthen financial sector supervision and soundness	**Cameroon** (2000 to present) 2000: Harmonization of national foreign exchange regulations and liberalization of capital flows within CEMAC Prudential limits on banks' net open foreign positions Residents' foreign exchange deposits prohibited Continued administrative restrictions remain on most capital outflows No immediate plans for further opening

Sequenced opening	**Nigeria** (1985–2006) Economic reforms initiated in the mid-1980s and subsequently reinvigorated in the mid-1990s, starting with treatment of dividends and profit repatriation, then later removal of controls in other areas such as derivatives and real estate; some remaining administrative restrictions Foreign exchange market reformed at various points from the mid-1980s to wholesale Dutch auction system initiated in 2006, along with growing importance of interbank market, and the effective unification of the parallel and official exchange rates	
	Tanzania (1990) 1990: start of FDI liberalization 1997: full liberalization of FDI flows 1998: supporting foreign exchange regulations Continuing restrictions on portfolio investments (government securities) FDI liberalization coinciding with privatization program, creation of one-stop shop, and investment promotion policy	**Senegal** (1999 to present) 1999: elimination of controls on inward FDI and foreign borrowing by residents Continuing administrative restrictions remain on capital outflows to non-WAEMU countries

Source: Murinde (2009).

Table 5.3 FDI inflows to SSA, 1980–2010 (millions of US dollars except for last two rows which are in percentages)

Yr.	1980–85**	1985–90**	1992–97**	2000	2005	2006	2007	2008	2009	2010
DCs	12,717	24,617	118,596	252,459	332,343	429,459	573,032	658,002	510,578	573,568
SSA*	974	1,461	4,035	6,202	28,229	26,550	40,783	51,968	44,381	39,714
2/1*	7.7	5.9	3.5	2.5	8.5	6.2	7.1	7.9	8.7	6.9
2/1	7.0		2.5	2.1	6.5	6.3	6.1	6.5	7.6	6.7

Notes: *includes South Africa.
**annual averages.
Source: UNCTAD (various years).

We can see that FDI flows to developing countries increased nearly twentyfold from the averages of the early 1980s to 2000. However, what is evident is that SSA was not initially part of this rapid proliferation. However, participation and recovery have been heavily driven by oil and has focused on a handful of countries. For example, during 1985 to 1990, two oil producers Angola and Nigeria, alone were attracting more than 50 per cent of the FDI to SSA excluding South Africa rising in 92 to 97 to 57 per cent. By 2005 there was a significant recovery of Africa's share of Developed Countries (DC) FDI flows excluding South Africa to around 8.5 per cent. However, the vast majority of the increase in inflows went to the traditional oil exporters Nigeria and Angola along with new oil producers like Sudan and Equatorial Guinea. In all roughly 78 per cent of the 16.1 billion increase in inflows to non-South African SSA from 2000 to 2005 went to these four countries. Similarly, between 2005 and 2008, 72 per cent of the increase of $21.4 billion to non-South African SSA countries went to just four oil-producing countries – Angola, Nigeria, the Republic of Congo and Ghana. Much of the rest went to countries with other extractive industries including Congo DRC (copper, cobalt etc.), Zambia (copper) and Tanzania (gas and gold).

The focus of the FDI flows was having a profound impact on the structure of exports, perversely returning SSA to a colonial structure of pure extraction. Such FDI has limited economic and developmental benefits because they usually do not stimulate general, broad-based development; significantly expand employment opportunities; diversify exports away from primary commodities; and facilitate meaningful transfer of technology to recipient countries except for the limited purpose of more profitable resource extraction. Moreover, due to the structure of taxation encouraged by the World Bank, the revenue generated tends to be rather limited. As Jomo and von Arnin (2012) aptly put it 'there is little evidence that the pattern of FDI in Africa is likely to bring the sustained, broad-based economic growth and employment generation desperately needed there' (p. 505).

Table 5.4 provides data on the structure of exports. We can see that fuel exports increased tenfold between 1995 and 2008, reaching 72.5 per cent of total exports. Overall primary exports encompassed nearly 93 per cent of the total a level similar to the 1960s before Africa began its early attempt to generate manufacturing.

We can see the impact on the structure of the economy more clearly in Table 5.5. By 2008, manufacturing had collapsed to a pathetically low 6.6 per cent of value added while mining was 27.4 per cent of the total, up from only 8.8 per cent in 1980. The contrast with Southeast

Table 5.4 Exports by Standard International Trade Classification (SITC), 1995–2010 (thousands of US$) SSA excluding South Africa

Year	1995	2002	2006	2008	2010
Total (SITC 0 to 9)	49,135,045	67,966,870	182,213,321	278,514,617	258,979,978
All food items (SITC 0 + 1 + 22 + 4)	11,187,789	11,731,173	16,901,366	22,325,079	28,031,885
Fuels (SITC 3)	**19,738,257 (40.2%)**	**34,621,616 (50.9%)**	**123,842,083 (68%)**	**202,055,278 (72.5%)**	**168,985,887 (65.2%)**
Primary commodities, including fuels and precious metals (SITC 0 + 1 + 2 + 3 + 4 + 68 + 667 + 971	**42,832,673 (87%)**	59,306,987	167,142,684	**258,682,813 (92.8%)**	**237,851,510 (91.8%)**
Manufactured goods (SITC 5 to 8 less 68)	**6,434,574** (13.1%)	**8,170,732** (12%)	**14,349,292** (7.9%)	**18,352,706** (6.6%)	**20,360,368** (7.9%)

Source: UNCTAD (2011a).

Table 5.5 Structure of economy, SSA and SEA, 1970–2008 (% value added)

Year	1970	1980	1990	2000	2006	2008
Ag-SEA	33.6	22.2	16	11.7	11.8	12.4
SSA*	35.8	23.9	28.9	28.1	28.1	25.3
Mi-SEA	4.3	14.1	7.8	8.5	9.2	10.1
SSA	8.8	19.9	15.4	24.0	25.6	27.4
Mf-SEA	15.4	18.2	22.8	27.2	27.7	26.4
SSA	15.6	24.1	15.1	9.4	7.7	6.6

Notes: *SSA does not include South Africa. Mining also includes utilities. Agriculture includes hunting and forestry.
Source: UNCTAD (2008, 2012).

Asia is striking: in that region FDI has flowed into manufacturing, helping to increase manufacturing exports to 70 per cent of the total in 2006. We can see how this has influenced the structure of the economy. Arguments about the centrality of manufacturing in the development process were prevalent and largely understood in African countries after independence. It was known at the time that manufacturing is subject to increasing returns, is a conduit for the transfer of technology, has higher income elasticities compared with other activities, generate employment, is very tradable, is more heterogenous and can allow for better market segmentation, and can stimulate extensive backward, forward and demand linkages. From the work of Prebisch (1950) and

Table 5.6 Development indicators

Year	1970	1980	1990	2000	2006
R.GDP-SEA	447	710	982	1363	1709
SSA	538	572	507	497	626
L.Exp-SEA	52	58	64	67	69
SSA	45	48	47	46	47
I.Mrt-SEA	105	76	51	34	28
SSA	136	119	111	101	94

Notes: *RGDP is in per capita figures in 2005 dollars for SSA excluding South Africa; life expectancy in years and infant mortality is per 1000; SSA does not include South Africa.
Sources: UNCTAD (2008, 2012).

Singer (1950), countries were aware of problems with continuing to rely heavily on unprocessed resource exports (Ajakaiye and Stein, 2009).

Table 5.6 compares the resulting trajectory of development in Southeast Asia and SSA. The contrast is striking. In 1970, SSA actually had higher per capita GDP but was only one-third of the level of Southeast Asia by 2006. Progress in key health focused indicators like infant mortality and life expectancy has been much higher in Southeast Asia.

5.6 Foreign bank ownership and its consequences

The relaxation of foreign ownership regulations has also had a substantial impact on the composition of banking in Africa. This selling off of banks to overseas investors of foreign ownership has been particularly rapid for countries in Africa and transitional countries in Europe – two regions heavily influenced by the Bretton Woods Institutions. In SSA, the change was quite rapid between 1995 and 2005. Foreign takeovers of banking where the World Bank and the IMF dominated policy are no coincidence. In many countries financial liberalization emphasized privatization to domestic banks that led to financial crises. In the aftermath of these crises, banks were often sold to foreign owners or new licenses were issued to them. Increasingly the Bank and Fund saw foreign ownership as the best route to financial stability (Stein, 2010). Table 5.7 provides examples from a selection of African countries.

What are the implications of the sale of banking to foreigners? Detragiache et al. (2006) develop a model that assumes foreign banks 'skim the cream', which erodes the quality of the remaining pool of borrowers. This result is higher interest rates on loans, which curtails borrowing and

Table 5.7 Foreign ownership trends by share of total banking assets in selected SSA countries

Country	1995	2000	2005
Ghana	34	71	65
Malawi	0	6	22
Mali	33	40	57
Rwanda	0	0	70
Tanzania	0	86	66
Uganda	29	59	80
Zambia	61	73	77

Source: Stein (2010).

Table 5.8 Banking asset structures in crises and non-crises countries in SSA

Years	Foreign assets/ loans	Claims on gov/GDP	Claims on priv. sector/GDP
Non-Crises Countries-1985–89	.13	.05	.15
Crises Countries-1985–89	.16	.03	.14
Non-Crises Countries-2000–04	.32	.08	.19
Crises Countries-2000–04	.49	.05	.11

Source: Stein (2010).

higher monitoring expenses which discourages lending leading to an overall fall in lending to the private sector. Micco et al. (2005), using data on 1,700 banks from 89 low- and middle-income from 1995–2002, find that foreign ownership has a significant and negative impact on private credit lending.

Independent of the 'cream-skimming' arguments, global financial institutions see entry into African and other emerging economies as part of a global strategy of accumulation with little interest in lending to the local private sector. Beyond purchasing government paper, working with resource-based multinationals and local wealthy elites, global banks are interested in moving funds out of the country as part of a broader strategy of asset accumulation. We can see the perverse increase in foreign asset ownership in Table 5.8. The rate is higher in the crisis countries where foreign ownership has frequently increased. Claims on government have also risen while claims on the private sector have declined. Clearly, the World Bank and IMF have helped multinational banks gain access to African markets by demobilizing the instruments of constraint at the national level that might deter their global accumulation strategies.

5.7 International reserves

An additional dimension of the perverse nature of global finance can be found in the statistics on reserves. The increasing and high level of global financial instability associated with globalization has driven countries toward a form of self-insurance by dramatically increasing reserves. African countries are no exception. Table 5.9 provides statistics on reserves and reserve ratios. We can see that reserves increased by more than 400 per cent in SSA between 2000 and 2009, reaching a ratio of nearly .5. The rule of thumb is for countries to keep at least three months of imports rather than nearly six months (Elhiraika and Nkikumana, 2007). The vast majority of these funds are kept in financial assets in developed countries, thus perversely financing the government and private sector debt of wealthy countries.

Based on the rule of thumb, one can calculate a rough measure of excess reserves which went from $10.9 billion in 2000 to $75.3 billion in 2009, or a more than sevenfold increase. This is not an insignificant amount and amounted in 2009 to roughly 40 per cent of gross capital formation in SSA or roughly $90 for every man, women and child in SSA. The averages hide enormous variations in the excess reserves particularly in oil producers.

In 2008, Nigerian reserves were $53 billion (peaking at $67 billion in June, 2008). Imports were approximately $23 billion for a reserve to import ratio of 2.3 or a total excess reserves of approximately $47 billion. This amounted to 270 per cent of gross capital formation or roughly $315 for every person in Nigeria in a country where 67 per cent

Table 5.9 SSA reserves, ratios and excesses (US$ billion except for ratio)

Year	2000	2005	2006	2007	2008	2009	2010
SSA total	36.8	84.9	118.4	146.6	158.4	160.1	165.7
Imports	103.6	216.7	263.6	324.7	390.2	339.3	393.1
Reserve/Imports	.36	.39	.44	.45	.40	.47	.42
'Excess'	10.9	30.7	52.5	65.4	60.9	75.3	67.4

Source: IMF, 2012, UNCTAD, 2012.

of the population live on less than a $1.25 per day (UNCTAD, 2012; World Bank, 2012; ODI, 2009).

5.8 Non-FDI capital flows

Equity and bond flows to developing countries exploded during the early 1990s, increasing more than twentyfold between 1990 and 1996 to roughly US$103 billion. How did Africa fare?

One can see from Table 5.10 that until recently equities have been focused overwhelmingly on one country, South Africa. This is not surprising given how small most stock markets are in Africa. In 2010 only Zimbabwe, South Africa, Nigeria and Mauritius had more than 50 companies listed. As we argued above, new stock markets tend to focus on mineral-extracting companies. In 2006 non-South African SSA equity flows began to rise and peaked at nearly $2 billion. However, we can see from the figures from 2008 that there was a significant net outflow from both SSA of nearly $5 billion and that there was still a net loss after 2009 in the case of equities excluding South Africa.

Overall, the figures for non-equity non-FDI private flows to SSA as a whole were dismal between 1996 and 2001. They amounted to an outflow of $4.9 billions as private banks stopped lending to SSA and loans were repaid. The most positive year was 2007 with Ghana issuing the first external bond of an Africa HIPC country for $750 million (in September). Gabon also issued its inaugural sovereign bond in December, 2007 for $1 billion and used it to prepay its Paris club creditors (World Bank, various years). However, it should be noted these have been issued at exceedingly high interest rates (above 8 per cent), creating a further long-term drain on the country's limited resources. The increasing volatility of the inflows is also noteworthy with a $22 billion swing between 2006 and 2008.

5.8.1 The perversities of debt-fuelled capital flight and odious debt

Table 5.11 provides details on the growth of debt to SSA, excluding South Africa. Ratios to GDP and exports are also provided. The proliferation of debt over the adjustment period was abundantly evident. The overall figures increased by nearly fourfold. By 1998 debt to export ratios exceeded 350 per cent with the figures above the nominal GDP level. By the IMF standard 200 per cent is considered to be the ceiling for exporting your way out. Most African countries were well above this. The biggest growth was in multilateral debt led by the World Bank generated by its failed structural adjustment programs.

Table 5.10 Net long-term private non-FDI capital flows to Sub-Saharan Africa, 1980–2009 (US$ billion)

	1980	1990	1996	1997	1998	1999	2000	2001	2004	2006	2007	2008	2009
Total Private Flows Non-FDI	2.2	–.1	1.5	5.0	7.2	8.5	4.4	–3.0	10.7	24.2	22.1	.3	5.6
Non-Equity	2.2	–.5	–.9	–.5	–1.4	–.5	.3	–2.1	4.0	7.4	12.1	6.0	–4.4
Equity	.003	.393	2.401	5.550	8.633	9.021	4.164	–.934	6.685	16.805	10.146	–5.7	10.198
S.Afr.			2.318	5.473	8.632	9.001	4.169	–.962	6.661	14.959	8.670	–4.707	9.364
Equity Ex. S.Africa			.083	.077	.001	.020	–.005	.028	.024	1.846	1.476	–.993	.834

Source: World Bank (various years).

Table 5.11 External debt of Sub-Saharan Africa, 1980–2009* (millions of US nominal dollars except for ratios)

Year	1980	1998	2001	2002	2004	2006	2007	2008	2009
Bilateral Concessional	12,374	45,208	33,213	35,700	50,288	31,335	34,275	35,593	36,983
Bilateral Non-conc.	5,695	36,680	39,723	39,798	30,105	12,996	11,087	10,017	11,778
Multilateral Conc.	3,936	45,015	46,249	52,850	66,605	36,852	40,911	44,458	48,488
Multilateral Non-Conc.	3,601	12,188	8,258	8,148	8,392	7,337	6,565	5,340	5,620
Private	20,778	27,512	20,375	20,397	20,686	18,402	21,370	23,689	24,563
Short-term	11,195	31,249	23,688	21,721	23,514	28,185	28,149	30,524	23,182
IMF	3,033	7,396	6,338	7,030	7,238	3,140	3,341	3,963	6,261
Total External Debt	60,612	205,271	177,532	185,644	206,556	137,977	145,698	153,584	156,875
Debt/GDP	0.33	1.08	.87	.86	.67	.30	.25	.21	.23
Debt/Exports	1.1	3.6	2.49	2.54	1.83	.66	.64	.51	.71

Note: *Figures do not include South Africa.
Source: World Bank (various years).

Debt relief from 1996 to 2010 amounted to $104 billion, a fraction of the total (IMF, 2010b). The prerequisites for relief has been good standing with the IMF and generating PRSPs with many of the same neoliberal targets of the adjustment era (Stein, 2004).

In addition, much of this debt was 'odious debt'[13] in the sense that they were incurred by regimes and leaders often for their personal enrichment rather than for the interests of the whole nation. Take the case of Nigeria which was not eligible for HIPC or MDRI. In October, 2005 the Paris Club wrote off $18 billion of $30 billion of debt but paid off a very onerous outstanding balance of $12 billion in April 2006. However, large amounts of this were penalties and compound interest not paid for by the military dictatorships of the 1980s and 1990s. Moreover, much of the debt was generated and not used for the purpose intended. The country had a long history of regimes that gutted the treasury. Abacha, for example, in the period 1993 to 1998 accumulated an estimated $2 to 5 billion in personal wealth by siphoning off an estimated $2.3 billion for the Treasury and another $1 billion by awarding contracts to front companies and by taking an estimated $1 billion in bribes from foreign contractors (Ndikumana and Boyce, 2011). Much of Nigeria's debt was odious but in the perverse world of international finance, nations are held responsible for debt that did not benefit them.

Moreover, the problem is systemic. The process that generates debt also fuels capital flight. There are willing participants both within African countries and in the private banks in the developed world who generate large fees and interest returns on the loans and deposits. International Financial Institutions are also driven by success criteria measured by the quantity of loans and by the political priorities of the USA to lend to corrupt military governments with ties to the West (Stein, 2008; Ndikumana and Boyce, 2011).

Ndikumana and Boyce (2003) examine data from 28 African countries covering the period 1970 to 1996 and estimate that every dollar of additional debt generates 80 cents of additional capital flight. Ndikumana and Boyce (2011) point to four different linkages between loans and capital flight debt-fueled capital flight; flight-fueled foreign lending; debt-motivated capital flight and flight-driven foreign lending. In the first case, loans from foreign sources directly finance the accumulation of private wealth. In the second case, African nationals send money offshore and then borrow back money from the same bank (round-tripping). The last two are more indirect. Money is sent abroad with the knowledge that exchange rates could rise with the inflow of new loans and then fall off as debt accumulates, allowing them to profit on exchange rate differentials or to avoid higher taxes that could follow the rise in debt. In the fourth case, capital flight undermines tax collection and forces governments to borrow abroad for replacement funds.[14]

They use updated data from 1970 to 2008 to examine the linkage between debt and capital flight. Every dollar of foreign loans from SSA leads to 60 cents of additional capital flight in the initial year of the loan and 2–4 cents of additional flight annually. They also look at data on the banking deposits held by African nationals overseas and find a 5.7 per cent deposit to capital cumulative debt relationship covering 33 African countries between 1970 and 2008. They find no relationship between funds held abroad and interest rate differentials between African and foreign countries and therefore dismiss standard portfolio explanations while pointing to a strong relationship between foreign aid, which is a lootable resource, and capital flight.

So how much capital flight has occurred and how does it compare to debt levels? Ndikumana and Boyce (2011) use a methodology to measure the degree of unrecorded capital flight from Africa. Their starting point arises from the observation of the huge divergence between the balance of payments data of African countries and the World Bank's Global Development Finance Data on changes in the stock of debt. To get the calculations of capital flight they examine a number of sources of errors and omissions. The first major adjustment is in trade misinvoicing. Both importers and exporters manipulate their invoices to hide foreign transactions. Exporters underreport (lower price or quantity exported) in order to avoid paying taxes and surrendering foreign exchange to authorities. Importers over-invoice (higher price or quantity imported) which increases the amount of foreign exchange they can obtain from the central bank while exaggerating their expenses to lower their tax burden. These are large sources of capital flight.

When exporters underreport they can retain abroad in foreign accounts the difference between their actual and recorded exports. Similarly, importers can send extra foreign exchange obtained from overinvoicing to their accounts abroad. On the other hand, imports can be understated through outright smuggling or to avoid duty. This can understate the outflows of foreign exchange. The overall net effect cannot be predetermined and will arise by comparing country data to the data of trading partners. The focus is on comparing the data on imports from and exports to industrialized countries. Imports recorded by industrialized countries subtract exports recorded by African countries with a positive difference indicating under-invoicing of exports. Similarly imports as recorded by African countries subtract exports to Africa as indicated in data from industrialized countries. A positive difference on imports indicates net over-invoicing and a negative net balance indicates under-invoicing. The number is adjusted for cost of freight and insurance and multiplied by the inverse ratio of the proportion of trade with industrial countries compared to total trade.

For remittances, they take the more accurate International Fund for Agricultural Development (IFAD) and compare it to the data in African balance of payments, which indicates a gross underestimation of remittances. The ultimate use of the money is not important since the calculation is a residual of the difference between foreign exchange inflows and all other usages of foreign exchange.

Overall, they start with changes in external debt in debt tables add net foreign direct investment subtract the current account deficit (surplus is negative) subtract change in reserves add adjustment for export misinvoicing (positive sign indicates underinvoicing) add adjustment for import misinvoicing (positive sign indicates net overinvoicing negative net underinvoicing – that is, smuggling) and adjust for unrecorded remittances. They then take the data from 1970 to 2008 adjusting for inflation and add interest rate returns (conservatively using the US T-bill rate).

Table 5.12 presents the results. The first figure is the cumulative total adjusted for inflation.[15] The second column provides the ratio of the total

Table 5.12 African capital flight 2008, including list of the top ten

Country	Total real capital flight (R2008 $B)	Capital flight/GDP (%)	Capital flight with interest 2008 ($B)	External debt ($B)	Net external assets ($B)
Nigeria	296.2	139.7	376.9	11.2	365.6
Angola	71.5	85.8	80	15.1	64.8
Côte D'Ivoire	45.4	194.1	66.2	12.6	53.7
S. Africa	36.2	13.1	36.4	41.9	–5.5
DRC	30.7	265.1	48.4	12.2	36.2
Zambia	24.4	170.5	35.1	3.0	32.1
Cameroon	24.0	102.8	33.3	2.8	30.5
Congo	23.9	223.4	26.9	5.5	21.4
Zimbabwe	22.6	807.6	31.3	2.2	26.1
Ethiopia	20.1	76	26.0	2.9	23.1
Total for 33 Countries	734.9	80.8	944.2	176.9	767.3

Source: Ndikumana and Boyce (2011).

to GDP and amounts to an average of 80 per cent of GDP. However, as we can see in the Zimbabwe case it can be as high as 8 times GDP. The third column provides figures on the total value including a return if it was invested in short-term US T-bills. The level is close to the estimated net worth of the richest Africans of $800 billion in 2008 according to the World Wealth Report (Capgemin and Merrill Lynch, 2009). The final column provides the difference between the two. Poor African countries are net creditors of nearly $800 or roughly $1,000/person where nearly 50 per cent of the population lives on less than $1.25 per day. This is perversion par excellence – a world where the rich live off the poorest of the poor.

Six of the top ten on the list are oil producers (Angola, Nigeria, Côte D'Ivoire, Republic of Congo, DRC and Cameroon) with extremely poor populations. The relationship between oil-producing countries and capital flight is particularly strong. For each extra dollar in oil exports from producing countries and estimated 11 to 26 cents leave the country. They point to three routes of accumulation, 'bonuses' for leaders for allocating oil development rights to multinationals, royalties or taxes on mineral exports which leak out of the country and resource backed loans which are deposited abroad. For example in 1999, Angola received an estimated $879 million for signature bonuses, $3 billion in oil taxes in 2000 and 2001 and $3.5 billion in loans in the same years all contributing to capital flight (Ndikumana and Boyce, 2011).

5.10 Alternative policy possibilities for African countries: toward new economic thinking

The literature on the governing of capital flows has been growing both in the wake of the 1997 Asian crisis and the global financial meltdown of 2008. Gallagher (2012) points to an expanding lexicon to replace the more pejorative 'capital controls' with terms such as 'capital management techniques', 'capital account regulations' and 'capital flow management measures'. The latter has become the preferred nomenclature of the IMF (2011).

Some authors tend to differentiate the regulation of capital inflows from outflows using price-based and quantity-based approaches (Gallagher, 2012). Price-based measures shift the price of foreign capital by taxing inflows or outflows, or by requiring the deposit of reserves without remuneration on transactions. Quantity-based measures include limits or prohibitions on certain transaction such as purchasing types of equities or setting minimum deposit periods for capital that comes into the country. Others prefer other ways to differentiate their approaches.

Davidson (2000), writing in the wake of the Asian crisis, is critical of focusing merely on simple price-based measures like Tobin taxes since they can increase the level of market volatility. More broadly, Davidson (op. cit.) utilizes a plumbing vs architecture metaphor to differentiate the policy recommendations that arise from an efficiency market perspective vs a liquidity view of financial markets. The plumbing perspective sees the current situation as basically sound, only requiring a bit of patchwork. In contrast, the liquidity view of markets and their associated volatility requires a rethinking of the structure of global financial markets. He places the Tobin tax alternative in the category of plumbing.

The most viable solutions, according to Davidson (2000), fall into the realm of architecture. They include a range of policy alternatives such as temporary administered controls on outflows (as in the case of Malaysia); permanent restrictions on types of foreign exchange transactions including foreign ownership of stocks as in the case of China; the differentiation of foreign exchange at different rates to the usage of a variety of different taxes on different kinds of transactions (not an across-the-board Tobin tax) like the kind used in Chile; and the differentiation of reserve requirements on banks, reflecting the extent of foreign exchange exposures.

Increasingly, the IMF has been moving away from dismissing all forms of capital account restrictions and interventions to embracing them under some circumstances. IMF (2010a), in line with the IMF of the 1990s (discussed above), generally welcomes capital inflows because they are 'providing lower-cost financing and indicating market confidence in the fundamentals of the economy' (as if speculation and herdism have no role). However, they recognize that surges in capital can lead to exchange rate appreciation with implications to the competitiveness of economies as well as asset bubbles. Under these circumstances controls might be possible where there is little ability to raise exchange rates, worries about reserve accumulation, insufficient room for sterilization and inability to sufficiently manoeuvre with monetary and fiscal policy. They do not choose between price vs an administrative approach options which would fall within Davidson's architectural realm. IMF (2011) buttresses the usage of controls (now called CFMs) but only as a last resort and they should be non-discriminatory (pp. 7–8).

Gallagher et al. (2012) challenge the IMF on a number of fronts. Capital account regulations (CARs) need to be on an equal footing with other macro tools and used for prevention as not simply a temporary last resort. Moreover, the IMF (2010a) position erroneously starts with the assumption that countries have open accounts and need to intervene which may not be the case. What is important is the continual adjustment of CARs to deal with changing circumstances while recognizing that each country has its own unique history.

There is also considerable evidence that quantity-based CARs may be more effective than price-based CARs particularly where central banks have weak capacities. Moreover, more focus needs to be placed on regulating outflows particularly when flows could better serve internal development. Moreover, it might be more useful to distinguish between residents and non-residents in order to make CARs more effective. CARs should be seen as an alternative to excess foreign reserve accumulation. More effort should be made on source countries to intervene to deal with destabilizing and speculative flows arising from their countries.[16]

Finally, they argue the IMF and others should expand policy space and help remove the punishing stigma still associated with capital account restrictions. Gallagher (2012) draws up a list of 'Nations with Most Policy Space for Capital Controls' (p. 20) to illustrate the continuing constraints on policy space from a variety of sources, including countries that have committed to GATS under the WTO. On the list are virtually all African countries which reflects a weakness in his categorization. Real policy space is also defined by the power embedded in international aid relations, the entrenched interests that gain from those relations, the will to push against prevailing doctrines and the institutions that need to be in place for generating policies that can better tap global finance for developmental purposes.

5.11 Institutions, global finance and development

To begin with there are no such things as 'institutions' in general, abstracted from history and the sedimentation of values and norms that history creates for a particular institutional form. From a cognitivist perspective, at a given point of time and space, institutions receive their conceptual content, their meaning, their legitimacy, the intensity of obligation of the rules associated with them, their scope of competence, because they coexist and are interlocked with other institutions. Each institution has specific and unpredictable rhythms of change. Any institution, whether it is endogenous (be it old and enduring or innovative) or exogenous (of external origin), develops specific meaning and function in its relationship with other institutions: it is the environment provided by the existence of other institutions that gives it scope, content and meaning. The relational nature of institutions, both with themselves and with other economic domains, greatly complicates efforts to transform institutions (Sindzingre and Stein, 2001).

This is particularly challenging in the world of finance which is infused with asymmetrical institutional relations and where the power to alter the essential can be circumscribed by extrinsic forces. From an institutional perspective financial flows can be seen as a series of domestic and international circuits that intersect among themselves and with the real flows of commodity and productive resources. Institutionally, each flow has a set of internally concatenating capacities, incentives, norms, regulations and organizations. Norms prescribe standards arising from social sanction and esteem and are generally built up from an established pattern of life and associated ways of thinking. Incentives are the rewards and penalties that arise from different forms of behavior. Material conditions are one of a broad array of social factors influencing behaviour. Regulations refer to the legal boundaries that constitute the rules of operations. Organizations are entities that concatenate the operation of groups of people with narrowly defined common rules and purposes. Regulations refer to the legal boundaries that constitute the rules of operations. Capacities refer to level or abilities of individuals, groups and organizations to operate effectively under rules to reach particular organizational and other goals.

The totality of these circuits constitutes a financial system. However, the existence of these circuits says nothing about the nature of their interaction which can be supportive or destructive due to both cyclical and secular trends. A shift in the institutional dimensions of any one flow such as shifting regulations in mortgage markets or the changing nature of the common rules and purposes inside large financial organizations has direct implications to the nature of the interaction with other flows and can create the problems described above.

For development to occur, financial flows need to feed into real sector circuits to enhance growth and investment expansion and national flows need to tap into international flows to complement the speed and capacity of the domestic flows to feed into the production of goods and services. As we have seen, international circuits have tapped financial and commodity flows to perversely direct resources away from the poorest African countries.

For SSA, the analytical framework of the 1980s has been marked by the disqualification of the state, and the stigmatization of developing country administrations – inefficient, oversized, corrupt – both in academia and in the literature of International Financial Institutions and aid agencies. The state was presented as the source of economic failure in SSA, for example, in the rent-seeking, rational choice and public choice literature. In the literature and in international agencies in the 1990s and beyond, there was some rehabilitation of the state through capacity building and improving governance. However, the focal point was overwhelmingly on ensuring property rights using an ideal Anglo-American system or what Mkandawire (2012) aptly calls 'institutional monocropping and monotasking' (p. 81). As a consequence the state is treated as institutionally extraneous rather than as the embedded political actor with the power that can impede, enhance or transform. They are relegated to 'a minimalist economic agenda to facilitate open capital accounts, deregulated labour markets, arms-length finance-and are hostile to intervention in general and in particular to industrial policies and financial arrangements that clearly facilitated rapid industrialization elsewhere' (Mkandawire, 2012, p. 93).

State and public institutions are embedded in even the most rudimentary markets. They provide infrastructure, licensing, regulations, and an array of related institutions such as legal systems. These are not simply supporting mechanisms; they are also generate constructs that are internalized in the operation of markets.[17] However, even more is needed. Financial transformation is a prerequisite for the increasing sophistication of production and exchange. There is little historical evidence for the spontaneous transformation of financial markets. For a state-assisted transformation of financial systems, one must first design a parallel track of institutions that have the potential to influence financial markets (such as corporate structures, industrial-financial ownership linkages, legal systems, international trading institutions and regimes and so on). Most of these are woefully underdeveloped in African countries partly due to their exclusion under the aid-driven policy regimes of the past three decades.

State finance is an essential part of any transformative strategy. At the heart of an industrial policy are state capacities to direct financial flows toward the productive private sector. Within the poorly formed financial markets of developing countries there will be a profound difference between the social value of lending and the private benefits. Banks in developing counties frequently gravitate to finance projects with short turnover, lower working capital, and lower risk (such as financing imports) while avoiding more developmentally-enhancing projects such as manufacturing which has higher working capital requirements, and much greater risk (Stein, 2008). As we have seen above, this has become all the more pressing in view of the growing dominance of foreign banks in developing countries who frequently have even less interest in lending to local private sectors (Stein, 2010). States must create incentives including risk-sharing to encourage private bankers to support loans which have greater social and economic benefit. State organizations, such as development banks, that have been discouraged and even closed down by the World Bank and IMF, need to be formed or strengthened.

Policies related to capital flows must transcend a focus on short-term stabilization issues towards creating conditions which ensure that international resources are tapped for development purposes. Take the issue of FDI with its focus on extractive resources. Inflows need not push economies into perverse economic structures, low rent-capturing and related pathologies such as Dutch disease and government boom and bust spending.

The Botswana government organized a Revenue Stabilization Fund and a Public Debt Service Fund in 1972, after the first diamond mine was constructed in order to sustain budget consistency. Their approach to FDI has been very different. Instead of going from the extremes of nationalization on one hand followed by the low royalty low regulatory approach of the World Bank on the other, the government went into partnership with foreign investors. The Debswana Mining Company was organized in 1969 as a joint venture between the government of Botswana and De Beers, with the government taking a 15 per cent share. In 1975, this was renegotiated to a 50 per cent share. It permitted the country to increase its revenues from diamonds and to have representation on the Board of Directors. In 2001, their position was further strengthened when they purchased 15 per cent of the parent company and a position on their board. After 1980, the government was able to capture about 76 per cent of the rents from mineral production.

Public expenditures were used wisely. The government was able to formulate and implement coherent policies through national planning which helped direct public investment towards improving the country's economic infrastructure, education and health care. To avoid white elephants, any approved projects required provisions for long-term recurrent costs. The country recognized that the diamond sector would not directly generate jobs. Emphasis was on creating parastatals and programmes to support the private sector. Examples included the Financial Assistance Policy to defray labour costs in firms engaged in production and the Citizens Economic Development Agency which provided subsidized interest to citizen entrepreneurs. In 1970, the government organized the Botswana Development Corporation Limited

(BDC). The BDC's primary objective is to assist in the establishment and development of commercially viable businesses in Botswana. Its roles include the financial assistance to investors and partnerships agreements (Poverty Environment Net, 2005; Siphambe, 2007; Taylor, 2005).

The capital account remained fairly closed until 1999 when exchange controls were abolished. Customers still must complete forms for any exchange exceeding 10,000 Pula (roughly $1,300) on the purpose and details of beneficiary prior to processing investors' transfer requests or loan applications. Various government agencies closely monitor capital flows for possible destabilization. Non-residents are able to hold bonds, but only with maturity periods of over one year, and are restricted from holding some types of savings certificates. To deal with the potential capital account volatility, Botswana built up very large reserves in a Liquidity Portfolio Fund. It also has a Pula Fund for long-term investment. Its total reserves peaked at $9.8 billion or 240 per cent of imports falling to $7.9 billion in 2010 and a still fairly high 140 per cent of imports (UNCTAD, 2012; Siphambe, 2007; Africa-Asia Business Forum, 2012; SADC Committee of Central Bankers, 2012). Still, opening the capital accounts has clearly had its costs during the current crisis.

Overall, Botswana's per capita GDP growth has been spectacular, averaging 8.1 per cent between 1970 and 89 and 4.1 per cent between 1992 and 2010. Compare that to an average annual decrease of 0.6 per cent in SSA between 1970 and 89 and 1.8 per cent between 1992 and 2010 (UNCTAD, 2012). Not surprisingly, Botswana has no history of lending from the IMF and therefore has been able to charter a more independent course.

5.12 Summary and conclusions

During the 1980s and 1990s, neoclassical economists, including those inside the World Bank and IMF, supported capital account liberalization in the belief that funds would flow from low marginal product of capital-rich countries to high marginal product of capital-poor countries. Deregulation was very much in line with developments in global capitalism with growing income inequality and the associated increase in the power and influence of finance capital. Like many emerging economies African countries embraced financial globalization. They removed restrictions on capital accounts, opened up to FDI, privatized state assets, sold off banks to foreign owners and built stock markets, often under the encouragement and supervision of the IFIs.

The promised gains of these policies have not only been unrealized; they have had a number of perverse effects. The poorest in the world are financially supporting the wealthiest. Capital flows have often reversed with funds flowing to rich countries from the poorest African countries. The system of debt generation and servicing has helped to fuel massive capital flight. Capital flows have pushed African economies into perverse economic structures aimed at unfettered resource extraction that can be readily financialized. Everywhere human needs have become subservient to the whim of the accumulation strategies of hedge funds servicing the needs of wealth and power. While orthodox economists, like Lucas (1990), have tried to provide explanations, most are aimed at rescuing their flawed axioms and few would admit to the basic cause of this perversion, the asymmetries of power inherent in the structures of international finance.

There are also complex multifaceted institutional requirements to integrate domestic and global financial circuit and for generating improved finance–development linkages. Integration must be circumscribed by high degrees of regulation governing the categories and terms of access to global finance. Since capacities and expertise are likely to be in limited supply, the organizational structures will move towards the creation of valve mechanisms that carefully control the linkage between internal and external financial circuits. The valve can also influence the direction of the flows in the sense of increasing the flows to the internal financial circuits that are propitiously connected to real circuits (for example, the policy loans of South Korea).

The orientation should be toward long-term sources of finance, primarily via state-guaranteed/sponsored bank loan syndication that avoids the rapid inflation or deflation of financial circuits. In global terms, emerging bond and stock markets are poorly formed and highly volatile. The most propitious but highly delimited usage of bond markets is likely to also arise from state-sponsored or co-sponsored issues that can extend the terms and lower the interest expense. Restrictions on the foreign ownership of stocks through term liquidation restraints or alternative issues are almost a universal necessity. Once again, the specific institutional design will vary from country to country, but there should be a common institutional purpose.

Notes

1. Earlier versions of this paper were presented at the Cambridge Trust on New Thinking in Economics Conference 'International Economic Policies, Governance and the New Economics', St Catharine's College, Cambridge University; at the African Studies Center, University of Leiden, Netherlands,

April, 2012; and at the '9th International Conference on Developments in Economic Theory and Policy', Bilbao, Spain, 28/29 June, 2012. I am grateful to Madelynne Wager for her research assistance, the comments from the discussant Prof. Meine Pieter van Dijk in Leiden, feedback from IPPE editors Philip Arestis and Malcolm Sawyer and the questions and suggestions from the audiences at the various venues.

2. Tabb (2012) refers to the period as the global neoliberal social structures of accumulation where finance has come to dominate global capitalism.
3. In Africa, this has not always meant increasing agricultural production for the market. Bryceson (2002) documents the growth of rural household labour income-generating activities outside of the cultivation of crops. Grand plans are now in place to increase agricultural commodities by handing large tracts of land to foreign investors for producing crops for world markets and including subsistence farmers contract farming. Tanzania, see, for example, SACGOT (2011), which is supported by the World Economic Forum and by a cast of interesting global players like Monsanto, Syngenta, General Mills, Dupont, Yara and banks like Stanbic. We learned from interviews at embassies in Dar es Salaam in May, 2012 that the government is considering incorporating 20 per cent of the land into the project which could only mean large scale peasant evictions.
4. Colbourn (2004) explores the linkage between health outcomes and different types of state regimes by focusing on an index of decommodification or the extent that citizens of a country have alternatives to decent livelihoods without recourse to the market. The index has a very higher negative correlation with measure like infant mortality than GDP/capita (for example, greater decommodification is associated with countries with lower infant mortality).
5. Many economists, including some on the more progressive end (like Paul Krugman), argue that speculation on futures markets cannot affect the price of commodities because they do not take physical delivery. The argument is not terribly cogent. Clearly the bidding up of future prices from speculative dollars forces end-users to lock in at a higher price, particularly if they believe even more speculation will result in further increases in prices. Food and other related end-user contracts are clearly influenced by futures prices as are spot prices, particularly given the arbitrage linkages between the two markets. Worthy (2011) outlines a plethora of linkages along with the obvious inability to explain price changes by movements on the production or user side.
6. Chwieroth (2007) also found that an IMF programme significantly increased the likelihood of capital liberalization in a sample of 29 countries covering the period 1977–99. Elsewhere, he argues that over this period, the IMF staff become increasingly neoclassical with a belief that capital account controls were 'ineffective' (Chwieroth, 2006, p. 8).
7. The sample is based on the Chinn–Ito index of capital account liberalization. The list includes Benin, 1990–94; Burkina Faso, 1990–94; Cameron 1993–95; CAR 1990–94; Chad 1993–95; Congo, 1995; Côte D'Ivoire, 1993–95; Gabon, 1990–94; The Gambia 1986–87 and 1990–94; Ghana 1994–95; Kenya 1996–98; Lesotho 1991–94; Madagascar 1997–98; Malawi 1995; Mali 1990–94; Mauritania 1989, 1893, 1996; Mauritius 1994; Niger, 1984; Rwanda 1994–95; Senegal, 1990–94; Sierra Leone 1986, 1995; South Africa 1982;

Tanzania 1993; Uganda 1984 and 1993–98; Zambia 1985–87 and 1996–98; and Zimbabwe 1994.

8. See ASEA, 2012 and various exchange websites, For example, SIDA supported stock exchanges in Zambia, Tanzania and Uganda and the IFC financed the formation of the exchanges in Ghana and the BRVM. BRVM is based in Abidjan and covers eight countries in West Africa (Benin, Burkina Faso, Cote D'Ivoire, Guinea Bissau, Niger, Mali, Senegal, Togo) (Mensah, 2004).
9. This list includes Kenya, Nigeria, South Africa, Botswana, Ghana, Ivory Coast, Mauritius, Mozambique, Namibia, Tanzania, Zambia, and Zimbabwe (T. Rowe Price, 2012a).
10. For example, Africa Mutual Funds Corporation also invests in Namibia (Africa Mutual Funds Corporation, 2012).
11. AngloGold Ashanti is the largest holding in T. Rowe Price's Africa and Middle East Fund and accounts for 4.3 per cent of their total portfolio (T. Rowe Price, 2012b).
12. The list of seven included Angola, Burkina Faso, Côte D'Ivoire, Kenya, South Africa, Swaziland and Togo. Angola was the only one that did not change. Unsurprisingly, Angola took no loans from the IMF during the period in question. Its first drawing on the GRA of the IMF did not occur until 2009 (IMF, 2012).
13. Odious debt is a legal term and refers to debt 'that was contracted against the interests of the population of a state, without their consent, and with full awareness of the creditor' (Jubilee, 2008, p. 2). Howse (2007) outlines a dozen cases where it was used to repudiate outstanding loans. A related measure is 'illegitimate debt', which is defined as 'debt incurred by undemocratic means, without transparency or participation by civil society or representative branches of government; debt that cannot be serviced without violating basic human rights; and debt incurred under predatory repayment terms, including situations where original interest rates skyrocketed and compound interest made repayment impossible' (Jubilee, 2008, p. 2). African debt incorporates both the narrow and broader dimensions. Arguably structural adjustment loans could be classified as illegitimate given their imposition with little or no democratic input and their basic violation of human rights by imposing user fees and cuts in social spending.
14. They estimate that there is a correlation coefficient of around .6 between capital flight stock and debt stock as percentages of GDP covering the period 1970–2008.
15. Ndikumana and Boyce (2011) estimate the unadjusted measure of capital flight at $432,159 billion, export overinvoicing of $311,838, billion, underinvoicing of imports of $–134,765 billion and remittance discrepancies of $125,699 billion.
16. As Gallagher (2012) points out that the two framers of Bretton Woods White and Keynes recognized the difficulties of unilateral actions without the cooperation of other countries. Interesting enough he states: 'After fierce push-back by Wall Street interests however, notions of "requiring" cooperation became watered down to simply "permitting such cooperation" indicating that even then Wall Street still had enormous power' (p. 5).
17. See Nissanke and Stein (2003, Table One) for examples of state driven changes in institutional constructs that could enhance financial development.

References

Africa-Asia Business Forum (2012) 'Botswana Investment Guide'. Available at: http://www.aabf.org/botswana_inv_guide.htm.

Africa Mutual Funds Corporation (2012) 'Funds'. Available at: http://africamutualfunds.com/.

Africa Stock Exchanges Association (ASEA) (2012) 'Statistics'. Available at: http://www.africansea.org/asea/Statistics.aspx.

Ajakaiye, Olu and Howard Stein (2009) 'Industrial-Led Development in Africa: Toward A Policy Framework', in Diery Seck and Sylvain Boko (eds), *Sector-Led Growth in Africa and Implications for Development*, Trenton, NJ: Africa World Press.

Alfaro, Laura, Kalemli-Ozcam, Sebnem and Volosovych, Vadym (2006) 'Why Doesn't Capital Flow from Rich Countries to Poor Countries? An Empirical Investigation', Weatherhead Center for International Affairs, Harvard University, Working Paper 06-04m April. Available at: http://dev.wcfia.harvard.edu/sites/default/files/1083__LA_PoorCountries.pdf.

Blackburn, Robin (2006) *Age Shock: How Finance is Failing Us*, London: Verso.

Bryceson, Deborah (2002) 'The Scramble in Africa: Reorienting Rural Livelihoods', *World Development*, 30(5): 725–39.

Campbell, Bonnier (2008) 'Regulation and Legitimacy in the Mining Industry in Africa: Where Does Canada Stand?', *Review of African Political Economy*, 35(117): 367–85.

Capgemini and Merrill Lynch (2009) 'World Wealth Report, 2009'. Available at: http://www.slideshare.net/Claudiodiniz/world-wealth-report-2009.

Chwieroth, Jeffrey M. (2006) 'Cheerleading for Liberalization: The International Monetary Fund and Financial Globalization in Emerging Markets', Department of International Relations, LSE. Available at: http://147.142.190.246/joomla/peio/files/Chwieroth_IMF.Financial.Globalization.Emerging.Markets.pdf.

Chwieroth, Jeffrey M. (2007) 'Neoliberal Economists and Capital Account Liberalization in Emerging Markets', *International Organization*, 61: 443–63.

Cobourn, David (2004) 'Beyond the Income Inequalities Hypothesis: Class, Neo-Liberalism and Health Inequalities', *Social Science and Medicine*, 58: 41–56.

Davidson, Paul (2000) 'Is a Plumber or a New Financial Architect Needed to End Global International Liquidity Problems?', *World Development*, June: 1117–31.

Detragiache, E., Gupta, P. and Tressel, T. (2006) 'Foreign Banks in Poor Countries: Theory and Evidence', IMF Working Paper No. 06/18, January. Available at: http://www.imf.org/external/np/res/seminars/2006/arc/pdf/tressel.pdf.

Elhiraika, Adam and Leonce Ndikumana (2007) 'Reserves Accumulation in African Countries: Sources, Motivations, and Effects', Economics Department, Working Paper 2007-12. Available at: http://scholarworks.umass.edu/econ_workingpaper/24/.

Epstein, Gerald (2002) 'Financialization, Rentier Interests, and Central Bank Policy', Political Economy Research Institute, University of Massachusetts. Available at: http://www.peri.umass.edu/fileadmin/pdf/financial/fin_Epstein.pdf.

Financial Times (2011) 'Hedge Fund Industry Assets Swell to $1.92 Trillion', 24 April. Available at: 24 http://www.ft.lk/2011/01/24/hedge-fund-industry-assets-swell-to-1-92-trillion/.

Fischer, Stanley (1997) 'Asia and the IMF', IMF Seminar, 19 September. Available at: http://www.imf.org/external/np/apd/asia/fischer.htm.

Gallagher, Kevin (2012) 'The Global Governance of Capital Flows: New Opportunities, Enduring Challenges', PERI Working Paper Series, No. 283, (May) Available at: http://www.peri.umass.edu/236/hash/5177c19e45bd73aaf9ae065db58a72cb/publication/512/.

Gallagher, Kevin, Griffith-Jones Stephany and Ocampos, Jose Antonio (eds) (2012) 'Regulating Global Capital Flows for Development', The Frederick S. Pardee Study for the Longer Range Future, Boston University. Available at: http://www.bu.edu/pardee/files/2012/03/RegulatingCapitalTF-March2012.pdf.

Gertler, Mark, and Kenneth Rogoff. (1990) 'North–South Lending and Endogeneous Domestic Capital Market Inefficiencies', *Journal of Monetary Economics* 26(2): 245–66.

Ghana Stock Exchange (2012) 'Profile of Listed Companies'. Available at: http://www.gse.com.gh/index1.php?linkid=46.

Gomme, Paul. (1993) 'Money and Growth Revisited: Measuring the Costs of Inflation in an Endogenous Growth Model', *Journal of Monetary Economics* 32(1): 51–77.

Gordon, Roger H. and A. Lans Bovenberg (1996) 'Why Is Capital So Immobile Internationally? Possible Explanations and Implications for Capital Income Taxation?', *The American Economic Review*, 86(5): 1057–75.

Howse, Robert (2007) 'The Concept of Odious Debt in Public International Law', UNCTAD Discussion Papers No. 185, July. Available at: http://unctad.org/en/docs/osgdp20074_en.pdf.

IMF (2007) 'Global Financial Stability Report', April. Available at: http://www.imf.org/External/Pubs/FT/GFSR/2007/01/pdf/text.pdf.

IMF (2010a) 'Capital Inflows: The Role of Controls', IMF Staff Position Note, 19 February. Available at: http://www.imf.org/external/pubs/ft/spn/2010/spn1004.pdf.

IMF (2010b) 'Heavily Indebted Countries (HIPC) Initiative and Multilateral Debt Relief Initiative (MDRI) – Status of Implementation, 2010'. Available at: http://www.imf.org/external/np/pp/eng/2010/091410.pdf.

IMF (2011) 'Recent Experiences in Managing Capital Inflows – Cross-Cutting Themes and Possible Policy Framework' (February). Available at: http://www.imf.org/external/np/pp/eng/2011/021411a.pdf.

IMF (2012) 'Angola: Transactions with the Fund from May 1, 1984 to May 31, 2012'. Available at: http://www.imf.org/external/np/fin/tad/extrans1.aspx?memberKey1=23&endDate=2012%2D06%2D09&finposition_flag=YES.

Index Mundi (2012) 'Commodity Food Price Index, April, 1997–March 2012'. Available at: http://www.indexmundi.com/commodities/?commodity=food-price-index&months=180.

Jomo. K.S. and von Arnin, Rudiger (2012) 'Economic Liberalization and Constraints to Development', in Akbar Noman, Kwesi Botchwey, Howard Stein and Joseph Stiglitz (eds), *Good Growth and Governance in Africa: Rethinking Development Strategies* (Oxford: Oxford University Press).

Joyce, Joseph and Noy, Ilan (2005) 'The IMF and the Liberalization of Capital Flows', East–West Center Working Papers, Economic Series, No. 84, August. Available at: http://scholarspace.manoa.hawaii.edu/bitstream/handle/10125/3658/ECONwp084.pdf?sequence=1.

Ju, Jiandong and Shang-Jin Wei (2006) 'Solution to Two Paradoxes of International Capital Flows', IMF Working Paper. WP/06/178. Available at: http://www.imf.org/external/pubs/ft/wp/2006/wp06178.pdf.

Jubilee USA Network (2008) 'Recent Development on Odious and Illegitimate Debt', Briefing Note Five. Available at: http://www.jubileeusa.org/fileadmin/user_upload/Resources/Policy_Archive/408briefnoteodiousilldebt.pdf.

Khan, Mustaq (2007) 'Governance, Economic Growth and Development Since the 1960s', DESA Working Paper Series, No. 54, August. Available at: http://www.un.org/esa/policy/backgroundpapers/khan_background_paper.pdf.

King, Robert, and Rebelo Sergio (1993) 'Transitional Dynamics and Economic Growth in the Neoclassical Model', *The American Economic Review*, 83(4): 908–31.

Knaup, Horan, Schiessl, Michaela and Seith, Anne (2011) 'Speculating with Lives: How Global Investors Make Money Out of Hunger', Spiegel, 9 September. Available at: http://www.spiegel.de/international/world/speculating-with-lives-how-global-investors-make-money-out-of-hunger-a-783654.html.

Lane, Philip, and Gian Maria Milesi-Ferretti (2001) 'The External Wealth of Nations: Measures of Foreign Assets and Liabilities for Industrial and Developing Countries', *Journal of International Economics*, 55: 263–94.

Lucas, Robert (1990) 'Why Doesn't Capital Flow from Rich to Poor Countries?', *American Economic Review*, 80: 92–6.

Mkandawire, Thandika (2012) 'Institutional Monocropping and Monotasking', in Akbar Noman, Kwesi Botchwey, Howard Stein and Joseph Stiglitz (eds), *Good Growth and Governance in Africa: Rethinking Development Strategies*, Oxford: Oxford University Press.

McIntosh, Bill (2012) 'How Big is the Hedge Fund Industry', *The Hedge Fund Journal*, September. Available at: http://www.thehedgefundjournal.com/news/8022.

Micco, A., Panizza, U. and Yanez, M (2005) 'Bank Ownership and Performance, 1995–2002: A Data Set'. Available at: http://www.iadb.org/res/files/data_app_mpy.xls.

McKinsey Global Institute (2008) 'Mapping Global Markets: Fifth Annual Report', October. Available at: http://www.mckinsey.com/Insights/MGI/Research/Financial_Markets/Mapping_global_capital_markets_fifth_annual_report.

McKinsey Global Institute (2011) 'Mapping Global Markets 2011', August. Available at: http://www.mckinsey.com/Insights/MGI/Research/Financial_Markets/Mapping_global_capital_markets_2011.

Mensah, Sam (2004) 'Capital Market Development in Africa: Selected Topics', Addis Ababa: UNECA. Available at: http://www.uneca.org/acmdp/CapitalMarketsDevptInAfrica.PDF.

Murinde, Victor (2009) 'Capital Flows and Capital Account Liberalization in the Post-Financial-Crisis Era: Challenges, Opportunities and Policy Responses', ADB, Working Paper No. 99, July. Available at: http://www.afdb.org/fileadmin/uploads/afdb/Documents/Publications/WORKING%2099%20Internet%20PDF.pdf\.

Machiko Nissanke and Howard Stein (2003) 'Financial Globalization and Economic Development: Toward an Institutional Foundation', *Eastern Economic Journal*, 29(2): 287–308.

Nkikumana, Leonce and Boyce, James (2003) 'Public Debts and Private Assets: Explaining Capital Flight from Sub-Saharan African Countries', *World Development* 31(1): 107–30.

Nkikumana, Leonce and Boyce, James (2011) *Africa's Odious Debt: How Foreign Loans and Capital Flight Bled a Continent*, London: Zed Press.

Obstfeld, Maurice and Ken Rogoff (1996) *Foundations of International Macroeconomics*, Cambridge, MA: The MIT Press.

ODI (2009) 'The Global Financial Crisis and Developing Countries: Preliminary Synthesis of Ten Draft Country Reports'. Available at: http://www.odi.org.uk/resources/docs/4245.pdf.

OECD (2011) *Divided We Stand: Why Inequality Keeps Rising*, Brussels: OECD. Available at: http://www.oecd.org/dataoecd/40/12/49170449.pdf.

Portes, Richard, and Helene Rey (2005) 'The Determinants of Cross-Border Equity Transaction Flows', *Journal of International Economics* 65: 269–96.

Poverty Environment Net (2005) 'Diamond-Based Growth in Botswana'. Available at: http://povertyenvironment.net/files/CASE%20Botswana.pdf.

Prebisch, Raul (1950) 'The Economic Development of Latin America and its Principal Problem', New York: UN Dept. of Economic Affairs.

Razin, Assaf and Chi-Wa Yuen (1994) 'Convergence in Growth Rates: a Quantitative Assessment of the Role of Capital Mobility and International Taxation', in Leonardo Leiderman and Assaf Razin (eds), *Capital Mobility: The Impact on Consumption, Investment, and Growth,* New York: Cambridge University Press.

Reinhart, Carmen, and Kenneth Rogoff (2004) 'Serial Default and the "Paradox" of Rich to Poor Capital Flows', *American Economic Review Papers and Proceedings,* 94: 52–8.

Rousseau, Peter and Richard Sylla, R (2003) 'Financial Systems, Economic Growth and Globalization', in Michael D. Bordo, Alan M. Taylor and Jeffrey G. Williamson (eds), *Globalization in Historical Perspective,* Chicago: University of Chicago Press.

Rutherford, Lucas and Michael Ofori-Mensah (2011) 'Ghana's Mining Code: In Whose Interest', *Governance Newsletter: A Publication of The Institute of Economic Affairs*, 17(4): 1–8.

SADC Committee of Central Bankers (2012) 'Bank of Botswana'. Available at: http://www.sadcbankers.org/Lists/News%20and%20Publications/Attachments/18/Fin%20Sys%20Botswana2011.pdf.

Schindler, Martin (2009) 'Measuring Financial Integration: A New Data Set', *IMF Staff Papers* 56(1): 222–38. Available at: http://www.palgrave-journals.com/imfsp/journal/v56/n1/pdf/imfsp200828a.pdf.

Sindzingre, Alice and Howard Stein (2001) 'Institutions, Global Integration and Development in Sub-Saharan Africa: A Theoretical Enquiry', African Studies Association, 2001 Annual Meeting, Houston, TX, November.

Singer, Hans (1950) 'The Distribution of Gains Between Investing and Borrowing Countries', *American Economic Review*, 40: 473–85.

Siphambe, Happy (2007) 'Growth and Employment Dynamics in Botswana: A Case Study of Policy Coherence', Working Paper No. 82. Policy Integration and Statistics Department. International Labour Office, October. Available at: http://www.ilo.int/wcmsp5/groups/public/---dgreports/---integration/documents/publication/wcms_088432.pdf.

Southern Agricultural Growth Corridor of Tanzania (SAGCOT) (2011) 'Investment Blueprint'. Available at: http://www.sagcot.com/uploads/media/Invest-Blueprint-SAGCOT_High_res.pdf.

Stein, Howard (2004) 'Fighting Poverty: Poverty Reduction Strategies, Employment and Accumulation in Africa', Occasional Paper, Centre for African Studies, University of Copenhagen, September. Available at: http://www.teol.ku.dk/cas/research/publications/occ._papers/stein_samlet.pdf/.

Stein, Howard (2008) *Beyond the World Bank Agenda: An Institutional Approach to Development*, Chicago: University of Chicago Press.

Stein, Howard (2010) 'Financial Liberalization, Institutional Transformation and Credit Allocation in Developing Countries: The World Bank and the Internationalization of Banking', *Cambridge Journal of Economics*, 34(2): 257–73.

T. Rowe Price (2012a) 'Africa and Middle East Fund: Prospectus'. Available at: http://individual.troweprice.com/staticFiles/gcFiles/pdf/trame.pdf.

T. Rowe Price (2012b) 'Africa and Middle East Fund'. Available at: http://www3.troweprice.com/fb2/fbkweb/composition.do?ticker=TRAMX#.

Tabb, William (2012) *The Restructuring of Capitalism in Our Time*, New York: Columbia University Press.

Taylor, Ian (2005) 'The Developmental State in Africa: The Case of Botswana', in Pamela Mbabazi and Ian Taylor (eds), *The Potentiality of 'Developmental States' in Africa: Botswana and Uganda* Compared. Dakar: CODESRIA, pp. 44–56. Available at: https://www.codesria.org/IMG/pdf/4-_Taylor.pdf.

Tornell, Aaron, and Andres Velasco.(1992) 'Why Does Capital Flow from Poor to Rich Countries? The Tragedy of the Commons and Economic Growth', *Journal of Political Economy* 100: 1208–31.

Ubide, Angel (2006) 'Demystifying Hedge Funds', *Finance and Development*, 43(2). Available at: http://www.imf.org/external/pubs/ft/fandd/2006/06/basics.htm.

UNCTAD (2008) 'On-Line Statistics'. Available at: http://unctad.org/en/Pages/Statistics.aspx.

UNCTAD (2011a) 'On-Line Statistics'. Available at: http://unctad.org/en/Pages/Statistics.aspx.

UNCTAD (2011b) *Price Formation in Financial Markets*, Geneva: UNCTAD

UNCTAD (2012) 'On-Line Statistics'. Available at: http://unctad.org/en/Pages/Statistics.aspx/.

UNCTAD (various years) *World Investment Report*, Geneva: UNCTAD.

Watson, Mathew (2009) 'Investigating the Potentially Contradictory Microfoundations of Financialization', *Economy and Society*, 38 (2): 255–77.

World Bank (1992) 'Strategy for African Mining, World Bank Technical Paper No. 181, Africa Technical Department Series, Mining Unit, Industry and Energy Division, Washington, DC: World Bank. Available at: http://www-wds.worldbank.org/servlet/WDSContentServer/WDSP/IB/1999/10/21/000178830_98101904142281/Rendered/PDF/multi_page.pdf.

World Bank (various years) *Global Development Finance*, Washington, DC: World Bank.

World Bank (2012) 'POVCALNET'. Available at: http://iresearch.worldbank.org/PovcalNet/index.htm?0.

Worthy, Murray (2011) 'Broken Markets: How Financial Market Regulation Can Help Prevent Another Food Crisis', World Development Movement. Available at: http://www.wdm.org.uk/sites/default/files/Broken-markets.pdf.

6
Capital Flows, International Imbalances and Economic Policies in Latin America

Luiz Fernando de Paula
University of the State of Rio de Janeiro and CNPq Researcher, Brazil

Fernando Ferrari-Filho
Federal University of Rio Grande do Sul and CNPq Researcher, Brazil

Aline M. Gomes
University of the State of Rio de Janeiro, Brazil

6.1 Introduction

Capital flows to emerging economies have followed a markedly pro-cyclical global pattern and tend to exacerbate economic booms, when they do not cause them. Empirical literature shows evidence that capital flows to Latin America have been mostly determined by push factors (for instance, the economic policies of the developed countries) rather than by pull factors (those associated with domestic factors). After a succession of currency crises, most Latin American countries have adopted floating exchange regimes but at the same time have made use of foreign exchange reserves accumulation policy in order to reduce the effects of capital flows volatility.

The 2007–08 international financial crisis, which induced the 'great recession', has substantially changed the dynamic process of the world economy. The countries of Latin America are no exception. The financial crisis generated mechanisms by which it was transmitted to these economies, including: (i) withdrawal of portfolio capital and foreign direct investment (FDI); (ii) interruption of credit, particularly for foreign trade; (iii) falling commodity prices; (iv) declining exports to developed countries; (v) volatile exchange rates; and (vi) rising levels of profit repatriation by transnational corporations. As a result, governments of developed and emerging economies have responded to the 2007–08 international financial crisis and 'great recession' with massive fiscal and monetary stimulus, by rescuing financial and non-financial corporations and by reintroducing a more hands-on approach to deal with the economic problems (Griffith-Jones et al., 2010; Arestis et al., 2011). In Latin America countries, alongside the counter-cyclical policies aimed at smoothing the negative impacts of the external environment, some central governments have been trying to implement more active developmental policies.

Moreover, the implementation of the 'quantitative easing' monetary policy in the United States, combined with the attraction of FDI, due to the commodities boom, capital inflows to Latin America have increased substantially. This trend has put pressure on the economic policy of the countries in the region and has had consequences in the real side of the economy (output, industry and so on). The responses of government, however, have differed in each country.

This paper aims to analyze the causes and consequences of the recent capital flows boom to Latin America, focusing on the major countries of the region, such as Argentina, Brazil, Chile, Colombia, Mexico, Peru and Venezuela. The main questions that we seek to discuss in this paper are: What are the specific determinants and features in the recent wave of capital inflows to Latin America? Why did Latin American countries succeed in preventing the contagious nature of the 2007–08 international financial crisis spreading to them? Have Latin American countries been successful in managing capital flows?

Following this brief Introduction, the paper is divided into six sections. Section 6.2 discusses the relationship between financial globalization, capital flows and economic policy in emerging economies. Section 6.3 analyses the adoption of 'Washington Consensus' policies during the 1990s in Latin America, as well as the implementation of the 'New Consensus Macroeconomics' policies in an important group of countries. Section 6.4 focuses on the recent trends and features related to capital flows, external vulnerability and economic policy in Latin America. Section 6.5 analyses specifically the contagious nature of the 2007–08 international financial crisis in Latin America and the economic policy responses. Section 6.6 shows some economic policy implications of the surge of capital inflows in the region. Finally, section 6.7 summarizes the paper.

6.2 Financial globalization, capital flows and economic policy in emerging economies

Financial globalization is a phenomenon that has intensified since the 1970s as a result of a set of factors that includes: (i) the development of the euro-dollars market, which was the 'embryo' of the international and deregulated financial markets; (ii) the end of the Bretton Woods system, with the end of the fixed but adjustable exchange rate regime; (iii) the development of technological innovations in telecommunication and informatics that allowed faster data computing and an online integration of different geographic regions; and (iv) the financial deregulation that happened initially in the context of the adoption of neoliberal policies in the United States and the United Kingdom and elsewhere. In other words, financial globalization is a process in which there is a greater integration among financial markets and capital flows cross-border at the global scale, a certain tendency to an erosion of the borders between countries, and an increase in the volume and velocity of financial resources in the international financial market. Other dimensions of financial globalization include: (i) the loss of hegemony of the banks as the main providers of finance to firms as a result of the growth of corporative securities market; (ii) the increased importance of big institutional investors, such as pension funds, investment funds, insurance firms and so on as important purchasers of securities; (iii) the spread of new financial instruments, such as debt securitization and derivatives; and (iv) the formation of financial conglomerates and brokers with global power (Ferrari-Filho and Paula, 2004).

Stiglitz (2000) states that capital flows in emerging countries are markedly pro-cyclical and exacerbate economic booms, and that financial liberalization exposes countries to the vicissitudes associated with changes in economic circumstances outside the country; so that such economies are exposed to sudden change in the perceptions of both lenders and investors. Such shifts can increase capital outflows. According to Stiglitz (2000): 'capital market liberalization is systematically associated with greater instability, and for good reason: capital flows are markedly pro-cyclical, exacerbating economic fluctuations, when they do not actually cause them (...) In addition, capital market liberalization exposes countries to vicissitudes associated with changes in economic circumstances outside the country: a sudden change in lenders' perceptions concerning "emerging market risk" can lead to huge capital outflows, undermining the viability of the entire financial system' (p. 1080).

One of the major drivers of capital inflows at the beginning of the 1990s boom and during the 2000s capitals flows' boom was the low interest rates in developed economies. Capital flows volatility can translate into huge macroeconomic instability in the domestic economies of main Latin American countries, complicating, in particular, the macroeconomic management and entailing trade-offs in attaining macroeconomic objectives (economic growth, financial stability, price stabilization, avoiding exchange rate appreciation and so on). Indeed,

> large surges in capital inflows can lead to strong upward pressure on the exchange rate and contribute to macroeconomic overheating, widening current account imbalances through an appreciating exchange rate as well as inflationary pressures and asset price bubbles to the extent that a nominal exchange rate appreciation is resisted and monetary sterilization is either not undertaken or is ineffective. The financial sector generally plays an important role in amplifying these asset price bubbles, and can exacerbate macroeconomic cycles. (Ghosh, 2010, p. 2)

Some analysts stress that with the process of financial liberalization and the emergence and spread of new financial instruments (such as derivatives), there is a substantial increase in the likelihood of the occurrence of speculative financial operations. Tobin (1978), for instance, states that the main macroeconomic problem related to integrated financial markets is not the choice of the appropriate exchange rate regime but rather the excessive short-run capital mobility that reduces the autonomy of national governments to pursue domestic objectives with respect to employment, output and inflation. According to Tobin (*op. cit.*), 'the mobility of financial capital limits viable differences among national interest rates and thus severely restricts the ability of central banks and governments to pursue monetary and fiscal policies appropriate to their internal economies' (p. 154). In the same contribution, Tobin also doubts whether a flexible exchange regime is a panacea: 'I believe that the basic problem today is not the exchange rate regime, whether fixed and floating. Debate on the regime evades and obscures the essential problem. That is the excessive international – or better, inter-currency – mobility of private financial capital' (p. 153).

In contrast with financial markets closed to foreign capital, capital flows in liberalized markets can have a disruptive effect on the countries' economies, damaging the autonomy of domestic macroeconomic policies, and even generating speculative attacks on domestic currencies. As Eichengreen et al. (1995) state, 'volatility in exchange rates and interest rates induced by speculation and capital flows could have real economic consequences devastating for particular sectors and whole economies' (p. 164). In other words, financial globalization has been a source of broader instability related to the occurrence of currency crises and speculative attacks, and also of the reduction in the degrees of freedom in the implementation of a more autonomous economic policy. Indeed, under the action of 'global players', in a more liberalized and integrated market, the operational way of working of the financial markets became a sort of large global casino. The high capital mobility of today's global economy has increased the arbitrage and speculative transactions in foreign exchange markets (Alves Jr. et al., 1999/2000).

Recent empirical studies undertaken by the IMF (2011b) and other economists, such as Cardarelli et al. (2009), found some findings that are line with Stiglitz's (2000) analysis of the effects of the capital flows to emerging economies:

(a) The volatility of capital flows has increased over time and fluctuations in net flows are much sharper for emerging economies than for developed economies – in the latter, gross outflows largely offset gross inflows, generating smoother movements in net flows. By contrast, in emerging economies, gross inflows and net flows both fell dramatically during the crisis and rebounded sharply afterwards (IMF, 2011b, p. 125).
(b) Episodes of large capital inflows are associated with the acceleration of the growth in GDP, but afterwards growth often drops significantly: over one-third of the completed episodes ended with a sudden stop or a currency crisis, which suggests that abrupt endings are not uncommon (Cardarelli et al., 2009, p. 5). Thus, there is an inverted V-shaped pattern of net capital flows to emerging economies that is outside the control of policymakers (IMF, 2011b).
(c) Fluctuations in GDP growth have been accompanied by large swings in aggregate demand and in the current account balance, with a strong deterioration of the current account during the inflow period and a sharp reversal at the end (Cardarelli et al., 2009, p. 5).
(d) The surge of capital inflows also appears to be associated with a real effective appreciation in the exchange rate, damaging the competitiveness of export sectors and potentially reducing the level of economic growth (Cardarelli et al., 2009).
(e) Historically, portfolio flows have been more volatile and their volatility has recently increased, and bank flows have been less volatile but their volatility rises sharply around times of crisis. FDI is only slightly more stable than other types of flow for emerging economies, and its volatility has increased recently due to increase of direct borrowing by a firm subsidiary (IMF, 2011b).

Grenville (2000) states that the problems related to exchange rate volatility are greater for emerging economies for the following reasons: (i) they have no long historical experience of a market-determined exchange rate; (ii) there are few 'Friedmanite' stabilizers speculators acting in the exchange rate market, that is there has been a lack of players willing take contrarian foreign exchange positions in emerging countries;[1] (iii) exchange markets are prone to exhibiting herd behaviour-generating swings in the exchange rate; (iv) these economies have much larger and volatile capital flows, in relation to the size of their capital markets and economies more generally; and (v) fundamentals cannot explain the behaviour of the exchange rate over a short-/ medium-term horizon.

In general, exchange rate volatility is higher in emerging economies than in developed ones as the former have small and less liquid foreign exchange markets that make such economies more vulnerable to one-way expectations and herd behavior. Indeed, such economies face problems related to 'asymmetric financial integration' as they have much larger and volatile capital flows compared to the size of their capital market and economies more generally. That is, markets in emerging economies are thin and subject to a high degree of uncertainty and information asymmetries. Foreign exchange markets in most emerging countries continue to be relatively small and have less liquidity than their counterparts in the industrial world. Countries with high debts, currency mismatches and/or fragile financial sector are particularly vulnerable (Moreno, 2005). Furthermore, the benchmark used to evaluate the performance of managers of global investors' portfolios does not include financial assets in emerging economies; so, '[they] can reduce or eliminate their positions quickly, at any signal of deterioration of expectations, or due to new and more attractive opportunity for investment in advanced markets or increase in the investors' risk aversion' (Freitas and Prates, 2001, p. 83).

In particular, exchange rates can influence inflation ('exchange rate pass-through') through the prices of traded final goods and imported intermediate goods, and their impact on agents' inflation expectations. Ho and McCauley (2003) show evidence that: (i) domestic income is negatively and significantly correlated with pass-through as lower-income economies have a larger portion of traded goods in the consumption basket; and (ii) 'exchange rate pass-through has tended to be stronger in Latin America than in Asia even though Latin American are not necessarily more open than their Asian counterparts' (p. 6). The explanation for such a difference is that countries with histories of high inflation – as is the case of many Latin American countries, especially in the 1980s – are more sensitive to exchange rate fluctuations, probably due to the existence of an inflationary memory (Eichengreen, 2002). Thus, considering the important influence of the exchange rate on domestic inflation in these economies, exchange rate considerations can be expected to play a more prominent role in emerging economies.

One important discussion in the literature about macroeconomic issues in emerging economies is which exchange rate regime is most appropriate for these economies. On the one hand, according to the 'bipolar view', intermediary regimes – which involve every type of intermediary exchange rate regime between a freely floating regime and a fixed exchange rate regime – are less appropriate for economies with substantial involvement in international capital markets. The main argument is that such exchange rate regimes make countries more vulnerable to speculative attacks (Fischer, 2001). On the other hand, the view labelled 'fear of floating' points out that many emerging economies that adopted flexible exchange rate regimes in practice sought to limit the level of exchange rate movements. Such resistance to floating arises from their low policy and institutional credibility and their high degree of pass-through of exchange rate changes into domestic prices, among other factors (Calvo and Reinhart, 2002).[2] Other reasons why monetary authorities seek to limit exchange rate movements are related to the effects of excessive exchange rate volatility (mainly devaluation) on the outstanding foreign currency debts of banks and the corporate sectors with un-hedged foreign currency liabilities, and also on governments with large amounts of foreign currency debt or debt indexed to the exchange rate, raising questions about their fiscal sustainability. In addition, exchange rate fluctuations may generate uncertainties that could impede trade. For instance, prolonged real appreciation associated with large capital inflows can have an adverse effect on export competitiveness and investment in the external sector (Bresser-Pereira and Gala, 2007).

Some flexibility in the way the floating exchange rate is managed can be helpful in absorbing the capital inflow, in buffering external shocks, and in responding to the changing productive capacity of their economies; it can also inhibit some short-term flows, by serving as a constant reminder that exchange rate volatility can outweigh the interest rate advantage of foreign currency borrowings (Grenville, 2000, p. 59). Moreover, some sort of administered floating exchange rates regime can be useful if the objective of the central bank is to reduce the exchange rate volatility and also somehow influence the real exchange rate for international trade purposes. The central bank intervenes in foreign exchange markets to achieve a variety of macroeconomic objectives, such as controlling inflation, maintaining competitiveness and/or maintaining financial stability. In contrast to a pegged exchange rate, authorities' interventions to limit exchange rate movements may not target a certain level of the exchange rate but may rather influence its path and/or volatility.

In order to enhance the possibility of achieving a successful management of the exchange rate regime in emerging economies it is necessary to introduce some measures to reduce the volatility of capital flows and the likelihood of speculative attacks on domestic currency. One possibility is the use of official intervention in the foreign exchange market, which may exert a direct influence on the nominal exchange rate as it alters the relative supply of domestic and foreign currency assets. On the one hand, the countries' ability to resist currency depreciation is limited by its stock of foreign exchange reserves and its access to potential credit lines. Thus, reserve accumulation can be seen as an insurance against future negative shocks and speculation against domestic currency, as emerging economies have only limited access to the international capital market. On the other hand, the ability to avoid currency appreciation may require the use of sterilized intervention. Monetary authorities have often sought to sterilize the impact of foreign exchange intervention through open market operations and other measures, such as increasing bank reserve requirements. If central banks have a target for the short-term rate, then they can attempt to offset increases in bank reserves by selling domestic assets or issuing their own securities (Mohanty and Turner, 2006). Moreover, sterilization often implies quasi-fiscal costs, as in general it involves the central bank exchanging high-yield domestic assets for low-yield foreign reserves (Cardarelli et al., 2009).

Another possibility to enhance the management of the exchange rate regime (that is, not excluding official intervention in the currency markets) in emerging economies is the use of 'capital management techniques' that include capital controls, in other words, measures that manage volume, composition, and/or the allocation of international private capital flows,[3] and/or 'prudential domestic financial regulations', which refer to policies, such as capital-adequacy standards, reporting requirements, or restrictions on the ability and terms under which domestic financial institutions can provide to certain types of projects (Epstein et al., 2003, pp. 6–7). Capital controls can be used for different, though related objectives, such as: (i) to reduce the vulnerability of a country to financial crises, including capital flight during currency crisis; (ii) to drive a wedge between onshore and offshore interest rates in order to provide monetary authorities with some policy autonomy at least in the short run; and (iii) to maintain some short-term stability of nominal exchange rate and to reduce exchange rate pressures derived from excessive capital inflows. Capital controls may be limited and temporary, which means that they should be used in the magnitude necessary to be effective, and dynamically adjusted to compensate the tendency of financial systems to elude them.

Magud and Reinhart (2006) review more than 30 papers that evaluated capital controls either on inflows or outflows around the world (the evaluation excludes those countries with comprehensive capital controls, such as China and India), making use of a capital controls effectiveness index in order to standardize the results of the empirical studies. They conclude that 'capital controls on inflows seem to make monetary policy more independent; alter the composition of capital flow; reduce real exchange rate pressures (although the evidence is more controversial)', but 'seem not to reduce the volume of net flows (and hence, the current account balance)', while 'limiting private external borrowing in the "good times" plays an important prudential role because more often than not countries that are "debt intolerant"' (pp. 26–7). Based on this, Magud and Reinhart (2006) argue for the enhancement of the effectiveness of controls by taking into account country-specific characteristics in their design.

To sum up, set against the adoption of orthodox economic policies is the perceived need to preserve the autonomy of developing countries' fiscal and monetary policies. This has reinforced the opinion of heterodox economists and some policymakers of the necessity of introducing capital controls and an exchange rate regime that prevents exchange rate fluctuations. These economists argue that such policy autonomy is fundamental to ensure sustainable economic growth and harmonious social development. This is particularly important given that emerging economies suffer from more volatility than developed countries and this contributes to recessions of longer duration (Hausmann et al., 2004).

6.3 'Washington Consensus' and the 'New Consensus Macroeconomics': The Latin American case

At the beginning of the 1980s most Latin American countries entered a deep economic recession in a context of the 'external debt crisis', which resulted from the combination of increasing external indebtedness during the 1970s and the increase in foreign interest rates after the implementation of a tightened monetary by the Federal Reserve (FED) in the United States in 1979, that contributed to an increase in current account deficits. The external crisis contributed to a deterioration in public finance, and also to the acceleration of inflation, due to the shocks caused by the large devaluations of the exchange rate in order to enhance export competitiveness. In particular, the economic crisis weakened the Latin American governments' ability to intervene in the economy.

At the end of the 1980s and beginning of the 1990s there arose a set of economic policies that aimed to promote a new strategy for growth to Latin America following a decade of stagnation ('the lost decade of the 1980s'). These economic policies were proposed by Williamson (1990) and they became widely known as the Washington Consensus, as they served as inspiration for the liberalizing economic reforms imposed by Washington-based institutions, particularly in Latin America. The 'Washington Consensus' originally consisted of ten propositions: (i) Fiscal discipline; (ii) A redirection of public expenditures priorities toward fields offering high economic and social returns, such as primary education; (iii) Tax reform; (iv) Interest rate liberalization; (v) A competitive exchange rate; (vi) Trade liberalization; (vii) Liberalization of inflows of FDI; (viii) the privatization of state-owned firms; (ix) Deregulation (to abolish barriers to entry and exit); and (x) Secure property rights. These policies were intended to stimulate economic growth through a set of economic policies and liberalizing reforms, notably macroeconomic discipline (exercised principally through price stabilization), trade openness, and market-friendly microeconomic policies. The proposal for the liberalization of the capital account was not included in the original Washington Consensus, but it was added to the proposals by the multilateral institutions, such as the World Bank. Liberal reforms, to a greater or lesser extent, were applied in a large number of Latin American countries in the 1990s, including Argentina, Brazil, Chile and Mexico.

Policymakers in Latin America and other emerging economies, following the Washington Consensus ideas, believed that structural reforms, such as trade and financial liberalization, capital mobility and privatization, were needed to reduce inflation and allow for the return of growth. Indeed, Latin American countries adopted liberal reforms (privatization, trade liberalization and capital account liberalization) during the 1990s, but with different styles. For instance, while Argentina adopted 'big bang' reforms, Brazil adopted a more gradual approach. Moreover, most countries experimented with a quick and deep process of capital account liberalization, including portfolio capital liberalization for both residents and non-residents.

The results of the implementation of the Washington Consensus strategy were largely disappointing, in particular with regard to economic growth and financial stability. Argentina, considered by IMF during the 1990s as an example of success of the Washington Consensus strategy, was in fact an enormous failure. Later, the Washington Consensus was criticized in various aspects by Stiglitz (1999) and Arestis and Sawyer (2005), who highlighted that: (i) in various countries domestic financial liberalization led to banking crises; (ii) capital account openness frequently stimulated speculation on domestic currency and currency crises, even when the economic fundamentals were sound, and had negative effects on real variables (such as output and employment); (iii) privatization failed in some countries because, on the one hand, it was not followed by economic policies for the promotion of competition and it did not improve market efficiency; and (iv) the excessive focus on inflation control was, in some cases, harmful to growth.

According to Kregel (2008), the Washington Consensus policies in Latin America during the 1990s led to the implementation of domestic policies (exchange rate anchor, high interest rates, and financial liberalization) that hindered the domestic productive and technological restructuring that could have contributed to a boost in economic and employment growth in the region. Moreover, price stabilization plans with the use of some exchange rate anchor were implemented in some Latin American countries, such as Argentina, Brazil, Mexico, and Peru.

As is well known, experience with stabilization programs involving some kind of exchange anchor shows that, in general, such plans at first generate an abrupt drop in the rate of inflation, accompanied by a marked appreciation in the exchange rate. The local currency appreciated in real terms as a result of differential evolution by domestic and foreign prices in a context where the nominal rate of exchange remains stable, causing the balance of payments current account to contract substantially, due principally to the increase in the value of imports. Normally, the resulting deficit is accompanied by a large capital account surplus, thus not only enabling the former to be financed, but also allowing for an increase in the volume of the country's international reserves. The latter increase occurs as a result of the surge of foreign capital entering the country drawn by the stabilization plan's initial success, combined generally with liberal structural reforms (Ferrari-Filho and Paula, 2003).

Higher domestic interest rates, an added attraction to external financing, are normally used to reinforce these factors. The introduction of tight monetary policies and greater freedom for foreign investors create an interest rate differential that is sufficiently large to attract arbitrage capital inflows. The increasing influx of foreign capital, however, can lead to a still greater real appreciation of the exchange rate, which leads in turn to a further increase in imports and also a downturn in exports. Thus, the need to maintain high interest rates in order to attract foreign capital, and efforts to sterilize the inflow of foreign capital (also requiring high interest rates), lead to an increasing in public internal debt and also a deteriorating fiscal balance, as was indeed the experience of the main Latin American countries.

In this context, a larger and growing current account deficit will only be sustainable if equivalent levels of long-term external funding are available, associated with productive investment capable of generating a future flow of exchange revenues that is sufficient to pay off outstanding debt. The precise nature of the capital inflow is fundamentally very important, since one of the great perils of stabilization plans with exchange rate anchors is that a reversal in the flow of foreign capital can lead to a balance of payments disequilibrium of such a magnitude that it becomes unfeasible for the government to maintain the existing exchange rate. As a result expectations for exchange rate devaluation are generated among international investors, leading in turn to further shrinkage in inflows of foreign capital and, consequently, a fall in the levels of reserves, leaving the government with no option but to carry out a substantial devaluation in the nominal exchange rate. This in turn may have a prejudicial effect on domestic prices.

Therefore, balance of payments disequilibrium (related to both current account deficits and capital account surplus) results from the fact that, in a world of globally mobile financial and productive capital investments, domestic stabilization policies are inherently destabilizing. This is because, under these conditions, the initially successful application of an internal stabilization policy comes to generate an endogenous process of deteriorating economic conditions (a growing public deficit, a growing deficit in its current account and a dependence on foreign capital, among other things), which may leave a country vulnerable to speculative attacks on its currency and thus subject to currency crises (Kregel, 1999).

Summing up, the 1990s were marked by economic openness (in both trade and financial spheres), the privatization of state-owned firms, and price stabilization with the use of the exchange rate anchor.

However, they were also characterized by the contagions of external crises under a context of high external vulnerability. The currency crises in Mexico (1994–95), in Russia (1998) and in Brazil (1999) and the collapse of Argentina (2001–02) showed that the evidence in support of these economic policies was weak and, sometimes, contradictory. This sparked a debate among economists about the virtue, for instance, of financial liberalization and capital mobility. On the one hand, some political economists (for example, Haggard and Webb, 2000) pointed to the absence of attention to institutions and argued that the rule of law, a competent judiciary and governability, among other things, were necessary to assure stability and economic growth. On the other hand, Rodrik (1998) led the charge against the blind support of liberalism and globalization, arguing that particular policy approaches might work better than a dogmatic set of policies. In a similar vein, Stiglitz (2002) suggested a number of economic policies and reforms, a 'post-Washington Consensus', which would be more likely to produce sustainable and equitable development.

The main outcome of this debate is that, on the one hand, according to the conventional view, the implementation of a free-floating exchange rate regime and ample capital mobility, even when backed by responsible or credible economic policy, in line with the Washington Consensus prescriptions, leaves emerging economies prone to the short-term logic of capital accumulation. The conventional argument on the difficulties facing such economies is to attribute the volatility of foreign financing to their adoption of irresponsible economic policies (Caramazza and Aziz, 1998). On the other hand, the heterodox view regards a floating exchange rate regime and high capital mobility as a destabilizing combination of factors that will intensify exchange rate crises in developing countries (Ferrari-Filho and Paula, 2006).

After the 1990s currency crises, some important Latin American countries adopted a regime of macroeconomic policy inspired by the 'New Consensus Macroeconomics', based on a floating exchange regime, an inflation targeting regime, and the implicit commitment to fiscal equilibrium. In Latin America five countries – Brazil, Chile, Colombia, Mexico and Peru – have adopted an inflation targeting regime.[4] In 1990 Chile became the first Latin American country to adopt such an inflation targeting regime, but since 1984 it had made use of a 'crawling band' exchange rate regime, based on purchasing power parity-adjusting moving bands. Brazil, Colombia and Mexico formally adopted an inflation targeting regime in 1999, and Peru, which had managed a floating exchange regime since the beginning of the 1990s, did the same in 2002.

Brazil, with the introduction of the Real Plan in July 1994, adopted an active crawling peg exchange rate regime, in which the nominal exchange rate was devaluated on a more or less fixed value: the exchange rate depreciated by about 0.6–0.7 per cent per month on average (Ferrari-Filho and Paula, 2003). Following the Brazilian currency crisis, in January 1999, the government authorities implemented a floating exchange rate regime.

Argentina and Venezuela did not adopt 'New Consensus Macroeconomics' policies. Argentina, which had implemented the Convertibility Plan in 1991 with a fixed exchange rate and a sort of currency board, after the 2001–02 crisis and the huge exchange rate devaluation that followed the beginning of the crisis, began to make use of a managed floating exchange rate regime that intended to maintain the real exchange rate at a competitive level.[5] Venezuela, since January 2002, has implemented a fixed dual exchange rate system of the *bolivar*.[6] Before the December 1994 crisis Mexico had a pegged exchange rate regime, where the *peso* exchange rate was stuck at the upper limit of a band. Beginning at the end of 1994, a floating rate policy has been maintained by the government, with the Central Bank of Mexico intervening in the foreign exchange market under exceptional circumstances to minimize volatility and to ensure an orderly market. However, since 1999 Mexico has opted for a 'cleaner float', that is a pure flexible exchange rate. Chile has also operated a floating exchange regime, although the government intervenes massively in the currency markets through the use of the stabilization funds.

Table 6.1 summarizes the main features of the monetary and exchange rate policies of the main Latin American countries.

Table 6.1 Main features of the monetary and exchange rate policies of the main Latin American countries

Country	Monetary policy regime	Exchange rate system
Argentina	Discretionary	Managed floating
Brazil	Inflation targeting regime	Floating exchange regime*
Chile	Inflation targeting regime	Floating exchange regime*
Colombia	Inflation targeting regime	Floating exchange regime*
Mexico	Inflation targeting regime	Floating exchange regime
Peru	Inflation targeting regime	Floating exchange regime*
Venezuela	Discretionary	Fixed dual exchange rate

Note: *Denotes dirty floating.
Source: Elaborated by the authors.

As is well known, the 'New Consensus Macroeconomics' maintains that the main focus of economic policy is on price stabilization, and that an inflation targeting regime is the best arrangement for economic policy, as it provides some elements of freedom to accommodate output fluctuations resulting from non-anticipated shocks (Bernanke et al., 1989). Under such arrangements, fiscal policy is no longer viewed as a powerful macroeconomic instrument, and should be aligned and subordinated to monetary policy (Mishkin, 2000). Monetary policy is a flexible instrument for achieving medium-term stabilization objectives, in that it can be adjusted quickly in response to macroeconomic developments. In most Latin American economies that have adopted the inflation targeting regime, this macroeconomic arrangement has been characterized by a three-pronged approach to economic policy: floating exchange regime, inflation target regime, and the generation of a primary fiscal surplus in order to achieve long-term fiscal equilibrium.[7] A certain and moderate autonomy of economic policy (for domestic purposes) is achieved under the context of capital account convertibility through the working of a floating exchange rate regime.

One should be careful in the adoption of the 'New Consensus Macroeconomics' style of economic policy in emerging economies, as it can inhibit some necessary flexibility in the economic policy and can simultaneously constrain economic growth. (Paula and Ferrari-Filho, 2010). Economic authorities have to face some policy dilemmas. One of these is that inflation and exchange rate developments can be such that they call for the introduction of divergent monetary policies. For instance, using monetary policy to counter adverse exchange rate movements may jeopardize the inflation target, although frequently, in emerging economies, inflation targets have in practice responded with some flexibility to the various challenges posed by exchange rate fluctuations, using not only monetary policy (Ho and McCauley, 2003). Mohanty and Scatigna (2005) report that a number of emerging economies relied on interest rate interventions to stem exchange rate volatility. The solution of some dilemmas of economic policy in emerging economies could be solved by the use of non-traditional tools of economic policy, such as credit controls and capital controls.

To sum up, the above debate suggests that the financial liberalization and capital mobility did not produce stability and sustainable economic growth that were expected while less liberalized systems grew more robustly in a context of price and external stability.[8] Moreover, the 'New Consensus Macroeconomics' model of economic policy, however, has been managed with some flexibility in Latin America, both before and after the 2007–08 international financial crisis, as we will see in the next sections.

6.4 Capital flows, external vulnerability and economic policy in Latin America: recent trends and features

Using the classifications outlined in the seminal paper of Calvo et al. (1993), the determinants of capital flows to emerging economies can be divided into *push factors* (global ones), which are related to global factors that affect almost all emerging economies across the board, such as developed economies' interest rates and global risk appetite, and *pull factors* (specific ones) which typically refer to domestic factors that attract capital inflows, such as capital account liberalization, domestic potential growth and high domestic interest rates. In this regard, Reinhart and Reinhart (2008) analyzed the macroeconomic implications of a large set of surges in capital flows that took place over the period 1980–2007 and concluded that global factors, including changes in commodities prices, international interest rates, and growth in developed countries are the driving forces of international capital flows. Indeed, abrupt and volatile outflows are one of the main reasons for emerging economies to be concerned about large inflows of capital.

Beginning in the 1990s we can identify, broadly speaking, three waves of episodes of capital inflows to Latin America: the first one was from early 1990 until the 1997–98 Asian and Russian crises; the second was from mid-2004 until the global contagious that followed the Lehman Brothers bankruptcy; and, finally, the third wave had begun by mid-2009, that is after the post-contagion recovery in Latin America.

Concerning the first wave of capital inflows, one distinguishing feature was the reintegration of Latin American economies into the international financial market, which occurred after the lost decade of the 1980s when such markets were virtually closed to potentially private borrowers. The reintegration was stimulated by the Brady Plan (1993–94), which renegotiated the external debt, towards the securitization of the debt that resulted in both the reduction in the interest paid and the lengthening of the debt. Considering the *push* determinant of the new surge of capital flows, the initial impulse was given by the expansionary monetary policy in the United States at the beginning of the 1990s, which eventually caused a boom in the liquidity of the international financial market, and combined with the global institutional investors' search for risk diversification to push large amounts of capital towards markets in emerging economies. As a *pull* factor one should consider that, as we have already stressed, since the end of the 1980s there has been in Latin America a process of capital account liberalization for both capital inflows and outflows.

In terms of the composition of capital flows, during the 1990s there was a predominance of portfolio flows, favoured by the interest differential and increasingly by the FDI, that was much more stable than other sources of capital flows, especially when compared to the portfolio investments. Compared with the wave of capital flows of the 1970s, where inflow derived mainly from lending by groups of banks, in the 1990s they came mainly from international bond issues. Consequently, there was a large shift in the composition of foreign liabilities, with a reduction in borrowing and an increase in securities portfolio liabilities (equities and bonds markets).

In the 1990s most emerging economies made use of some sort of intermediary (or semi-pegged) exchange rate regimes. In the case of Latin America, the use of fixed or semi-pegged exchange rates by most countries, including Argentina, Brazil, Chile and Mexico, for the purposes of price stabilization, generated current account deficits financed by external indebtedness that contributed to an increase in the external vulnerability of such economies, which very often faced speculative attacks on their domestic currencies. Indeed, capital flows were very volatile in Latin America: following the surge of capital inflows from 1991 to 1994, they were briefly interrupted in December 1994, because of the Mexican crisis, began again quickly in 1995, and ended abruptly with the 1997–98 Asian and Russian crises. Brazil, the biggest economy in the region, was the main recipient of capital flows in Latin America, followed by Mexico and Argentina, which increased capital inflows between 1996 and 1998. Figure 6.1 and Figure 6.2 show, respectively, the capital inflows to the Latin America countries and, especially, Argentina, Brazil, Chile, Colombia, Mexico, Peru and Venezuela.

From 1999 to mid-2004 net capital flows in Latin America reduced dramatically, due to both the deterioration in the supply of funds by international financial markets (as a result of the increase in the investors' risk aversion) and the macroeconomic instability that was predominant in the region during this period, marked by the 1999 Brazilian currency crisis and 2001–02 Argentinean Convertibility Plan collapse. Indeed, the reduction in the net capital flows, with a substantial exit of capital outflows, was experienced by Argentina and Brazil, while Mexico had the highest flux of capital inflows in the region.

A new surge of capital inflows to emerging economies, that began in the middle of 2004, appears to mark the beginning of the exuberance

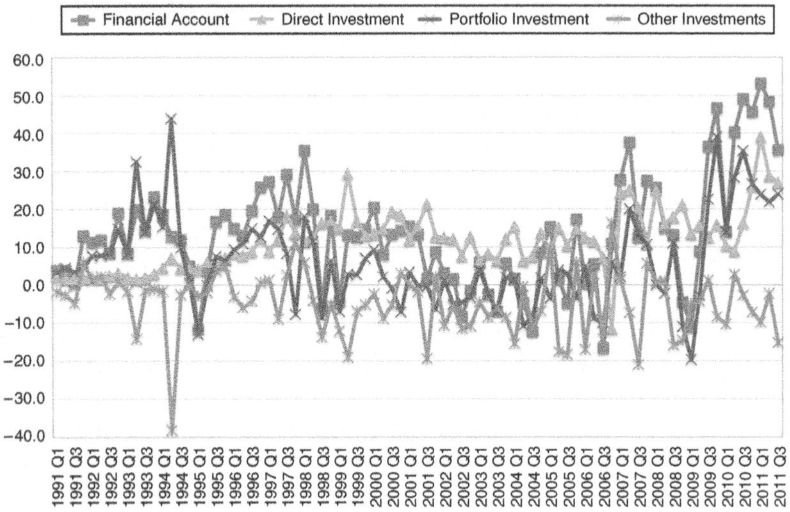

Figure 6.1 Financial account of Latin American countries (net balance in US$ billion)

Note: Latin America figure is calculated by the simple average of the seven major economies.
Source: ECLAC/Data Bases and Statistical Publications (2012) and IMF/International Financial Statistics (2012).

in international financial markets. It was related to both push factors, such as the low United States interest rates due to the loosening of FED monetary policy, and the reduction in the levels of global risk aversion, and a set of pull factors, which included high emerging economies potential growth and an increase in the commodities prices that contributed to an enhancement in the exports of those emerging economies that are exporters of commodities. Indeed the 2000s was known until the 2007–08 international financial crisis as the period of 'great moderation': low interest rates that accompanied the decline in the inflation indexes around the world and a commodities boom, both in part due to the positive shock derived from the 'China's effect'. From the 2000s economic growth in the emerging economies was no longer entirely connected to the growth in the developed countries. Greater GDP growth contributed somehow to attract FDI to both productive sectors oriented to exports or domestic market.

The surge in commodities prices was an additional cyclical force pushing capital toward commodity exports, which was an important factor for some Latin American countries including Brazil, Chile, Colombia,

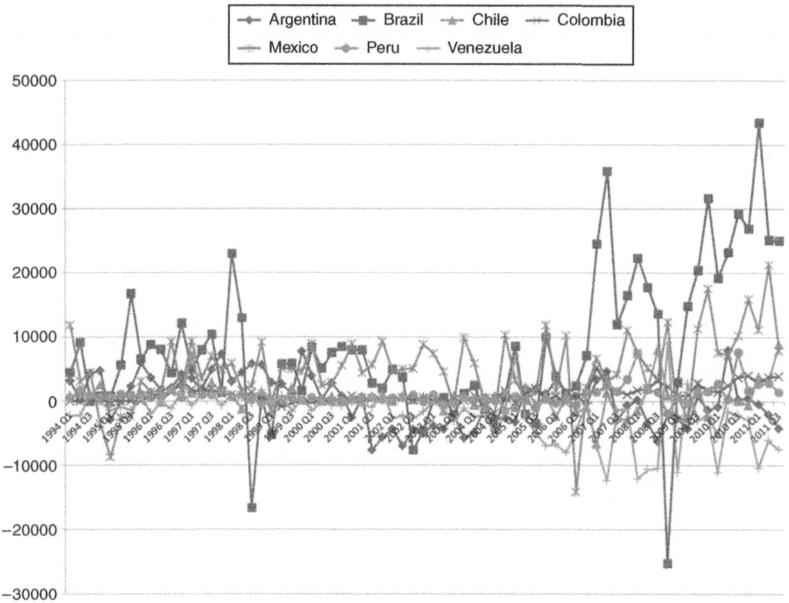

Figure 6.2 Financial account of the main Latin American countries (net balance in US$ million)

Source: ECLAC/Data Bases and Statistical Publications (2012) and IMF/International Financial Statistics (2012).

Peru and Venezuela. Indeed, the strong improvement in the terms of trade resulting from high world metal prices has attracted FDI to the mining sectors in Brazil and Peru. As we can see from Figure 6.3, the price of commodities increased gradually and sharply since the beginning of 2003, with a peak after mid-2007 due to the rise in the price of energy. After August 2008 there was a sharp decline in the commodities prices until the beginning of 2009. The improvement of the terms of trade was particularly favorable for Venezuela and Chile as a result of the increase in the oil and cooper prices, respectively. However, other major Latin American countries – Argentina, Brazil, Colombia and Peru – all of them exports of commodities, were also favored by this improvement in the terms of trade. As a result, with the exception of Colombia, the ratio of current account to GDP increased substantially in the 2003–07 period, which eventually resulted in a surplus for most countries, including Argentina, Brazil, Chile, Peru and Venezuela.

During the 2004–08 period of surges of capital flows in emerging economies, there was a predominance of net FDI flows relative to net

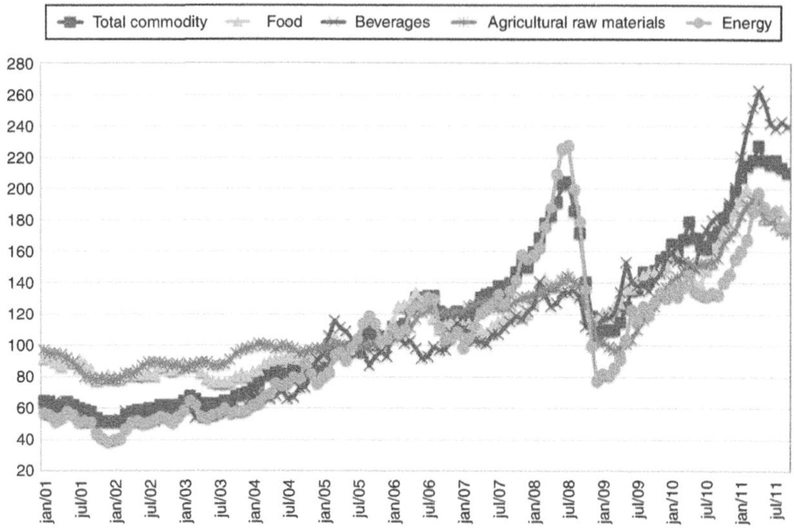

Figure 6.3 Commodity price index (2005 = 100)
Source: ECLAC/Data Bases and Statistical Publications (2012).

financial flows (portfolio and other flows) in all emerging regions, and such cycle involved a larger set of countries.

Brazil again was the most important recipient of capital flows in Latin America. It should be stressed, however, that foreign investment abroad (that is commanded by domestic firms) increased significantly during the 2000s as there was a trend towards the internationalization of Brazilian domestically-owned firms. This movement started to gain momentum following an initiative by a few large firms with significant direct investment abroad, mainly in natural resources-intensive sectors (mining, energy, steel makers and so on). Resource-seeking strategies helped these firms to control their supply of raw materials, as well as to place them in a stronger competitive position in the international market (Baumann, 2010).[9]

Other countries also increased their capital inflows significantly, as in the cases of Mexico, Peru and Colombia, while net capital flows have been low or negative in the case of Argentina, a country that had to renegotiate, compulsorily, its external debt after the colapse of the 2001–02 Convertibility Plan, which left international financial markets somehow closed to Argentina since then. The most striking case is Venezuela, where since 2005 net capital flows have predominantly been negative with significant amounts, evidence that this country has had an almost permanent capital flight driven by residents. The performance of this country and its balance of payments depend crucially upon the conditions of the oil market.

From the figures a number of new features of the international financial integration of the emerging economies in the 2000s can be stressed: much stronger current account positions for most of the emerging economies with a surplus or a reduction in the deficit, and a substantial acceleration in the accumulation of international reserves. The combination of net capital inflows and current account surpluses contributed to the generation of significant foreign reserve accumulation. As can be seen in Figure 6.4, international reserves increased in all the major Latin American countries, with the exception of Venezuela. Brazil, in particular, experienced a sharp increase in its reserves by US$ 50 billion in 2004–05 to more than US$ 200 billion in 2009.[10] The availability of international reserves reduced the default risk of public and private debts because of the lack of international liquidity in case of a sudden stop, and at the same time provide additional instruments to the central banks to intervene in the foreign exchange market (Frenkel and Rapetti, 2011).

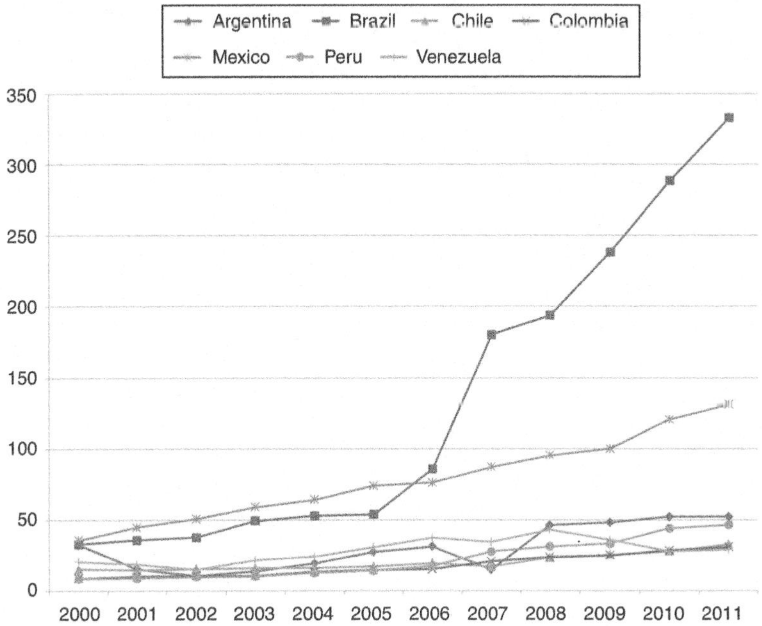

Figure 6.4 Foreign reserves (US$ billion)
Note: 2011 data are the position in May 2011.
Source: ECLAC (2011) and ECLAC/Data Bases and Statistical Publications (2012).

There was a marked reduction in the external vulnerability of the emerging economies during the 2000s because of the combination of massive self-insurance through foreign reserve accumulation, the reduction in public external debt, the implementation of a flexible exchange rate regime that allows the absorption of external shocks, and the development of domestic financial markets which made some governments less dependent on external financing (Ocampo, 2012).

The second wave of capital inflows ended in 2008 as the flows of international capital have been curtailed due to the global financial crisis – in particular, after the collapse of Lehman Brothers. The financial contagion of the collapse that followed the Lehman Brothers bankruptcy was deep and short, but in 2009 many emerging economies resumed their access to international credit with low interest rate.

The third wave of capital flows to Latin America began in the middle of 2009, with a quick recovery of capital inflows. The main drivers behind of this wave are: (i) the loosening of monetary policy in advanced economies due to the 'quantitative easing' monetary policy of the FED, and later of the European Central Bank (ECB) which expanded the liquidity of the financial system, widening interest rate differentials and creating abundant global market liquidity; (ii) the improved economic performance of the emerging economies and the slow recovery of the developed countries; (iii) the sound fiscal and debt position of the emerging economies relative to advance economies; and (iv) the prices of commodities recovered quickly and continually until May 2011, after the sharp decline of the prices after the spread of the global financial crisis to emerging economies in 2008. By mid-2011, however, the prices started to decline. So, all of these factors, along with an improved appetite for global risk, have attracted capital inflows, especially portfolio debt capital flows.

The recovery of capital flows was driven primarily by portfolio flows, and secondarily by FDI. The current episode is characterized by the predominance of volatile portfolio inflows, much more than in the previous wave. According to IMF (2011a, p. 13), '[t]he larger role played by portfolio flows, especially compared to banking flows, could persist in the coming years and likely reflects that international banks that intermediate cross-border flows are still in the process of balance repair'.

In the case of Latin America, portfolio investments commanded the wave of capital flows with a sharp and unprecedented increase in the flows (net flows of more than US$50 billion in some quarters according to Figure 6.1), followed by the FDI that have increased in 2011. Indeed, the smaller share of bank and other private capital flows compared to portfolio debt flows for most of the regions of emerging economies may reflect deleveraging in external asset positions by the banks in

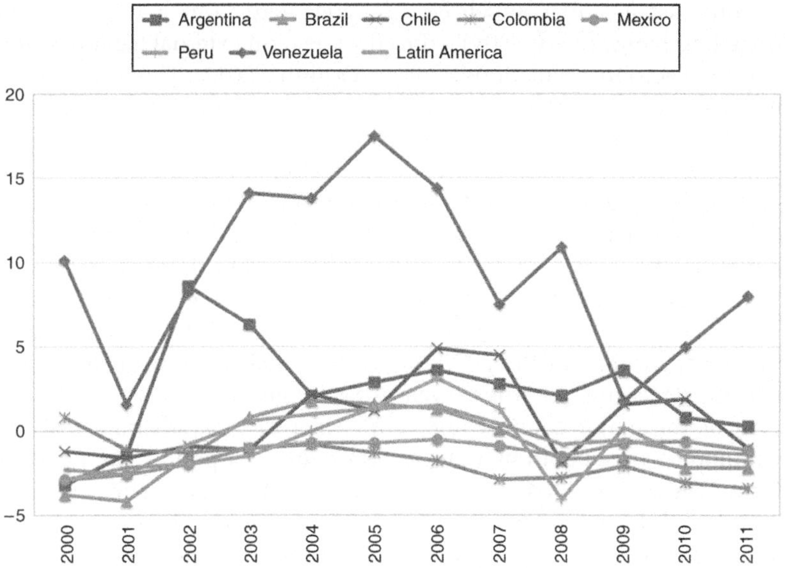

Figure 6.5 Current account to GDP ratio (%)
Note: Latin America is calculated by the simple average of the seven major economies.
Source: ECLAC/Data Bases and Statistical Publications (2012).

developed economies. Historically, portfolio flows have been more volatile than other types of flows and their volatility has risen recently. The largest recipients of capitals among the emerging economies are the Asian and Latin American ones, South Africa and Turkey. Brazil had records of capital inflows in the recent wave, followed at a considerable distance by Mexico, Colombia, Peru and Chile (see Figure 6.2).

Despite significant accumulation of international reserves, with the levels before the crisis quickly restored, in most cases the real exchange rate has appreciated back to the pre-crisis level or even higher. Figure 6.5 shows that the current account to GDP ratio decreased in 2010–11 due to both the rise in the imports and in the current account' incomes services, but has not reached critical levels.

6.5 The contagious nature of the 2007–08 international financial crisis and policy responses in Latin America

Reduced external vulnerability was the principal reason for the better performance of emerging economies during the recent global financial crises, and it is associated empirically with a set of factors: (i) lower current account deficits; (ii) competitive exchange rates; (iii) a high level of foreign exchange reserves; (iv) reduced short-term external liabilities; and (v) capital account regulations in place (Ocampo, 2012). The combination of stronger external accounts, the accumulation of international reserves and the flexibility of the exchange rate showed that the most emerging economies were prepared to face the contagion of the global crisis. Thus, with the exception of some Western European countries, most emerging economies did not have an external and financial crisis, although all regions in the world showed high levels of stress in the final quarter of 2008. In particular, financial stress in emerging economies – that rose in response to capital outflows initiated by investors in advanced economies – was much stronger in the 2007–08 international financial crisis, in line with the larger impulse from developed economies.

All of the major countries of Latin America took advantage of the commodity price boom by reducing their levels of public external debt during the period 2004–07, and building up international reserves. In 2005 Brazil, Chile and Mexico decided to restructure its external debt and to reduce the external debt stock and its costs, as C-Bonds[11] had been issued when the level of the country risk was very high, that is with high premium risk. Later, Argentina used part of its foreign reserves to reduce the external debt, a dramatic event that eventually caused the resignation of the chairman of the Central Bank of Argentina. Figure 6.6

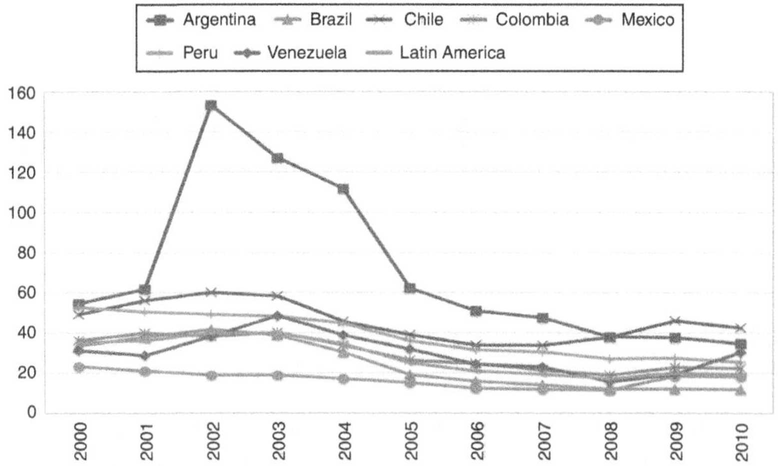

Figure 6.6 Public external debt (% of GDP)
Note: Latin America is calculated by the simple average of the seven major economies.
Source: ECLAC/Data Bases and Statistical Publications (2012).

presents the public external debt to Latin American countries and the main emerging economies of the region.

The contagious effect of the 2007–08 international financial crisis on the economies of Latin America, in terms of the growth rate of GDP, was deep, short and synchronized, as can be seen in Figure 6.7. Indeed, not only Latin America, but also all of the other regions of the world recovered quickly. All of the major Latin American economies, with the exception of Venezuela, recovered sharply in 2010.

Latin America was affected both directly by the 2007–08 international financial crisis (capital outflows) and indirectly (international trade) in the fourth quarter of 2008. The international financial crisis translated internationally to the emerging economies through the following channels: (i) a reduction in external credit; (ii) capital flight due to increase of risk aversion; (iii) lower levels of global economic growth (mainly in the case of the developed economies); and (iv) a fall in the price of the commodities (CEPAL, 2009). Specific countries' factors are related to the domestic and external vulnerabilities and the degree of trade and financial integration. In particular, the 'significant reversal in capital flows, the collapse in commodity prices and the deterioration of

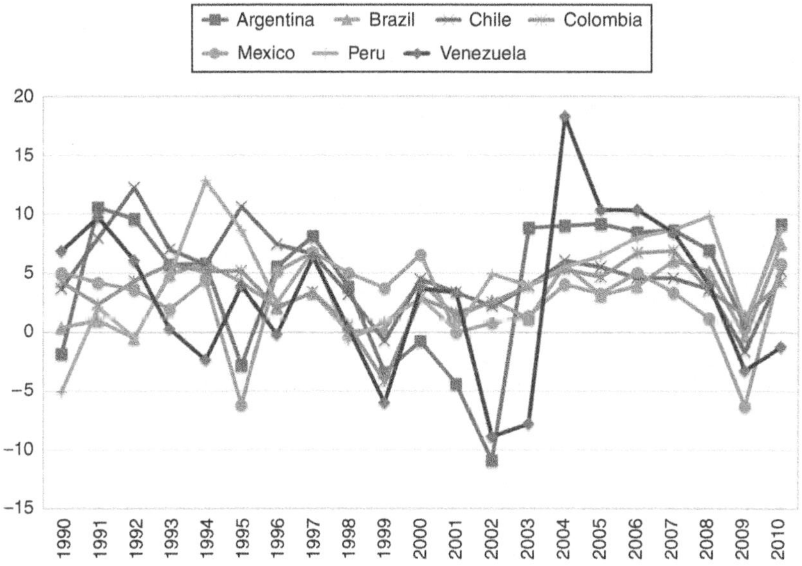

Figure 6.7 GDP growth rate (%)
Source: ECLAC/Data Bases and Statistical Publications (2012).

confidence following the Lehman Brothers bankruptcy triggered sharp currency depreciations and higher costs of external financing across the region' (Jará et al., 2008, p. 57). However, although the size of the exchange rate adjustment was very large, its effects were limited, due to the widespread use of flexible exchange rate regimes and lower currency mismatches.

In the case of the major economies of Latin America, in most countries the reduction of public external debt, the previous policy of international reserves accumulation and the reduction and improvement in the composition of public debt (increase of domestically denominated debt) provided some policy space for counter-cyclical and stabilization policies. Actually, the combination of the reduction of public external debt (external liabilities) with the increase in the foreign reserves (external assets) meant that most countries had a positive net balance in foreign currencies, so that the immediate and direct impact of the exchange rate devaluation on the public finance was positive, instead of negative – as it was the case in other previous occasions. Consequently, governments could make use of some counter-cyclical fiscal policy to face to effects of the financial crisis, when in other occasions they made use of tightened policies. As can be seen in Figure 6.8 the overall fiscal balance did not deteriorate in 2008, and it was only in 2009, with the

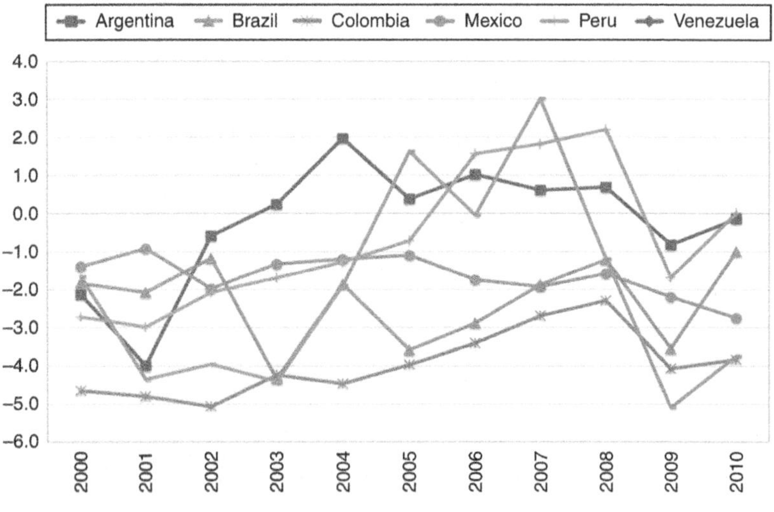

Figure 6.8 Overall fiscal balance (% of GDP)
Source: ECLAC/Data Bases and Statistical Publications (2012).

combination of short recession and some expansionary fiscal policy, that there was a reduction in the fiscal balance, that quickly improved in 2010.[12]

The countries in the region had a variety of reactions to the crisis and employed different tools of political economy. The economic policy responses include a large range of tolls that included (Jará et al., 2009; CEPAL, 2009):

(i) Central banks provided foreign currency liquidity to the private sector, to ensure both the continued operation of foreign exchange markets and the continued availability of external financing.
(ii) External resources provided significant additional support to Latin American countries during the global financial crisis: the central banks of Brazil and Mexico established reciprocal currency arrangements, with the FED totalling US$30 billion each, while IMF created FCL financing facilities, that was used by Mexico (US$47 billion) and Colombia (US$10.5 billion).
(iii) Some central banks increased the range of assets accepted as collateral to improve access to short-term funding, such as Argentina, Brazil, Mexico and Peru. Many central banks also relied heavily on lower domestic currency reserve requirements (Colombia, Brazil and Peru).
(iv) However, central banks delayed lowering rates until late 2008 or early 2009, due to concerns about inflationary pressures and the potential impact of the exchange rate depreciation, and such behaviour contributed negatively to a reduction of economic growth in 2009.
(v) Some countries made use of counter-cyclical fiscal policy, by the reduction of the taxes to stimulate consumption (Brazil and Chile) and/or by the increase in the public expenditures (Argentina, Brazil and Colombia).

Specifically considering the economic policy responses of the Brazilian government to the contagion effect of the 2007–08 international financial crisis, it is important to mention that, on the one hand, before the onset of this crisis, the Brazilian government adopted some structural initiatives – including the expansion of the social protection and income transfer programs, the real increase in the minimum wage, the expansion of the credit supply by state-owned banks (mainly the Brazilian Development Bank – BNDES), a reduction in the public external debt, and some expansion of investment expenditures – which contributed to a prevention of a greater drop in economic activity and also facilitated the policy response to the 2007–08 international financial crisis. On the other hand, in 2008, as a result of the adoption of previous policies oriented toward the reduction of the external vulnerability (reserve accumulation, reduction of public external debt, and so on), Brazil had some degree of freedom in adopting counter-cyclical economic policies.[13]

In 2010–11, the main economies of Latin America resumed economic growth, in part because many of them had some capacity to implement policies that helped to sustain demand, favoured by a set of macroeconomic factors that include: foreign reserve level was restored, public accounts in general improved with low levels of indebtedness,[14] inflation stopped rising, and still the fact that '2008 global financial crisis left the region a legacy of experience in coordinating countercyclical fiscal and monetary policies and measures for heading off a liquidity crisis in domestic financial markets' (ECLAC, 2011, p. 27). On the external front, however, the worsening terms of trade and the lower volume of exports has caused a deterioration in the balance of payments current account.

6.6 Some economic policy implications of the surge of capital inflows

As we have already seen, there was a quick and deep contagion of the 2007–08 international financial crisis in Latin America, but the recovery was also quick. The previous policy of reducing external vulnerability plus the adoption of a floating exchange rate regime provided some space for the introduction of counter-cyclical economic policies. In several countries the economic recovery in 2010 and 2011 was sustained in part by the counter-cyclical policies implemented to offset the impact of the economic and financial crisis of 2007–08 (ECLAC, 2011, pp. 13–14).

One of the main challenges of the Latin American economies is the 'entry of large capital inflows in the form of both FDI and portfolio investment, fuelled by interest rate spreads between markets in the region and in developed economies traditionally perceived as low-risk, together with the positive growth outlook and limited risk perception for the Latin American countries' (ECLAC, 2011, p. 23). In part due to this, most currencies of the region came under strong upward pressure in 2010–11.

Concerning monetary policy, emerging economies – including Latin American countries – have more recently refrained from tightening aggressively, despite emerging inflationary pressures, out of fear that a tightening would pull more capital flows. A further reason is the increase of uncertainty related to the performance of the global economy, due to the slow recovery of the United States economy, the unknown future of the eurozone, and the reduction in the level of Chinese economic growth in 2012. Some emerging economies have complemented macroeconomic policy with other measures to manage capital inflows, such as taxes on certain inflows, minimum holding periods, macroprudential measures and currency-specific reserve requirements, motivated by concerns about economic aspects such as export competiveness, financial stability and sterilization costs.

As we have already stressed, intervention in the currency markets, including the accumulation of reserves, has been massive in Argentina, Brazil and Chile and very high in Colombia and Peru. However, for some economies there was a gradual trend towards the real appreciation of the exchange rate due to massive capital flows. This was the case for Brazil and Colombia, who, together with Venezuela, are the countries whose currencies had a strong upward pressure in real terms. According to Figure 6.9, Argentina, Chile and Colombia have maintained more or less stable real effective exchange rates (REER) from 2005 to 2011, while Mexico had its REER depreciated in the period 2009–11[15] – although Mexico is the only one of the seven largest countries of the region where official intervention in the foreign exchange market has been limited. Argentina is the only country where there is an implicit exchange rate target – indeed, the maintenance of a competitive exchange rate is one the cornerstones of macroeconomic policy (Ocampo, 2007).[16] Venezuela, a big exporter of oil, suffers typically what is called as 'Dutch disease' – that is, the chronic overvaluation of the exchange rate when compared with its real exchange rate average in the 2000s, caused by the abundance of cheap natural and human resources compatible with a lower exchange rate than the one that would pave the way for the other tradable goods.[17]

Although the improvement in the terms of trade can contribute to the appreciation of the currency, the strong currency appreciation in Brazil and Colombia was clearly associated with capital inflows, under an environment of exuberance in international financial markets. In both countries, exchange rate appreciation has contributed to a deterioration of the current account. Brazil was one of the emerging countries that had a stronger trend of currency appreciation until February 2012, due to the combination of huge capital inflows, the commodities boom, high domestic interest rates, and the existence of a sophisticated and deep foreign exchange derivatives market totally open to foreign investors that provides space for speculation on the exchange rate. However,

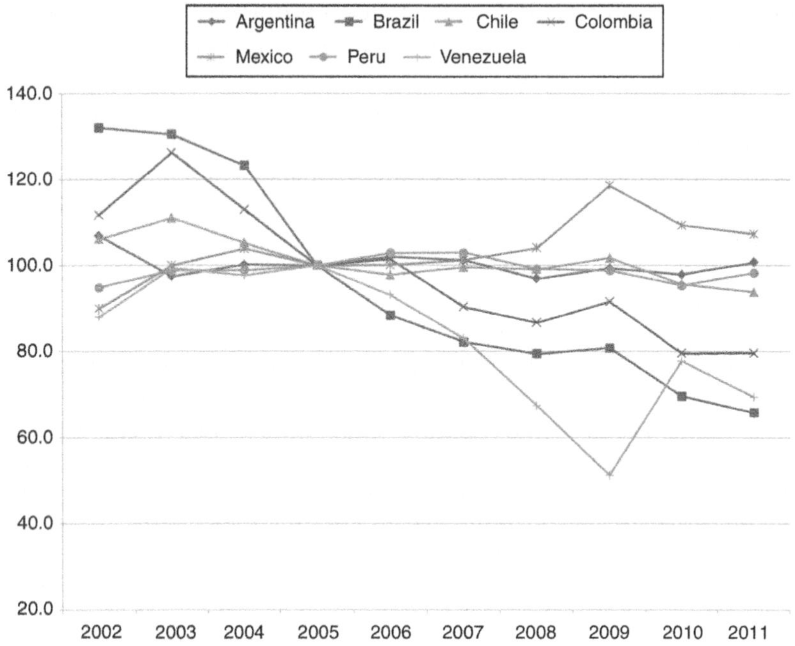

Figure 6.9 Real effective exchange rate (2005 = 100)
Note: Annual averages. A country's overall real effective exchange rate index is calculated by weighting its real bilateral exchange rate indices with each of its trading partners by each partner's share in the country's total trade flows in terms of exports and imports. A currency depreciates in real effective terms when this index rises and appreciates when it falls.
Source: ECLAC/Data Bases and Statistical Publications (2012).

since the beginning of March 2012, due to, basically, the effects of the European crisis, the *real* has been devaluated.

Large capital inflows can help to reduce the cost of capital, but can also complicate macroeconomic management. In the region the current account deficit widened more recently (1.4 per cent of GDP on average in 2011, according to ECLAC, 2011), due to an increase in imports and income deficit, but it is still not too high, and can be managed as the economies have combined a flexible exchange rate, with low external indebtedness and the accumulation of foreign reserves.

The degree of sterilized foreign exchange interventions has varied from country to country. As we have seen in section 6.2, these interventions can allow countries to manage exchange rate volatility, while allowing the authorities to keep monetary aggregates under control in order to determine the short-term interest rate. Sterilized intervention has been used in Brazil and Peru as a dominant response against surging inflows, in order to smooth exchange rate volatility and slow the rate of appreciation, at least in the short term (IMF, 2011a, p. 26). Sterilization costs, however, is high in some countries that have high domestic interest rate as it has been the case of Brazil, and can pose a constraint especially where fiscal positions are already weak. Rodrik (2006) argues that if sterilization costs are high, it can be the case of using alternatively capital controls in order to face the consequences of the surge of capital inflows.

In the face of rapid exchange rate appreciation, in October 2009 Brazil reinstated the Tax on Financial Transactions (*'Imposto sobre Operações Financeiras'* in Portuguese – IOF) to discourage carry trade operations. In October 2010, IOF was also extended to cover margin requirements in derivatives transactions. After implementing some slight capital controls in 2009 and 2010,[18] it was only after January 2011 (when the first prudential financial regulation tool was implemented and the Brazilian government imposed reserve requirements on banks' short foreign exchange positions in the cash market) and, mainly, after July 2011 (when the Brazilian government adopted a broader regulation of the foreign exchange derivatives operations) a more comprehensive regulation has been launched, encompassing both capital controls, prudential financial regulation and foreign exchange derivatives market regulation.

In Argentina, although there had been a considerable devaluation in 2009, the country's exchange rate policy continued its trajectory of the REER (Figure 6.9). The stable and competitive real exchange rate strategy was a result of the exchange rate administration by the Central Bank of Argentina and its intervention in the monetary market to control the interest rate. In this connection, both the continuing trade surpluses (even with world GDP and trade growth slowing from 2008 onwards) and the policy of accumulating foreign reserves helped to stabilize the exchange rate market and assure a relatively comfortable external situation. However, since 2011 there has been a deteriorating trend in the trade surplus due to both the decline in the prices of agricultural commodities (Figure 6.3) and also the appreciation of the real exchange rate (Figure 6.9) in consequence of the deterioration of the terms of trade and the increase in the domestic prices. Argentina's government has responded to such a situation by implementing administrative controls on foreign currencies, in order to seek to avoid a further deterioration of the exchange rate.

In respect of the Chilean economy, throughout 2008 and 2009 the Central Bank of Chile continued to intervene in the exchange rate market, either to prevent the *peso* from appreciating or depreciating, or to buy foreign currency so as to strengthen Chile's foreign exchange reserves. Thus, in a context in which the exchange rate was being held stable in real terms, added to a significant reduction in imports and a slight improvement in copper prices on the international market, the current account balance of payments was reversed from a deficit in 2008 to a situation of surplus in 2009 and 2010 (Figure 6.5).

As we have already seen, since 2004 Colombia has had a steady trend for exchange rate appreciation, one of the highest among the major Latin American economies. *Banco de la República*, the central bank of Colombia, has implemented a flexible exchange rate scheme with the following objectives: '(i) To maintain an adequate level of international reserves that will lessen the economy's vulnerability to external shocks (...); (ii) To limit excessive volatility of the exchange rate in the short term; and (iii) To moderate excessive appreciation or depreciation of the nominal exchange rate that could jeopardize the achievement of future inflation targets, as well as the economy's external and financial stability' (Banco de la República, 2012). To prevent currency appreciation, in September 2011 Central Bank of Colombia replaced the reserve purchase program involving daily actions of up to US$20 million with options auctions in an effort to control volatility (ECLAC, 2011, p. 80).

Like other emerging economies, the Central Bank of Mexico, in an attempt to contain the currency appreciation of the *peso* against the dollar, and to reduce the risk of a possible capital flow reversal, implemented some measures in the exchange rate market, for example, the international reserve accumulation was expanded and capital flows were limited (Banco de México, 2012). In addition, the flexible line of credit with the IMF was increased in January 2011 from US$48 billion to US$72 billion for a period of two years.

Peru also introduced a wide range of measures to tackle rapid capital inflows, and reduce upward pressure on the exchange rate. Among other measures, in July 2010 the government implemented additional capital requirements for foreign exchange credit risk exposure, and in September 2010, the reserve requirements were raised, including 120 per cent reserve requirement for non-residents' deposits in domestic currency. The highly restrictive reserve requirements on domestic and foreign currency deposits and active intervention have helped to maintain low exchange rate volatility and restrain credit growth in Peru (IMF, 2011a, p. 31).

In Venezuela, because of the possibility that an inflationary shock might result from the global trend towards exchange rate devaluations, the monetary authorities adopted an essentially restrictive monetary policy characterized by high basic interest rates and higher levels of compulsory deposits to be held by banks, which reduced the levels of liquidity and credit in the economy. More recently, the Venezuelan government has decided to control the exchange rate, to avoid the 'exchange rate pass-through' mechanism, and to continue as the only administrator of the foreign currencies and executor of this devaluation. Indeed, the high level of inflation in Venezuela has resulted in some difficulties for the economic authorities to avoid the appreciation of REER.

Some authors (Bresser-Pereira, 2008; Frenkel and Rapetti, 2011) have warned of the risks of a sustained trend of exchange rate appreciation in countries such as Brazil and the other Latin American economies: it can lead to the end of industrial firms and the destruction of human capital, technical and entrepreneurial know-how, horizontal and vertical integration with other firms, and a reduction in the access to external trade markets. Real exchange rate appreciation and the contraction of the industrial sector can have negative consequences for the long-term growth of the economies. Indeed in semi-mature countries that have a manufacturing sector, a trend of real exchange rate appreciation can translate into a gradual process of the reduction of the aggregate value of the industrial sector and industrial employment – an effect that can only be felt in the long term (Frenkel and Rapetti, 2011). Thus, it may be the case that some of the Latin American economies may be going through a sort of 'early de-industrialization'.[19] Furthermore, there is some evidence that shows that Brazil, Chile, Colombia and Peru have been in a process of 'primary sector exports priorization',[20] – that is, the economies become specialized in exporting commodities goods in which they have natural comparative advantage, while at the same time they reduce the share of manufacturing good in total exports.

6.7 Summary and conclusions

Capital flows in Latin America have been volatile and have exhibited pro-cyclical behaviour, following a pattern that has been described in the literature on capital flows. In particular, we have seen that capital flows to Latin America have been mostly determined by push factors (for instance, the economic policy of developed countries) than to pull factors.

Brazil was the main recipient of capital inflows, but other countries, such as Colombia, Mexico and Peru, took part in the surge of capital flows in the 2000s. Commodity price boom in the 2000s was an opportunity to reduce external liabilities and build up international reserves. In most major Latin American countries the reduction of public external debt, the previous policy of international reserves accumulation, and the reduction and improvement in the composition of public debt (increase of domestically-denominated debt) provided some policy space for counter-cyclical and stabilization policies during the contagious period of the 2007–08 international financial crisis. In 2010–11, the main economies of Latin America resumed their period of economic growth, in part because many of them had some capacity to implement policies that could help to sustain demand, but there are a large number of concerns about the performance of the economy of the region due mainly to the uncertainties related to the global economy, such as the euro crisis, semi-stagnation of the American economy, the slowing in the growth of the Chinese economy and so on.

After the 1990s currency crises, some important Latin American countries – notably Brazil, Chile, Colombia, Mexico and Peru – adopted a regime of macroeconomic policy inspired by the 'New Consensus Macroeconomics'. Some countries, such as Argentina and Venezuela, did not adopt such a model of economic policy. The 'New Consensus Macroeconomics' model of economic policy, however, has been managed with some flexibility in Latin America, both before and after the 2007–08 international financial crisis. In future it would be useful to evaluate whether or ot a sustained and stable economic growth in Latin America is compatible with the 'New Consensus Macroeconomics' model of economic policy – indeed, the region has underperformed when compared with the most dynamic Asian economies (China, South Korea and India, among others), and there is some concern that some Latin American economies may be going through a sort of 'early de-industrialization', due to the currency appreciation caused by the 'Dutch disease' that resulted from the commodities boom.

Two lines of thought can be crystallized from the 2007–08 international financial crisis. On the one hand, as highlighted by Prates and Cintra (2009), in previous crises – more particularly the contagious periods of the currency crises of the 1990s (Mexico, 1994–95; East Asia, 1997; Russia, 1998; and Brazil, 1998–99) and the Argentinean Convertibility collapse in 2001–02 – most emerging countries adopted pro-cyclical (restrictive) measures, in line with IMF principles and approval, in an attempt to regain the confidence of the financial markets as a necessary condition for foreign capital to flow back to those emerging economies. However, in view of the systemic nature of the 2007–08 international financial crisis, emerging economies' monetary authorities decided that such policies would be ineffective. Rather they would contribute to an aggravation of the developments from the crisis by setting off a vicious circle of exchange depreciation, credit squeeze, asset deflation, and crises of effective demand and unemployment. In that light, these economies countered the contagion effect – as did the developed countries – by putting in place anti-cyclical measures to render their currencies less volatile, prevent a balance of payment deterioration, ensure liquidity for their domestic financial systems, stabilize prices and bring growth back on track. Thus, most of the world's monetary authorities responded to the 2007–08 international financial crisis by operating counter-cyclical economic (fiscal, monetary and exchange rate) policies in order to mitigate the effects of the crisis on both the financial and the 'real' dimensions of their economies.

On the other hand, in contrast to the financial and exchange rate crises of the 1990s, where the emerging economies suffered most from the repercussions on the economy, the economic impacts of the present crisis have been much more damaging to the developed economies.

Finally, massive capital inflows – in consequence of large capital inflows in the form of both FDI and portfolio investment, fuelled by interest rate spreads between markets in the region and in developed economies – have caused some macroeconomic problems for the main emerging countries of the region, including exchange rate appreciation and a rapid increase in domestic credit. The relevant question is: What is to be done in the face of massive capital inflows? Capital controls can be a useful tool as a complement of macroeconomic policy, but in order to be effective they need to be comprehensive and should be dynamically adjusted to compensate for the tendency of financial markets to elude them. Capital account regulations should be seen as an essential part of the macroeconomic policy toolkit and not regarded as measures of last resort. In particular, during the boom periods, they can help authorities to manage economic policy by avoiding exchange rate appreciation, reducing the risks associated with rising current account deficits and contributing to foreign exchange reserve accumulation. Furthermore, in pursuit of a multiplicity of policy objectives – economic growth, a reduction in external vulnerability and the promotion of financial stability, among others – economic authorities should actively search for more instruments, such as capital controls, prudential measures on credit and so on.

Another relevant question is: How could inflation targeting and exchange rate targeting be compatible? Frenkel and Rapetti (2011) and Ocampo (2012) suggest a mix of administered exchange rate flexibility with active foreign exchange reserve accumulation, the regulation of capital inflows and the active sterilization of international reserves combined with low domestic interest rates and a policy of fiscal restraint. To evaluate deeply the macroeconomic problems and their consequences, to identify the trade-offs of economic policy, and to choose the right economic strategy is the main challenge for economic policy in the Latin American countries.

Notes

1. Friedman (1953) argues that a speculator who consistently earns profits must stabilize the exchange rate, as profits can be made only by buying when the price is low and selling when it is high. Such purchases increase the prices while the sales lower them, so that speculation can reduce the magnitude of exchange rate fluctuations.
2. Emerging economies as a group have a higher pass-through than developed economies since lower-income economies have a larger portion of traded goods in the consumption basket so that the significance of the exchange rate in the evolution of domestic inflation tends to be greater in such economies (Ho and McCauley, 2003).
3. Capital controls can target inflows and outflows, and can be *tax-based* (for instance, reserve requirement taxes against certain types of investments) or *quantitative* (for instance, outright bans on certain investments, restrictions or quotas, or license requirements).
4. Latin American countries that adopted inflation targeting regime (ITR) plus floating exchange rate system implemented an institutional arrangement of ITR that includes a range for the inflation target, the use of the headline inflation index as reference and the calendar year as commitment horizon.
5. According to Frenkel and Rapetti (2010), the Central Bank of Argentina, however, never made an explicit statement regarding the existence of a real exchange rate target.
6. The new system offered a 2.6 *bolivar* per dollar rate for imports of essential items such as food, medicine, and industrial machinery, and a 4.3 *bolivar* per dollar rate for imports of other products, including cars and telephones. *Comision de Administracion de Divisas* (CADIVI), the government body which administers currency exchange, continues as the only administrator of the foreign currencies and executor of this devaluation.
7. Primary fiscal surplus is understood as necessary to enable government to pay interest expenses related to public debt.
8. See, for instance, Ferrari-Filho and Paula (2006).
9. Carvalho and Senne (2009) present details of the main abroad investments of some Brazilian transnational companies. According to them, the Brazilian steel, mining, energy and food major companies (Gerdau, Vale do Rio Doce, Petrobras and JBS) have invested, respectively, in 13, 25, 26 and 14 countries around the world.
10. In the beginning of 2012, the Brazilian foreign reserves reached US$370 billion.
11. 'Capitalization-Bonds' (with front-loaded interest rate reduction) of external debt issued by the main emerging countries in the mid-1990s as part of the Brady Plan, in which some countries restructured their external debts.

12. According to CEPAL (2009), countries with high percentage of non-taxes resources related to natural resources, low tax burden and/or greater trade aperture suffered major reductions in the governments' revenues, as it was the case of Venezuela.
13. The counter-cyclical implemented by the Brazilian government produced the expected impact, because from the second half of 2009 onwards the Brazilian economy began to show signs of recovery, in turn encouraging expectations among consumers, businesses and the financial system, even to the point of persuading them to take decisions, respectively, to spend (consumption and investment) and borrow. As a result, the Brazilian economy grew by 7.5 per cent in 2010.
14. However, public revenue is some countries of the region is highly dependent on commodities prices, what can eventually endanger fiscal accounts and lead to the deployment of pro-cyclical public policies.
15. Mexico has REER similar to the real exchange rate bilateral with United States due to the high concentration of trade with this country.
16. The maintenance of a competitive exchange rate requires the build-up of foreign reserves during upturn be matched by measures to sterilize their monetary impact – that is why fiscal surplus is essential complement to this sort of policy, what has been relaxed more recently in Argentina.
17. According to Bresser-Pereira (2008), 'Dutch disease is a market failure resulting from the existence of cheap and abundant natural resources used to produce commodities which are compatible with a more appreciated exchange rate than the one that would be necessary to make competitive the other tradable industries. By using cheap resources, the respective commodities cause the appreciation of the exchange rate because they can be profitable at a rate which is incompatible with the rate that other goods using the best technology available worldwide require' (p. 50).
18. The IOF was too low to stem the derivatives carry trade due to its high leverage degree, and private agents found loopholes to circumvent the regulations. One of the main channels of circumvention after October 2010 was the increase in bank's short dollar positions in the spot currency market. In fact, the IOF on portfolio inflows encouraged the build-up of long real/short dollar positions in the onshore derivatives market, that is, the derivatives carry trade supported by resident banks which take the other side of non-resident investors in the derivatives market. For more details, see Prates (2012).
19. Classic de-industrialization is seen in the literature as a secular decline in the share of manufacturing employment in the advanced economies, in part due to the shift in domestic expenditure from manufacturing to services caused by the increase in the average per capita income. For more, see Rowthourn and Ramaswamy (1997).
20. This process is also called as 're-primarization'.

References

Alves Jr., A., Ferrari-Filho, F. and Paula, L.F. (1999/2000) 'The Post Keynesian Critique of Conventional Currency Crisis Models and Davidson's Proposal to Reform the International Monetary System', *Journal of Post Keynesian Economics*, 22(2): 207–25.

Arestis, P., Sobreira, R. and Oreiro, J.L. (2011) *The Financial Crisis – Origins and Implications*, Basingstoke: Palgrave Macmillan.

Arestis, P. and Sawyer, M. (2005) 'Financial Liberalization and the Finance Growth Nexus: What Have We Learned?', in P. Arestis and M. Sawyer (eds), *Financial Liberalization: Beyond Orthodox Concerns*, Basingstoke: Palgrave Macmillan.

Banco de la República (2012) *Exchange Rate Policy*. http://www.banrep.gov.co, access in April.

Banco de México (2012) *Annual Reports*. http://www.banxico.org.mx, access in April.

Baumann R. (2010) 'Brazilian External Sector So Far in the 21st Century', *Revista Brasileira de Política Internacional*, 53: 33–53.

Bernanke, B., Laubach, T., Mishkin, F. and Posen, A. (1989) *Inflation Targeting: Lessons from the International Experience*, Princeton: Princeton University Press.

Brazilian Central Bank – BCB (2012) *Séries Temporais*, http://www.bcb.gov.br, access in April.

Bresser-Pereira, L.C. (2008) 'The Dutch Disease and Its Neutralization: A Ricardian Approach', *Brazilian Journal of Political Economy*, 28(1): 47–71.

Bresser-Pereira, L.C., and Gala, P. (2007) 'Por Que a Poupança Externa Não Promove Crescimento', *Brazilian Journal of Political Economy*, 27(1): 3–19.

Calvo, G. Leiderman, E. and Reinhart, C. (1993) 'Capital Inflows and Real Exchange Rate Appreciation in Latin America: The Role of the External Factors', *IMF Staff Papers*, 40(1): 108–51.

Calvo, G. and Reihart, C. (2002) 'Fear of Floating', *Quarterly Journal of Economics*, CXVII (2): 379–408.

Caramazza, F. and Aziz, J. (1998) *Fixed or flexible? Getting the exchange rate right in the 1990s*, Washington, DC: International Monetary Fund.

Cardarelli, R., Elekdag, S. and Kose, M.A. (2009) 'Capital Inflows: Macroeconomic Implications and Policy Responses', *IMF Working Paper 09/40*, Washington, DC: International Monetary Fund, March.

Carvalho, C. E. and Senne, R. (2009) 'Integração Financeira e Internacionalização de Empresas Brasileiras na América do Sul', *Nueva Sociedad*, December: 17–32.

Comisión Económica para América Latina – CEPAL (2009) *Estudio Económico de América Latina y el Caribe 2008–2009*, Santiago del Chile: CEPAL.

Economic Commission for Latin America – ECLAC (2011) *Preliminary Overview of the Economies of Latin America and the Caribbean – 2011*, Santiago del Chile: ECLAC.

Economic Commission for Latin America – ECLAC (2012) *Data Bases and Statistical Publications*, http://websie.eclac.cl/infest/ajax/cepalstat.asp?carpeta=estadisticas&idioma=i, access in April.

Eichengreen, B. (2002) 'Can Emerging Markets Float? Should They Inflation Target?', *Working Papers Series*, Brasília: Banco Central do Brasil, February.

Eichengreen, B., Tobin, J. and Wyplosz, C. (1995) 'Two Cases for Sand in the Wheels of International Finance', *Economic Journal*, 105(428): 162–72.

Epstein, G., Grabel, I. and Jomo, K.S. (2003) 'Capital Management Techniques in Developing Countries', *Working Paper Series no. 56*, Cambridge, MA: University of Massachusetts.

Ferrari-Filho, F. and Paula, L.F. (2006) 'Regime Cambial, Conversibilidade da Conta de Capital e Performance Econômica: A Experiência de Brasil, Rússia,

Índia e China', in J. Sicsú and F. Ferrari Filho (eds), *Câmbio e Controle de Capitais*. Rio de Janeiro: Campus-Elsevier.

Ferrari-Filho, F. and Paula, L.F. (eds) (2004), *Globalização Financeira: Ensaios de Macroeconomia Aberta*, Petrópolis: Vozes.

Ferrari-Filho, F. and Paula, L.F. (2003) 'The Legacy of the Real Plan and an Alternative Agenda for the Brazilian Economy', *Investigación Económica*, LXII(244): 57–92.

Fischer, S. (2001) 'Exchange Rate Regimes: Is the Bipolar View Correct?', *Journal of Economic Perspectives*, 15(2): 3–24.

Freitas, M.C. and Prates, D. (2001) 'A Abertura Financeira no Governo FHC: Impactos e Consequências', *Economia e Sociedade*, 17: 81–111.

Frenkel, R. and Rapetti, M. (2011) 'Fragilidad Externa o Desindustrialización: Cuál Es la Principal Amenaza para América Latina en la Próxima Década?', *Serie Macroeconomia del Desarrolo no. 116*, Santiago del Chile: CEPAL, November.

Friedman, M. (1953) 'The Case for Flexible Exchange Rates', in *Essays in Positive Economics*, Chicago: Chicago University Press.

Ghosh, S.R. (2010) 'Dealing with the Challenges of Capital Inflows in the Context of Macrofinancial Link', in *World Bank – Poverty Reduction and Economic Management Network no. 19*, Washington: World Bank, June.

Grenville, S. (2000) 'Exchange Rate Regimes for Emerging Markets', *Reserve Bank of Australia Bulletin*, November: 53–63.

Griffith-Jones, S., Ocampo, J.A. and Stiglitz, J. (2010) *Time for a Visible Hand: Lessons from the 2008 World Financial Crisis*, New York: Oxford University Press.

Haggard S. and Webb, S.B. (2000) *The Political Economy of the Asian Financial Crisis*, Washington, DC: International Institute of Economics.

Hausmann, R., Pritchett, L., and Rodrik, D. (2004) 'Growth Accelerations', *NBER Working Paper* no. 10566, June.

Ho, C. and McCauley, R. (2003) 'Living With Flexible Exchange Rates: Issues and Recent Experience in Inflation Targeting Emerging Market Economies', *BIS Working Papers no. 130*, February.

International Monetary Fund – IMF (2010) *Global Finance Stability Report: Meeting New Challenges to Stability and Building a Safer System*, Washington, DC: IMF, April.

International Monetary Fund – IMF (2011a) *Recent Experiences in Managing Capital Inflow – Cross-Cutting Themes and Possible Policy Framework*. Prepared by the Strategy, Policy, and Review Department, February, Washington, DC: IMF.

International Monetary Fund – IMF (2011b) *World Economic Outlook 2011 – Tensions from the Two-Speed Recovery: Unemployment, Commodities, and Capital Flows*, Washington, DC: IMF, April.

International Monetary Fund – IMF (2012) *International Financial Statistics*, http://www.imf.org, access in April.

Jara, A., Moreno, R. and Tovar, C.E. (2009) 'The Global Crisis and Latin America: Financial Impact and Policy Responses', *BIS Quarterly Review*, June: 53–68.

Kregel, J. (1999) 'Was There an Alternative to the Brazilian Crisis?', *Brazilian Journal of Political Economy*, 19(3): 23–38.

Kregel, J. (2008) 'The Discrete Charm of the Washington Consensus', *Journal of Post Keynesian Economics*, 30(4): 541–60.

Magud, N. and Reinhart, C. (2006) 'Capital Controls: An Evaluation', *NBER Working Paper no. 11973*, January.

Ministry of Finance (2012) *Brazilian Economic Outlook no. 14 – Special Edition*, Brasília: Ministry of Finance, http://www.fazenda.gov.br, access in April.

Mishkin, F. (2000) 'What Should Central Banks Do?', *Federal Reserve Bank of St. Louis Review*, 82(6): 1–13.

Mohanty, M. and Scatigna, M. (2005) 'Has Globalization Reduced Monetary Policy Independence?', *BIS Papers no. 23*, May.

Mohanty, M. and Turner, P. (2006) 'Foreign Exchange Reserves in Emerging Countries', *BIS Quarterly Review*, 24: 39–42.

Moreno, R. (2005) 'Motives for Intervention', *BIS Papers*, no. 24, May.

Ocampo, J.A. (2007) 'The Macroeconomics of the Latin America Boom', *CEPAL Review*, 93: 7–28.

Ocampo, J.A. (2012) 'Balance of Payments Dominance: Its Implications for Macroeconomic Policy', https://www.mtholyoke.edu/.../Ocampo_Macro_Mount_Holyoke.pdf, access in April.

Paula, L.F. (2011) *Financial Liberalization and Economic Performance: Brazil at the Crossroads*, Abingdon: Routledge.

Paula, L.F. and Ferrari-Filho, F. (2010) 'Arestis and Sawyer's Criticism on the New Consensus Macroeconomics: Some Issues Related to Emerging Countries', in G. Fontana, J. McCombie and M. Sawyer (eds), *Macroeconomics, Finance and Money: Essays in Honour of Philip Arestis*, Basingstoke: Palgrave Macmillan.

Paula, L.F. and Prates, D. (2012) *Capital Account and FX Derivatives Regulation in Brazil: The Recent Experience*, Conference on Compatibility Review of the Trade Regime and Capital Account Regulations, 28–9 June, Buenos Aires: CEDES.

Prates, D.M. (2012) *How to Evaluate Financial Regulation in Brazil?*, Paper prepared to the workshop 'Growth with Financial Stability and New Developmentalism in Brazil', São Paulo: FGV-SP, March.

Prates, D.M. and Cintra, M.A.M. (2009) 'Os Países Emergentes Diante da Crise Financeira Global', *Proceedings of II Encontro Internacional da Associação Keynesiana Brasileira*, Porto Alegre: AKB.

Reinhart, C.M. and Reinhart, V.R. (2008) 'Capital Flow Bonanzas: An Encompassing View of the Past and the Present', *NBER Working paper* 14321, September.

Rodrik, D. (2006) 'The Social Cost of Foreign Exchange Reserves', *NBER Working Paper no. 11952*, January.

Rodrik, D. (1998) 'Who Needs Capital-Account Convertibility?', *Essays in International Finance*, 207: 55–65.

Rowthourn, R. and Ramaswamy, R. (1997) 'Deindustrialization: Causes and Implications'. *IMF Working Paper* No. 97/42, April.

Stiglitz, J. (2002) *Globalization and Its Discontents*, New York: W.W. Norton.

Stiglitz, J. (2000) 'Capital Market Liberalization, Economic Growth, and Instability', *World Development*, 28(6): 1075–86.

Stiglitz, J. (1999) 'More Instruments and Broader Goals: Moving Toward the Post-Washington Consensus', *Brazilian Journal of Political Economy*, 19(1): 94–120.

Tobin, J. (1978) 'A Proposal for International Monetary Reform', *Eastern Economic Journal*, 4: 153–9.

Williamson, J. (1990) 'What Washington Means by Policy Reform', in J. Williamson (ed.), *Latin American Adjustment: How Much Has Happened?*, Washington, DC: Institute for International Economics.

Williamson, J. (2000) 'What Should the Word Bank Think About the Washington Consensus?', *The World Bank Research Observer*, 15(2): 251–64.

Index

Printed and bound by CPI Group (UK) Ltd, Croydon, CR0 4YY

The manufacturer's authorised representative in the EU is Springer Nature Customer Service Centre GmbH, Europaplatz 3, 69115 Heidelberg, Germany. If you have any concerns regarding our products, please contact ProductSafety@springernature.com

Printed and bound by CPI Group (UK) Ltd, Croydon, CR0 4YY
10/10/2026
02231221-0009